ACTING IN REAL TIME

ACTING IN REAL TIME

Paul Binnerts

TRANSLATED BY
PAUL BINNERTS AND
STEPHEN WANGH

THE UNIVERSITY OF MICHIGAN PRESS
ANN ARBOR

For Nancy

English translation copyright © by Paul Binnerts 2012

Originally published in Dutch as *Toneelspelen in de tegenwoordige tijd—een veldboek voor het vertellende toneel* © by IT & FB, Amsterdam, 2002

Published in the United States of America by
The University of Michigan Press
Manufactured in the United States of America
♾ Printed on acid-free paper

2015 2014 2013 2012   4 3 2 1

A CIP catalog record for this book is available from the British Library.

Library of Congress Cataloging-in-Publication Data

Binnerts, Paul.
    [Toneelspelen in de tegenwoordige tijd. English]
    Acting in real time / Paul Binnerts ; translated by Paul Binnerts and
    Stephen Wangh.
        p. cm.
    ISBN 978-0-472-11794-9 (cloth : alk. paper) — ISBN 978-0-472-03503-8 (pbk. :
    alk. paper) — ISBN 978-0-472-02856-6 (e-book)
    1. Acting. 2. Method acting. I. Title.
    PN2061.B44513   2012
    792.02'8—dc23   2012011049

The translation of this book has been made possible by a generous subsidy of the Dutch Performing Arts Foundation (Nederlands Fonds voor de Podiumkunsten) in The Hague, The Netherlands.

Cover photo: Peter de Kimpe's set design for *Allein das Meer (The Same Sea)*, Neues Theater, Halle, Netherlands, 2005. Photo by Peter de Kimpe.

CONTENTS

ACKNOWLEDGMENTS

Writing this book has been quite a journey, which started when my son, David, told me that I "should write that down." This was in Holland, where I spent most of my professional life as a director, acting teacher, and writer. From the moment I started writing I was surrounded by friends, colleagues, and wise counselors, whom I wish to acknowledge, especially my dear friend Rudy Engelander, who helped me to edit the first drafts of the book; Ben Hurkmans, who supported me with a stipend from the Dutch Performing Arts Council; and publisher Marlies Oele of International Theatre & Film Books who, in 2002, made the Dutch publication possible.

By that time I was teaching an acting workshop for Kevin Kuhlke's International Theater Wing (ITW) of New York University's Tisch School of the Arts (the Summer School Program in Amsterdam), and started teaching in Michael Cadden's Theater Program at Princeton University. The contact with the students of these excellent schools made it clear to me that my book would be welcomed in the United States. I decided to translate it into English, and I asked Stephen Wangh, my friend and colleague from Tisch, to be my co-translator. It was again Ben Hurkmans of the Dutch Performing Arts Council who supported the idea and provided me with a grant.

Translating is editing, and I can't say how grateful I am to Steve for initiating a unique discussion—we called it "a walk on the beach," although we mainly talked through email—about the content of the book: definitions needed to be refined, notions about acting and acting styles needed to be clarified, cultural gaps needed to be bridged. We acting teachers, theater professionals in general, rarely have such an opportunity to talk at length and in depth about the principal issues of what we love the most: the theater, its form and its content, how to tackle the questions it poses, and how to teach it. In this process the book gradually underwent a transformation.

My own development also expanded: the book was no longer an end point but became in many respects a new exploration, which helped me further in my teaching and directing. I am forever grateful to the many acting and directing students, professional actors, stage designers, and composers I had the honor to work with, in Holland as well as in the United States, in Germany, and in Japan: I learned from them, as much as I hope they learned from me.

When the translation was finished after several years of steadily interrupted work, I was delighted that the University of Michigan Press decided to publish the book. Editor LeAnn Fields has helped me enormously, by encouraging me to make the necessary rearrangements to make the book meet the standards of the Press. Again the book underwent a transformation. The result is an almost entirely new book. I am very grateful for LeAnn's diligence, her professionalism, and patience. I also want to thank the editorial staff, especially Marcia LaBrenz, for the excellent work they have done to make this book happen. Writing a book is one thing, but producing one is quite a different ballgame.

I have always seen my work as a director and a teacher as an exploration, a practical research as in a laboratory: you might have an idea about how the performance should be, but *you don't know what you don't know*—and that's what you want to discover. Creating theater and teaching actors is a process, of which the final result cannot (and, as I strongly believe, should not) be known beforehand. I wish to thank the drama schools, the theaters, the ensembles, and the producers I have worked with in all these years, for giving me the space to set up my workshops and performances as exploratory projects.

The literal English translation of the title of the Dutch book does not cover its meaning entirely. But the English title Stephen Wangh and I came up with, *Acting in Real Time,* does. It refers to the *presence of the actor as himself,* performing in the "here and now" of the theater. The term also represents the new acting convention, which has been developed by Dutch actors and directors from 1970 onwards. I had the honor to be one of them, and today this form is applied by many theater artists and ensembles, and is taught in schools. I especially want to mention actor, director, and stage-designer JanJoris Lamers, and his company *Discordia*, to whom I, like many others, am deeply indebted for their inspiration, their ceaseless questioning of existing theater conventions, and their continuous pursuit of radical new forms.

Everyone has his teachers, who allow him to stand on their shoulders. For me they are Benjamin Hunningher and Bertolt Brecht. As my drama professor, and later my friend, Hunningher opened my eyes to the wealth of dramatic literature and the history of the theater. He taught me how to analyze a dramatic text. And, most important, he passed his passion for the theater on to me. Yet, with pain in my heart, I had to leave him, when I decided that I had to find out for myself, in the practice of the theater, what it *really* was he had taught me. And with pain in his heart he let me go, but this book bears the fruit of his wise teachings.

Brecht put me on the track of the "epic theater," but it was only after many experiments and exploratory performances that I understood his vision. Reading his theoretical texts puzzled me at first, but re-reading them after many years was an "Aha-Erlebnis," an eye-opener. A teacher wouldn't be a good teacher if his students can't say goodbye to him. From the concept of epic theater I was able to develop, with a deep bow of gratitude to my master Brecht, the concept of real-time theater.

Nancy Gabor, my wife, friend, and colleague, is and has been my deepest and permanent inspiration. She has been the witness of my struggles and joy, while I was writing the book in Dutch. But only when I was working on the English translation could she read every word. With her critical eye, not only for the language but also for its content, she kept encouraging me. Her insightfulness, her love, patience, and trust, accompanied me with every step of the process. I am delighted to dedicate this book to her.

Paul Binnerts, New York, May 2012

Introduction: Human Behavior
Is the Core Business of Theater

Two acting styles and techniques dominated Western theater in the twentieth century. At the beginning of the century, the Russian actor-director Konstantin Stanislavski[1] developed the convention of *psychological realism* (also referred to as *naturalism, realism,* or *naturalistic realism*[2]) based on the idea that actors,[3] by accessing their own emotions, *transform* themselves into the characters they play: the actor *identifies* with his character by living through him. By applying the elements of the *identification technique,* the actor becomes the character he plays to create a psychologically based, truthful reality on the stage.

In the 1930s, German playwright and director Bertolt Brecht[4] developed the convention of the epic theater and the technique of the *alienation effect,* based on the idea that actors should approach their tasks in quite the opposite way: by keeping a distance from the character he plays, by looking at him in the same way the artist studies his model. Through imitation of *social examples,* using technical and physical skills, the actor gives shape to reality in a stylized form. By applying the elements of the *alienation technique,* the actor *demonstrates* the character he plays, instead of *becoming* him, and creates a no less truthful, purely theatrical reality.

Theater is about human behavior, and human behavior was the main concern of both of these giants of the theater, but from different points of view. Stanislavski wanted to show the inner life of the characters in a play, their thoughts and feelings, and the motives for their actions.

Brecht wanted to show how human behavior is influenced and some-times even dictated by social and political circumstances. Stanislavski wanted to involve an audience emotionally, Brecht intellectually.

Brecht did not originally conceive his epic theater in response to Stanislavski's psychological realism, but it is often considered an alter-native to realism. Although the two acting conventions are in many re-spects diametrically opposed, they have more in common than is gen-erally assumed. The fact is that the theater communities in most Western countries have accepted Stanislavski's psychological realism, which remains the most practiced theater and acting convention, whereas Brecht's epic theater, since its inception, has been controversial and often misunderstood.

The 1960s and 1970s brought a new wave of ideas, challenging the existing conventions in the arts in Western culture. Theater concepts were changing, particularly in English-speaking countries, but also in Holland, where I lived and worked. Through experimentation, new ideas were emerging, especially outside the world of traditional theaters with their tested production techniques. Some of these ideas crystal-lized into new ways and methods of acting. *Real-time acting*, as one of them, is the subject of this book.

The Measures Taken

When I began as a director, acting teacher, and playwright in 1971, I wanted to understand what "epic" theater and acting is, and more im-portantly, how one does it. I chose to work on one of Bertolt Brecht's most controversial plays, *The Measures Taken*,[5] with a small group of di-recting students at the Amsterdam Theater School. Composer Louis An-driessen wrote new music, replacing the original score by Hanns Eisler.[6]

I chose this play because in Brecht's own assessment it was a proto-type of epic theater. In the assessment of some critics, it is the only true communist tragedy ever written. Yet still others think the play is about blind obedience to a rigid Communist Party.

The Measures Taken tells the story of a group of Communist Agitators who penetrate into China in order to "bring the revolution." Their guide is a Young Comrade "whose heart beats for the revolution," but who is so passionate about the cause of social justice that he makes a series of strategic and tactical blunders that threaten to jeopardize the entire secret undertaking. In vain the Agitators try to rein him in, so that when the Young Comrade wants to proclaim the revolution, they are forced to seize and kill him, throwing his body into a lime pit so that it will burn and all traces of him will be wiped out. In a heartbreaking scene, the Agitators, who have been patient with him but now see that their mission is imperiled, ask him if he agrees with this ultimate "measure." The Young Comrade admits his fault and bows his head, preparing to be shot.

But this is not the whole play. The Agitators report the story of the Young Comrade, his tragic fate, and their role in his death to what is called the Control Chorus, which stands for the Central Committee of the Party. In order to succeed in their mission, they had to kill a comrade in the process. They want to hear the judgment of the Party: was it right what they did, or was it wrong? First ignoring the moral dilemma of the Agitators, then acknowledging it, the Chorus concludes that they did the right thing, because "the revolution advances." And that is the only thing that counts, no matter what.

The dramaturgical structure of the play is exceptional, and deceivingly simple: the Agitators report to the Chorus about their mission, and engage in discussion; in the reenacted scenes the Agitators and the Young Comrade, engaging other characters, try to carry out their mission; the comments of the Chorus often end with, or are interrupted by, a song. Together these actions constitute three levels of play.

Theory and Practice

Right from the start of our theater company's practical exploration, we bumped into a series of contradictions and seeming contradictions—*paradoxes*—about the actor's identity and craft, and about time and space in the theater. Whatever we tried, the result was at best some sort of a reproduction of a reality, which didn't go beyond what we had learned from the play when we were reading and analyzing it. We might have understood theoretically what epic theater was, but we couldn't bring it into practice.

However simple the construction of the play seemed, once we began to act out the scenes we encountered problems in each level of play. The main problems were in the reenacted scenes between the Agitators, the Young Comrade, and the other characters. It took us quite a while before we began to understand that they were caused by the prevailing concept of the actor's *identification* with the character. Simply by lack of *practical* understanding of what Stanislavski's and Brecht's techniques meant and implied, we automatically *associated our own feelings* with those of the characters we were playing, and created *realistic situations* that were supposed to represent the reality of prerevolutionary China. This, of course, brought us immediately into conflict with Brecht's ideas about *alienation*. And, when we tried some sort of stylization through sharply defined physical gestures and formal blocking, we found that it simply didn't work. It was obvious that this was not what Brecht wanted.

How We Solved Our Problems

Only after we looked closely again at the three levels of play did my students and I realize that the main dramatic action of the play is between the Chorus and the Agitators, who discuss their mission and its outcome. In between these discussions the Agitators show the actions of the Young Comrade in the reenacted scenes as *illustrations* of the case they are presenting. In the characters' list the Young Comrade is one of nine characters, *to be performed by the Agitators*.[7] We concluded that the only real characters of the play are the four Agitators and the Chorus. They have an argument about the justness of the Agitators' actions. This is what the play is really about.

To establish the relationship between the Chorus and the Agitators did not seem difficult. Their dialogues are short and simple and often evolve into song. We had to make sure, however, that we didn't play these dialogues as *commentary*, taking place outside the action of the play. They *are* the central action of the play. So when we had to find a place for the Chorus, we positioned them in the center of the stage. In front of them, downstage, were the Agitators, who mainly operate as one character, speaking with one voice when they speak with the Chorus, but split up as individual characters when they play their scenes with the Young Comrade. When they dialogued with the Chorus they stepped to the side of the limited playing area. It was a simple and transparent staging.

Two Time Frames: Play within a Play

We also realized that we had to deal with two time frames. The first is the dialogue between the Chorus and the Agitators, which is the *present time of the play,* and the second consists of all the scenes about their mission in China some time before, *in the past.* The second time frame takes place within the first: it is a *play within a play:* the narrative of the Young Comrade interrupts the narrative of the four Agitators and their discussion with the Control Choir. And the two time frames, in the way they were acted, needed to be very clearly separated from each other.

The two time frames have two different casts of actors. In the first, the present, there are four Agitators and the Chorus. In the second, the past, there are in fact only the four Agitators, who play the Young Comrade and others, for example the Merchant and the Supervisor. The first time frame facilitates the second, and if it were not for the urgency of the questions the four Agitators put before it, the Chorus would have dismissed them without listening. In the first time frame the Young Comrade is dead, he is simply not there: the four Agitators report to the Chorus *in retrospect,* after the death of the Young Comrade. *Therefore his role is not a role for one actor, but for one of the Agitators,* which implies that four agitators and a chorus in both the time frames were all we needed. Traditional casting, especially for the role of the Young Comrade, who appears in all the reenacted scenes, is in this situation impossible, and even undesirable.

The fact that we were a small group of seven players helped us enormously: four of them were the Agitators, and three of them the Chorus, which was different from the play's original intention.[8] Once we understood this, we additionally decided to have the role of the Young Comrade performed not by one "chosen" Agitator, but by all of us. This resulted in a permanent changing of all the roles from scene to scene, and even in switching the parts of the Chorus and Agitators. Eventually each one of us got to play the Young Comrade. As a consequence, each one of us played all the roles, and sang all the songs, although not in the same performance. Each one of us could play the whole play, and stand in for each other, if necessary. Through this device, we were able to keep a distance from the characters, step back to look at the characters, and truly *demonstrate* the Young Comrade's actions. Brecht's idea of alienation was certainly served by this approach to the play. This was a major step, but it was not enough to prevent full identification of the actor with the characters, particularly in the reenacted scenes.

Agitprop: A Theatrical Metaphor

The reenacted scenes with the Young Comrade and other characters still tended to be "realistic," "psychological," and "emotional." We decided to bring in a *theatrical metaphor* from outside the play, a vehicle for *images*, with which we could create the desired stylization, an even bigger distance, and tell the story of the play effectively. We chose the form of "agitation propaganda" (agitprop), a political educational theater form widely used by the Soviet propaganda machine, which seemed appropriate for this particular play.

With this as inspiration we found for every scene almost cartoon-like *images*, which could have been taken from any "agitprop" piece of that time. This approach gave us the freedom to use our theatrical imagination, and get away from emotional identification with the characters. The images forced us to play the situations and the roles in a non-realistic manner. The sketchlike form of "agitprop" enabled us to present situations without realistic detail, and helped us to stage the actions of the characters without delving into the full depth of their being. The actions explained themselves through the form. And through the form we created real people.

We had found an honest, convincing, and therefore "truthful" form for the scenes, through which we could explore the moral dilemmas of people who become torn and crushed between believing in an ideal/ideology and the cruel realities of Communist Party discipline. And this is what Brecht wanted. In the first place he wanted to show the dilemma, not the tragedy of the Young Comrade, nor the dogmatism of the Communist Party. He wanted the audience to think about this dilemma.

With the device of the second theatrical metaphor, it seemed that we had solved most of our problems, except for one: *what do we do between the dialogues of the Agitators and the Chorus and the songs on the one hand, and the reenacted scenes with the Young Comrade on the other?*

The Actor Is Essentially a Performer

One of the most instructive moments during this project was the discussion about the position of the piano and, more importantly, of the piano player. We had placed the piano in the middle of the stage because of the central role we had given to the Chorus, singing from behind it. Louis Andriessen himself played the piano. The question arose whether he had to exit after every number, or if he could stay at the piano and watch while the scenes were played—and perhaps even smoke a cigarette (we didn't ask questions about smoking cigarettes back then). Finally we opted for the second choice.

It was significant that, as a musician, Louis didn't have any problem with his presence on the stage, while we, as actors, were always looking for a *justification* of our presence, especially during the songs some of us were singing, while the others were . . . doing what??? Again it took a while before we understood that we as actors did not need any justification to be on stage: we could *watch* the others while they were singing, just as Louis and the Chorus were *watching* when the others were playing. But if this was true for the musical numbers in *The Measures Taken*, then perhaps the actors *never* needed a justification for their presence on stage—beyond the fact that they were there to play a role. This means, that their presence *doesn't need to be justified by the dramatic situation, but by the theatrical reality*. So this is what we had to do in the time between actions, and in between the three levels of play: we had to be *present as ourselves*, and *watch*. And from there we would jump into the different roles we were playing. This realization was the first step toward the birth of the *real-time actor:* he or she is essentially a *performer,* just as a musician is.

The Basic Elements of Real-Time Acting and Theater

This incubator project was the beginning of a long exploration of the possibilities of this way of acting and making theater. Through our experimentation with *The Measures Taken,* we stumbled upon a theater form that I now call *real-time theater,* touching upon the basic elements of what became not just another acting style, but a new theater convention in its own right, one that affects all of theater's elements.

In retrospect this is what we discovered:

1. The way we dealt with the roles allowed us to *dissociate our own feelings* from those of the characters, while still being able to play them.
2. The dramaturgical structure of *The Measures Taken* allowed us to take the play apart in three levels of performance. This opened up the play, and allowed us to introduce other elements than Brecht had provided in the text, that is, the theatrical metaphor of "agit-prop." I realized later that before it was a word and a concept, that this was a true *postmodern* moment: we *deconstructed* the play—we took it apart and put it together again.
3. The space in between the three levels of play allowed us to be *present as ourselves* on the stage. The presence of the actor as himself became over the years the basis of the *technique of real-time acting.*

A fourth element, to which we didn't pay too much attention in this project, was the *performance space.* Ours was a classroom. This elementary setting in a theater school—basically a bare room—helped us to make our discoveries.

Real-Time Acting for Postmodern Theater

Real-time theater is more than just an extension of Brecht's epic theater, although his form has helped me greatly to discover and define its principles. It uses the *alienation technique,* but without the one-sided political didacticism Brecht often is accused of. It leaves room for important elements of Stanislavski's *identification technique* just as it is open to other styles and forms of theater.

In real-time theater the key is this: what is *real is the acting itself, not what is acted.* What is acted—the play and the characters—are and remain an *illusion*—a fantasy, created by the imagination of the playwright, the director, and the actors, and all the other contributors to the creative process of a performance. The actor, when he is acting, is in the *here and now,* in the *present time,* in the *reality of the stage and the theater,* and not in an illusionary time or space. This requires *the presence of the actor,* first as himself, then as the character he plays, and often both at the same time. The "real-time" actor creates the *reality of an illusion,* instead of the *illusion of a reality.* His presence as himself expands the palette of his acting, and doesn't limit his activities to acting his role.

Acting in real-time is the *technique* required for the aesthetic demands of *postmodern theater,* in which other, sometimes alien, theatrical elements break up, or *deconstruct,* the text of a play, and the usually closed theatrical spaces, approaching these elements from a different point of view. It reconciles Stanislavski's psychological realism with Brecht's epic theater, adding the *presence of the actor as himself.*

The presence of the actor as himself also implies the *reality of the stage itself* and of the theater as the place in which he performs his dramatic illusions. In our time, changes in theatrical space have played a major role in spurring new approaches to acting and other theater practices. And different approaches to acting and making theater have spurred changes in theatrical space. The many forms and styles of real-time theater usually live outside the traditional theater and are especially suited to *empty spaces, black box theaters,* and *site-specific* settings. In these venues, all the production elements take on new functions— the acting, the performance space itself, and the audience.

Through my practical work as a director and acting teacher, I have been able to fathom the secrets of epic acting and of psychological realism. It has taken me a lifetime to realize the full consequences of my early discoveries, which I expanded in many experimental theater productions, and which finally led to writing this book about real-time acting and all its implications. I wasn't alone in my quest: other theater-makers, directors, and actors came up with similar results from their experiments, along different routes and in different ways. Today real-time theater is being practiced in many forms and styles, and applied to various modes of theatrical expression.

The notion of the actor's presence is not my invention alone. Joseph Chaikin, one of the three giants of modern theater,[9] explored the phenomenon with his experimental group, the Open Theater of New York.[10] He once formulated it like this: "The actor has to be present in the role he plays, so that he can mean what he says." The actor's presence as himself goes back to the original meaning of *play*, which is what we do when we are children, and what our ancestors did in primitive rituals. *Acting evolved out of play.*

What Is in This Book?

To fully understand the technique of real-time acting, it is necessary to include a description and an analysis of the acting techniques from which it is a departure. This book also contains a detailed description of the workshop that I teach and have developed over the years, followed by practical exercises. The book concludes with an analysis of the historical context of real-time acting, with an emphasis on how it relates to its origins in play, and the development of the theater space.

Part I of the book is titled "Premises and Inspirations." In chapter 1 I describe the manifold identity of the actor, the paradoxes and contradictions he encounters, and what he does when he acts. Chapters 2 and 3 put this in the context of the acting conventions initiated by Stanislavski and Brecht. In a comparative manner I analyze Stanislavski's *psychological realism* and the technique of *identification*, and Brecht's *epic theater* and the technique of *alienation*.

Part II, "Acting in Real Time," is primarily a practical guide, describing the tools the actor needs to act in postmodern theater. In Chapter 4, I describe the main skills of real-time acting, and compare them with Stanislavski's psychological realism and Brecht's epic theater. As often as possible, I use examples from my own experience as illustrations. Chapter 5, "The Workshop," presents a series of exercises designed to help the actor play a role using the real-time acting form. The actors tell a story from their personal lives, take and maintain a distance from it, and create first a solo-performance and then a montage of all stories. These exercises can increase the actor's awareness of his identity as an actor and the natural distance between himself and the roles he plays. At the same time he can gain more precise command of the technique of real-time acting. The physical exercises described in Chapter 6 are designed to help the actor become truly *present* in performance.

Part III is titled "Real-Time Acting and Theater in Historical Perspective." Beginning with its earliest origins of *play*, *ritual*, and *story-telling*, Chapter 7 presents a broad overview of the history of acting, specifically relating the developments in acting to the history of theater architecture and stage design. Chapter 8 explores the origins of realism as a theatrical convention. The two major acting conventions of twentieth-century theater—Stanislavski's psychological realism and Brecht's epic realism—are also put in this context, eventually leading up to real-time acting, where the distinction between *play* and *acting* is restored.

How to Use It

This book can be used in different ways: the reader or student can read it from start to finish or can, according to where his or her main professional interest lies, choose what to read, even select sections from every chapter that are particularly useful.

With this book I hope to enlarge the understanding of the essential elements of real-time theater and the real-time acting technique. It aims to make this relatively new form available and workable for theater students and theater practitioners—actors, directors, acting and drama teachers, stage designers, and even architects—and to make a permanent place for the convention of real-time theater within our variegated theater culture.

You don't learn acting from a book—you learn acting by doing it. But reading about it can help actors to understand what they do when they act, and to become better actors.

Part I

Premises and Inspirations

1   The Dilemmas of the Actor: Who Is He and What Is His Task?

The Actor's First Paradox: What Is Real?

If the presence of the actor is the most important feature of real-time theater, we want to know who the actor is. By this I don't mean the glossy, glamorous, biographical gossip on actors in the media, and not the Who's Who of Broadway's *Playbill*, but his *identity*.

As far back as the eighteenth century, the French philosopher and playwright Denis Diderot put his finger on the problem of the actor's identity, and what he is doing when he acts. In search of truthfulness in acting, Diderot discovered what became known as "the paradox *of* the actor."[1] He asked: are the tears of the actor *real*, or does he only act *as if* he cries? Should the actor make us believe his tears are real? And must the tears be real tears, or is it all right if he simulates them? In fact there is a seeming contradiction here, a paradox indeed, for the actor himself may not be sad when he plays a sad character, who sobs and has tears rolling down his cheeks. The actor knows this, and so does the audience. So the "paradox of the actor" lies in the *conflict between the actor and the character, existing together within one body*. This complicated problem might also be formulated like this: Can an actor embody a character *truthfully* without using his own emotions? Is that permissible? Is it even possible? These questions seem to boil down to the question: what is "real" on the stage, and what is "not real?" And does it matter, if the audience wishes to believe it is real?

Acting Is a Mysterious Craft . . . but It *Is* a Craft!

Perhaps nothing is more difficult to describe in concrete terms than what an actor is doing when he is acting. How can we express it clearly, so that we can really imagine it, truly understand it, and put it into our own words? A shoemaker can tell you exactly what he is doing when he makes a shoe. But many actors cannot articulate what acting is. Yet acting, like making shoes, or baking bread, or designing clothes, or building ships, is a craft. Then why is it so hard to describe? And why do so many people question whether this craft of acting can be learned?

The art of acting is shrouded in mystery. Either you have the talent—the disposition, the natural ability—or you don't. Those who embrace the ideas of Konstantin Stanislavski say that acting is a kind of *transformation,* a metamorphosis. According to these ideas, the actor turns himself into someone else, the fictional character in the play. The idea that the actor "identifies" with the character he is playing is not far-fetched or strange, since the actor and the character share one physical body, and one physical appearance. The audience can easily be persuaded to identify the actor with the character he plays: after all, they see only one body on the stage.

But of course the actor does not change in the way a fairy-tale character does. He may "transform" himself a great deal, but he never entirely loses himself, the way a prince in a fairy tale "becomes" a frog. In fact, such a feat, say the followers of Bertolt Brecht, is not only impossible, but also undesirable. Acting, they maintain, is not the mystical unification of the actor with another person. According to Brecht's ideas, the actor merely *demonstrates* a character.

In other words, the Stanislavskian "transformative" actor acts *as if* he had turned into another person. He imagines himself to be someone else by identifying with the character. The Brechtian "demonstrative" actor, on the other hand, may *imagine* and then *demonstrate* the character, but he refrains from acting as if he were transformed into that character.

The truth, it seems to me, lies somewhere between these two approaches—or rather it is an extension of them: the art of acting lies in the actor's ability to *embody a fictional character without becoming that character.* Just as a musician plays upon his instrument, the actor plays upon his body as an *instrument,* and the body, being the container of the brain and the heart, includes the mind and the soul. Thus there is always a separation and a distinction between the actor and the character. It is exactly this separation that enables the actor, using his *imagination* and his *skill,* to embody the character with all that person's behavioral characteristics. In this way, the actor can channel whatever talent he may have through the *instruments* of his body, voice, and mind to form and shape a character: acting is a craft. The technique of playing upon his "instrument" can be learned. The talent itself cannot. So, if there is any mystery to the art of acting, it lies only in this innate talent.

The Simultaneity of Acting and of What Is Acted

During the history of acting, many terms have been used to describe what an actor is doing when he acts. The result has been a Babel-like confusion of words. There are different words for the same phenomenon, and there are the same words for different phenomena. The word *intention,* for example, meaning "purpose," is often used as if it meant "emotion." The word *action* is used for both a physical action and a dramatic action. This confusing vagueness of language contributes to the mystery of acting.

Perhaps the mystery—and its confusion of words—also arises because the actor, while he is acting, while he is creating something (as a shoemaker creates a shoe) *simultaneously experiences* the very thing he is creating. In other words: while the actor performs, he simultaneously experiences *what* he is performing. Or, to put it even more precisely: the actor experiences *what* he plays *only at the very moment* of his playing it. This is something he shares with dancers and musicians.

Because of the simultaneity of the act of creation and what is created, the actor, in the perception of the audience, often coincides with the character he plays. The audience sees only one body on stage and hears only one voice. Yet all of us—audience and actors alike—know that this is just an outward appearance; we know that *the actor is not the character, but that he plays him;* that what we see is not real, but an *illusion,* or rather real *and* an illusion at the same time. This convention is essential to what we call theater.

A painter can take a few steps back to look at the brushstrokes she just put on the canvas and a writer can read back what she has written. But an actor cannot do that—there is no distance between his acting and what he plays. The simultaneity of acting and what is acted makes it difficult for him to be aware of what he is doing while he is doing it. It slips through his fingers before he can grasp it. And as soon as the performance is over, his creation disappears. For the actor—and for the audience that has witnessed this remarkable trick—the magic has become merely a memory, an event recorded only in the Book of Time. Thus, what the actor plays, the role he creates, the performance . . . does not exist except during the very moment of performing. Afterward, it is gone. Then, the following evening, the actor must re-create his role. One proof of how hard it is for an actor to know what he is doing is the common disagreement between the actor and his colleagues or the director as to whether a performance went well. Often the actor is convinced that his performance went badly, while those around him think he was brilliant. And just as often he feels his performance is "on," while his colleagues think he's "off."

The shoemaker's shoe is something real and tangible. It is something you can put on your foot. It is a *thing*. But the actor, like the musician and the dancer, is making something elusive, something abstract—something that evaporates into thin air. And yet, paradoxically, acting itself is an utterly concrete activity.

This is only the first of several problems in understanding what acting is. But it begins to explain just why it is so difficult to describe what an actor precisely is doing when he is acting.

Who Is the Actor?

Try this test: Look in the mirror. We look at ourselves at least a few times each day, so it won't hurt you to do it once more. No, not a quick glance; don't look away as if you knew what you looked like. Look again. That nose, that mouth, those eyes. . . . Are those my eyes? Is that my nose, my mouth? Do I really look like this? I had a different picture of myself in my mind.

Apart from the slight distortion of the mirror, you may become aware that your image in the mirror is different from your internal image of how you look. The same thing may happen when you look at a photograph of yourself, or—even more shockingly—when you hear your voice on a tape or see yourself on a video. Many people cannot even look at themselves at all. Why is that? Is it that they are afraid of themselves? Or is it that they don't want to see or hear the truth? Or is it just a matter of perception?

And what about when others look at us? What do they see? Do they all see the same thing? Do they see the same person that we see when we look in the mirror—or do they see us, as we *believe* we look? And what about the internal qualities of our being, what we call our soul? Does the same distinction exist there, between the self that we believe ourselves to be and our real being—and between our being and what others perceive? So then: What is real, what is the reality? In the face of these questions it may seem very difficult, perhaps impossible, to be sure of our real identity. Perhaps we can only approximate it. Or perhaps we have more than one identity; perhaps we have more identities than anyone could count.

How complicated it must be, then, for actors to embody the emotions and the characteristics of the characters they play so that these characteristics and emotions will be perceived and understood by the audience in the way the actor intended. Luigi Pirandello, the Italian playwright of the early twentieth century, wrote several plays about the tragicomic discrepancy between how we see ourselves and how the outside world sees us.[2] In each of these plays, he poses more questions than he answers. And now, in what is called "postmodernism," we've grown accustomed to the idea that several participants in the same event will tell us different versions of that event, each in his own words.

For example: We are told that someone is arrogant. No, another disagrees, he is not arrogant; he is in fact very shy and modest, it is just that he hides his shyness behind the arrogance: it is a mask. But whether the person is, in fact, arrogant or shy, both of these ways of being can be seen as forms of insecurity about himself. It is as if we needed to justify how someone expresses himself or is perceived.

In the end, we can never be entirely sure. Perhaps, at bottom, we are all insecure because we can never be certain of who we really are. Of course we all find ways of coping with this problem, ways of behaving that give us something to hold onto. And maybe we experience these coping behaviors differently than they are perceived by others . . . until, for a moment, standing in front of a mirror, we may look ourselves in the eye and see behind the mirror of our souls. Then, for a brief moment, a split second, we may catch a glimpse of our real selves, and suddenly we are startled, or relieved or perhaps even pleased. A moment later we realize that the image of ourselves that we thought we had captured and understood has already vanished—it is so fleeting, so volatile, so indefinable.

This is, then, a second set of problems, problems that exist for everyone but are infinitely more complicated for the actor, who must deal not only with himself, but also with the characters he plays.

Quadruple Identity

While some acting teachers believe that the actor undergoes or brings about a mysterious transformation within himself when he plays a character, they contend that in order to do so, the actor must first know himself. Other teachers, however, contend that it is not necessary for the actor to know himself in order to play someone else—because he does not "become" that other person, he merely "plays" him by using his skills and acting technique.

But some things are undeniable: It is the actor who does the playing, and whether he transforms or demonstrates, he needs an instrument upon which to play. Moreover, he himself *is* that instrument: his voice, his body, his mind, his imagination, his intuition, his feeling, and his intellect—these are the tools with which he embodies the character he plays. And finally, at least for the duration of the play he is performing, the actor is also the *product* that he creates, the "gestalt" or form of the character he takes on.

So, there are the four levels on which the actor operates—his *quadruple identity:*

- The actor as himself: a person in his own right with his own identity
- The actor as an instrument
- The actor as the player of that instrument
- The actor as the character he embodies, and to which he gives form

Intuition

The shoemaker always remains who he is—although it is true that when he is concentrating on making a shoe he behaves differently than he does when he sells the shoe to a client. But the actor has to be a kind of acrobat, an acrobat of the mind at least, not to get caught in the confusing web of his quadruple identity. No wonder he is often so inarticulate about his profession. And directors, sensing the actor's confusion, often resort to vague language filled with associations, metaphors, and literary references rather than speaking to the actor in concrete and specific terms. For directors also have a hard time grasping the art of acting.

In the face of this situation, the actor's recourse is often to rely on his *intuition,* the antennae of his soul. With the help of these antennae, he tackles the difficulties of the matter at hand—the text, the psychological makeup of the character he is playing, the dramatic situation of the play, and the theater space itself. He listens to his feelings rather than his intellect, for rationalization, too, can be an obstacle to his work. He sometimes simply relies on that mysterious, unspeakable "something": his "talent." He becomes an adventurer, a hopeful—and sometimes desperate—romantic who is always on the way, but never arrives, or who can't quite remember how he got there.

Different Acting Conventions

The actor's difficulties do not end here. He must also contend with differing ideas about form and style, and about what the audience is to understand from his performance. First he encounters the ideas the playwright has given him in the play, offered perhaps in the form of philosophical thoughts about the world in which we live. Then he must contend with the concepts of the director, the dramaturge, and the designers who barrage him with their thoughts about theatrical form, about how to approach the text, about acting styles, and about the world that the set design creates. Now, under this onslaught of input from others, the actor must re-create his role, transforming the written words of the text into a three-dimensional, visual form.

In every production, the artistic collaborators develop an idea, a concept about how the play should be performed and how the stage should look. They work together to relate all the separate elements of the production to this overall concept. In this process, the actor is the key figure: it is his task to integrate himself and the character he is playing into the theatrical environment created by the lights, the set, the costumes, and the sound. And he must do so in such a way that he rises above them and seems to be in command of them, for in the end, it is he who controls the performance. During the process of rehearsal, the original concept is tested. Then, when the audience sees the result, it undergoes its own re-creation process. And most of this final process depends on the actor.

The artist-collaborators usually devise their concepts in relation to the work of other artists and cultural trends, which manifest themselves in other art forms as well. The contemporary philosophical and aesthetic ideas about the world are usually not private. Moreover, during one historical period, different ideas can appear simultaneously—this was the case with naturalism and symbolism at the end of the nineteenth century.

The concepts for the theatrical form are based on existing conventions, the aesthetic rules of the age that determine how the director directs, how the designer designs the set and the costume designer the costumes, and even how the audience watches the performance. The actor becomes part of this cultural debate, and consciously or unconsciously he must integrate this debate into the way in which he acts.

Embodiment

When an actor *embodies* a character, he embodies an imaginary person, in an imaginary situation, often in an imaginary time and an imaginary place. This imaginary character is usually the creation of a playwright's imagination—even if the character is supposed to be a "real" person who once was alive or is living now. Until an actor embodies him, this imaginary person remains a paper character, a being that waits patiently on the pages of the script, until the actor brings him to life. The actor's task is to *animate* the character: on the stage, in public, in the presence of an audience who watches him do so. This has been the essential task of actors since the very beginning of theater. Over time, the forms and conventions by which actors perform have changed, but this principle has remained the same.

The actor has to be able to describe the character he embodies, he has to know him, to understand him, to "read and write" him, to tell his story. To do so, he must engross himself deeply in the character, regardless whether this is a character in a written play, a character that comes into existence within an improvisation, or a character in a play without words.

In the case of a written play, the actor receives a great deal of information from the text of the play about the physical and psychological makeup of the character he is playing. He learns about the character's actions, the decisions he makes, what secrets he keeps and which ones he divulges, how he devises his plans and with whom, with which of the other characters in the play he does—or does not—get along (his friends and his enemies), whether he is a vain person and domineering or modest and shy, whether he is a go-getter or a loser.

And of course, the text often provides the actor with information about the character's external characteristics: how old he is, how he looks and moves, whether he is small or big, the color of his hair, what clothes he wears, whether he is married, or in love.

Much of this information from the text may be hypothetical. It gives the actor clues about how to play his role, but it doesn't give all the answers he needs; nor do the stage directions fill in the gaps. In fact, the answers must usually be discovered during the practical work, and sometimes they must simply be invented. In the case of an improvised play, or a play without words, the actor must provide all the "information" and make up all these "characteristics" himself. Whatever the source, all this information helps the actor to embody the character he plays.

To "embody a character" is certainly an adequate way of describing the art of acting, for it implies that the actor uses his own body to give shape to an imaginary person. But one doesn't solve the mystery of acting by simply using another term, which is still no more than a general description. The question remains: what does the actor *do* when he acts?

2   The Heart and Soul of the Actor: Stanislavski's Approach

Drama Is Action

The core of all theater is *drama*. In the classical dramaturgy recorded by Aristotle in his *Poetics*,[1] the word *drama* means "action"—it is "something that happens," an event, or a situation told as a story. (Many people nowadays use the word *drama* as if it meant "tragedy," but tragedy is simply one form of drama, a *genre* . . . just as comedy and tragicomedy are genres of drama.)

Dramatic action is that which a character does in a play—whether it is tragic, or comic, or tragicomic. The dramatic actions of the characters bring about what happens in a play. A play is made up of a series of dramatic actions, recorded in the text. Often, what happens is a *change of situation* brought about by the action of a character. Then friction arises between the existing situation and the new situation that the character has created with his action. Because of this, one character will often clash with another character. This is what we call *conflict*. In a play, this conflict is often resolved—or it may lead to a new conflict, or it may remain unresolved but reappear in a new form.

The process by which the characters struggle through such conflicts is what we call the *dramatic development* of the play, or the dramatic *course of events*. It is a process created by all the characters-in-action, all of who operate according to their own interests within an old or a new situation. Often these interests involve deep, existential needs upon which the future lives of the characters may depend. So the dramatic action and the outcome of the play may depend upon the characters' personal needs. But whether or not a conflict is resolved, the way it develops within the dramatic course of events always shows some change.

Physical Action and the Four *W*'s Plus Two: Who, What, Where, When, Plus Why and What For

If the dramatic action is that which happens in a play, then the actor who embodies a character *plays actions*. All actions of a character are accompanied by *thoughts* and *feelings*. Most actions are preceded by a *decision*—sometimes a well-considered, conscious decision, but often an impulsive, rash decision, made in a split second or in a frenzy. These decisions, often not spoken, bear what the character wants to achieve (what he is after)—his *intentions,* and *why*—his *motives.*

To achieve a truthful representation of the actions of a character in a dramatic situation, Stanislavski[2] designed the system of the four-plus-two *W*'s: *who, what, where, when, why, what for: Who* is the character (his identity)? *What* does he do (his action)? *Where* and *when* does the play take place (place and time)? *Why* does he do it (his motives), and *for what purpose* does he act (his intentions)? These are the canon of questions an actor always must ask himself about the character he is going to play. In addition, he must answer another question: Under what (outer and inner) *circumstances* does the action of the play takes place? To find the answers to all of these questions, he must look behind the text.

The identity of the character is in the first place defined by his actions, by what he does. Stanislavski defines an *action* first of all as a *physical action,* that is: a physical event, not an inner state of mind. But for an actor to open a door in a truthful manner, for example, he must have a reason, a *motive,* and a goal, an *intention: a why* and a *what for.*

Every action can be defined by a *verb,* which connects the physical action with the psychological meaning of that action. The verb defines the *dramatic action,* which *includes* motives and intentions, feelings and thoughts. By *physically playing the verb,* the actor embodies the dramatic action of his character. One can draw up lists of verbs that reflect an action. Every verb expresses something else, and has in the hands of the actor a different expression. To *encourage* is something else than to *pro-*

voke. To *console* is something else than to *appease.* Every actor encourages, provokes, consoles, and appeases in a different way.

Interpretation: Text and Subtext

Action, feeling and *thought, motive, intention,* and *objective* are the elusive qualities of the character, which can be found in the lines of a play, or rather beneath the lines. Together they constitute what Stanislavski calls the "subtext." The words of a play are just the tip of the iceberg, but what is *not* said is almost more important than what *is* said. Let us look at how the subtext informs the text.

At the beginning of *King Lear,* Lear asks his daughters how much they love him. It is a silly question, a question that only children or lovers would ask, a question that can only be answered with an equally silly answer: "a million dollars' worth" or "from here to Tokyo," because love is immeasurable. But, purposefully or not, Lear is testing his daughters' loyalty because he doesn't know whether he can trust them—or more particularly, whether he can trust the men they are married to or are marrying. Are they loyal to the kingdom? Are they willing and able to keep the realm together? So the actor playing the king must address a host of questions: What lies behind the king's plan to split the kingdom in three parts? Is it a precaution, good statesmanship, a risky gamble, or a recipe for trouble? Is his intention to "divide and rule"? Or does he really want to give up control? Or does he hope that the king of France, who is about to marry Cordelia, his dearest daughter, will be the real inheritor of his power? Does he act out of fear or out of confidence? Does he behave boyishly and naively, or is he shrewdly pretending to be the childish innocent? "Testing" is Lear's action, but Lear never says it: *to test* is the verb the actor uses to embody the action.

All the possibilities for action, emotion and thoughts, motive, intention, and objectives linger under the text, waiting to be activated by how the words are spoken, and by how the actors embody their characters. They are up to the actors' and director's *interpretation,* and therefore they are entirely subjective. In the hands of other actors and directors, they can be replaced by other meanings. "Testing," for instance, can be replaced by "inviting," and we will have an entirely different scene, played in a different tone.

Reading and "breaking down" the text of the play can uncover hidden meanings, but the words only spring into life by active, physical action on the rehearsal floor, and later in performance. The actors may start rehearsing with one verb for the action, but soon they may discover a wealth of possibilities that lie under a text.

Objectives, Superobjectives

Stanislavski says, quite correctly, that no character shows up in a situation without a reason and an intention. Every character wants something, even if it is only the house key. What he wants is part of, and becomes evident through, the action. The outcome of the play depends on it. Stanislavski calls this the *objective,* the *purpose* of an action. The actor has to make sure that his physical actions serve the *objectives* of the character's dramatic actions. The objective gives an intentional charge to the physical action, makes sense of its content and meaning, and helps the actor make it believable and truthful. The words *objective* and *intention* are closely related in their meaning: objective has a more rational and concrete value, intention a more emotional value. The actor can use these distinctions in connection with thought and feeling.

Objectives can be defined for the smallest unit of action in a play, the largest elements of action, and for the whole play: the *superobjective* for the whole play connects all the consecutive actions of the play and helps the actor make clear what the play is about, and to play a *through-line of action.*

Imagination, Magic If, and Emotional Memory

In order to speak not as himself, but as the character, and yet to be truthful at the same time, the actor must use his *imagination,* which must always serve the *story* and the *given circumstances* of the play: the facts and events that happen in the play, the historical time period, the time and place, and the life circumstances of the character. If the actor can imagine all these circumstances, he can create a believable physical form for them.

All the actions on stage must be *justified* within the actor. He must feel that what he is doing is logical, coherent, and true. If he must enact things that are impossible on stage, like igniting a fire or dying, the actor must find a substitute: he must act *as if* he were building the fire or *as if* he were dying, for it is his inner justification that makes the character's action truthful. The rest is theater pyrotechnics. Inner justification, Stanislavski believed, can make even the agony of death believable, devoid of false pathos and theatrics.

In fact everything that happens in the performance of a play, is based on what Stanislavski calls the *magic if*, because none of it is really real or true; it is all a fiction, enacted by actors who act *as if*, creating a fictitious world through their *imaginations*. In this act of imagination, the actor has to be truthful, true to life; he is not a magician, and he wants the audience to experience what they see as true and real. This is why the actor must employ his own emotions and the *emotional memories* that were created by similar events in his own life. Using his own emotional resources, he must embody the emotional state of his character in a truthful manner, *substituting* his own emotions for those of the character he plays. (Later in his work, Stanislavski puts a greater emphasis on the actor's imagination than on the technique of emotional memory.) With the help of this substitution technique, the actor could lend his character's actions a sense of naturalness and reality.

The Actor's Second Paradox: Acting Consciously

Activating the "emotional memory" of the actor is a matter of activating his consciousness, his awareness, or his senses, a process the actor must consciously control. He must be able to consciously embody the character he plays, and this ability must be a repeatable process. But, Stanislavski warns—as Diderot had long before—as the actor embodies his character, he must avoid the dangers of completely identifying with him. The actor must search within himself for authentic feelings, but then he must apply them in a controlled and conscious manner. This is the confusing, gray area of the actor's paradox.[3]

For a young child, the world is undivided (see also Part III, Chapter 7): there is no great distinction between "play" and "reality," the "real" events of daily life—the activities of eating, drinking, or cleaning up. Similarly there is no great distinction for him between physical sensation and feeling or thinking. But we adults are aware of these distinctions. As we grow up, we learn to differentiate "play" from "real life," and we start to take conscious control of our lives . . . to such an extent that, after a while, we stop playing entirely.

And yet, even though as grownups we are aware of these distinctions, few of us ever really act as consciously as the actor does on stage, and no normal human being is aware of the "meaning" of his real-life actions while he is "performing" them. That is not how we live. We reflect after the fact. But unlike other people, the actor must, on the one hand, keep alive at least the memory of what it is to "play," and, on the other, he must become aware of the "meaning" of his actions: he must reflect before the fact. Moreover, he must develop the ability to play and to perceive meaning at will.

Perhaps this is the real nature of the *paradox of the actor:* that in his daily life the actor—like everyone else—is rather unaware of what he is doing, while on stage, within the totally fictional world of the theater, he must be aware of all the actions of his character, even unto the smallest details of motive and intention, for otherwise he cannot "push the buttons" in his conscious mind that allow him to express them. At the same time—*paradoxically*—the character he plays, like the actor in his daily life, must remain only vaguely aware of what he does and of what mood he is in. *On stage, the actor acts consciously—even if his character does not!*

So the "paradox" is that the actor must hide the things that he "knows" because his character cannot know them. It is a paradox that exists in the consciousness of the actor, and it can be confusing to him when he must perform in a theatrical form in which the reality of the play is identical to—and therefore confused with—the reality of the actor, as is the case particularly in realism. Within this convention this "paradox" is reinforced by the material imitation of reality on the stage.

The Actor's Third Paradox: The Difference between Rehearsal and Performance

The actor learns what he "knows" during the rehearsal process. Looking for the truth of his character, he must search for what the character is actually "doing," how he behaves, and what he feels and thinks in the

dramatic situations in which he finds himself. In rehearsal the actor often acts out of *impulse,* and probably more than half of his actions con-
sist of *reactions.* He is not alone in this search: there are the other actors
who play other characters, and to whom he responds; there is the text,
which challenges him to come up with ideas and images; there are certain givens for the arrangement of the stage—a set and props and costumes—that he must deal with; there is a director who has his own
ideas about the form and the possible outcome of the searching process.

In order to clarify his character's actions within this complicated
process, the actor must work to create a conscious progression of
thoughts, which will then underlie each action of his character's development. Regardless of the theatrical convention in which he is working, the actor needs to be *specific.* The more specific he becomes in his
choices as to the nature of his character's actions, feelings, and
thoughts, the more conscious he will eventually be on stage.

What he finds in his search the actor memorizes, just as he memorizes his text. He stores it all in the back of his mind, in the computer of
his brain and nervous system. In this process, the indispensable thing is
repetition. By repeating and repeating and repeating in rehearsal, the
actor becomes able to re-create in performance what he "knows" in his
mind and body.

Then in performance, the actor is able to invoke consciously what
he needs: text, actions, emotions, thoughts, and the theatrical form.
The actor's awareness or consciousness is both mental and physical: he
looks and sees, he listens and hears, he moves, he knows where he is or
has to be on stage, and in relationship to the other actors.

As long as he is in rehearsal, discovering his role, the "paradox" is
much less paradoxical. The actor is constantly aware of the rehearsal situation: he can be stopped by the director at any given moment; he can
stop or interrupt himself; he can start all over again or try something else;
he can forget or skip a text; or he can deal with a new prop the director
might throw in for him to use. But especially within the convention of realism, this "consciousness" can become an obstacle during performance:
What the actor "knows" about the dramatic situation of the play and the
character he's playing is all contained within the theatrical "illusion of reality" he himself has created during rehearsal. Within the "rules" and
givens of this theater convention, he creates his own paradox.

Feeling and Thought

To embody his character, to play his action, the actor must discover how the character feels and thinks. No action is neutral. Nobody does something without having thoughts and feelings that go along with it. In daily life, these feelings often remain unconscious, unless the emotions are particularly fierce. Moreover, in daily life we rarely think deliberately about each step we take. In fact, it may seem that we become aware of our thoughts and feelings only a moment *after* we have made a subconscious decision to do something, as if our conscious thought were an afterthought to something we did unthinkingly. But even when our actions are based on subconscious decisions, they are not simply senseless, purposeless, uncontrolled, or impulsive. They are (subconsciously) accompanied by what we feel and think.

These processes of feeling and thinking give substance, weight, color, sense, and meaning to what might otherwise be senseless actions. The same is true for a character in a play. So the actor who plays a character must activate the thoughts and feelings of his character in order to give sense and meaning to the character's actions. Thus, feeling and thought are always implicitly part of the action.

In rehearsals, in classes he taught, and in interviews and talks, Dutch actor and acting teacher Ton Lutz often said that "acting is thinking," and that "feelings are inappropriate" for an actor.[4] But the actual situation is not that simple. If it were, it would be taboo for an actor to have feelings while he acts, and his acting might be reduced to a thought-filled, mechanical activity. But what Lutz really means is that an actor doesn't have to engage *his own personal feelings* in order to give form to the feelings of the character he plays. In other words, he need not evoke within himself feelings he doesn't really have—which would be a kind of lie.

Moreover, what Lutz is pointing to is the fact that the actor, in order to play the action of a character, must make conscious decisions about which feelings and thoughts he wants to bring into play, and about how to give them shape. In other words, Lutz is not saying that acting is purely a cerebral matter, but rather that the actor must *think about* what he does and how he needs to do it.

Feelings and Thoughts Are Intertwined

Feelings and thoughts are interconnected processes—initiated in our central nervous system and the brain—which influence each other. A thought can provoke a feeling, and a feeling can provoke a thought. Sensations, like smell and taste, can also provoke feelings and thoughts. We do not have thoughts without having feelings, even if we are not always aware of this. For instance, we cannot think of chocolate ice cream without experiencing the sensory experience of its taste. If we could, our mouths wouldn't water at the thought, nor would that same thought remind us of the images and emotions of some long-forgotten birthday party. Similarly. we cannot feel pride about the accomplishments of our children without thinking of them. And feeling that pride, we become consciously aware of it, for it is not just a vague, nondescript glow in our chest, but a feeling that inspires us to describe our children's achievements to others. Or the other way around: the description of their achievements informs our feeling of pride. No matter how abstract and elusive these processes of thought and feeling may seem, they are, at the same time, very concrete because they actually take place in our bodies: they are physical events, activities that take place within our nerves and flesh and blood. And this means that they can also be provoked by physical actions. They entail mental and physical changes, which, with training, actors can become more and more aware of.

Playing the Result: Misunderstandings about Feeling and Thought . . .

Stanislavski's method of substitution and his technique of emotional memory have contributed to a misunderstanding: an acting mistake in which the actor identifies so entirely with his character that he *substitutes* his own feelings for those of the character. This method[5] is meant to be of help to the actor, but can sometimes lead instead to a real confusion between the feelings and thoughts of the actor and those that belong to the character. If the actor attempts to use his own feelings and thoughts while playing the character's action, he will often find himself playing the *effect* that the action had on him—rather than enacting the character's emotional life. This is exactly the sort of emotional mistake that Lutz has called "inappropriate," for if the actor allowed this to happen, his own feelings would mask the emotional life of the character. This error can occur because what happens in a play inevitably evokes feelings and thoughts in the actor. In fact, it is not only what *happens* in the play that evokes feelings in the actor, but also the *meaning* that the actor perceives in the play.

For instance: if the fate of a character evokes pity and sympathy within the actor playing the part, he may try to play the part "out of pity" or "with sympathy," but if he does so, he will end up playing a feeling instead of an action belonging to the character that had this effect on him. He is playing the *result*, instead of the original action—which may have included feelings and thoughts, which were quite pitiless and unsympathetic. This error can lead to sentimentality in the performance. Of course, an actor tends to look kindly upon a character. It's hard not to. After all, the actor is the one who embodies him. *The lesson here is that the actor can play actions, which will generate feelings and thoughts, but not feelings per se, when these are separated from or not connected with the action.*

Many acting teachers have suggested that an actor must love his character in order to play him. Perhaps this is necessary if he must completely identify himself with his character, as is the case in psychological realism. But it seems to lead to another misunderstanding. Film actor Russell Crowe said in an interview: "I don't love my role, I love my work." It is only necessary for the actor to *understand* the character he plays, from inside out and outside in. Does the actor understand his character better if he loves him? I think not. In fact, it is often a very good idea for the actor to be a little critical of the character, and a little mistrustful of his own emotional reaction to the character, and to search for emotions opposite those that the character's actions first evoke in him.

. . . and How to Avoid Them

In order to discover the feelings and thoughts of his character, the actor must first and foremost focus on the character's actions, not on his feelings and thoughts. He can begin by defining his character's actions with a *verb*, or a sentence with a central verb in it, that describes the action. Of course, such definitions are just hypotheses based on interpretation—a more or less abstract supposition about what the characters exactly are doing. It is during the rehearsal process that the actor will discover whether these hypotheses are right or need to be corrected—or perhaps even replaced—by others.

"Breaking down" the text bit by bit, as Lee Strasberg called it,[6] helps the actor to find a sense of the dramatic dynamics and structure of the play. By simply speaking a text, the actor can begin to understand the character's actions. He also will begin to experience the feelings and thoughts that go along with these actions. This doesn't mean that the actor immediately knows what these feelings are, or that he instantly is aware of the thoughts of the character. But even the simple act of speaking the text without knowing exactly what it means, or reading the text tonelessly and without interpretation, will evoke emotions in the actor because no action is neutral. *Speaking is an action itself, and actions produce emotions!* Moreover, these feelings and thoughts are not just the private feelings of the actor. If we consider the actor's voice and body to be his instruments, then reading and speaking a text is like striking a chord upon that instrument. The trained actor has an ear for this. He "hears" how the action resonates with certain feelings and thoughts within him, feelings that are not simply his own private feelings. And if he wants to try out another interpretation, or another take on the action, he will strike another chord and "hear" different tones and rhythms, which will produce different feelings and thoughts. This process is even more marked when the actor begins to move and to discover the physical dynamics of the character's dramatic action. As he does so, he will sense in his own body how his character is acting, not only what he is "doing," physically and dramatically, but also how his feelings and thoughts correspond with his movements, and vice versa. Thus, the actor begins to discover the physical and dramatic actions of the character. At this point he begins to use his body as the instrument he plays on; he "meets" his character and gets slowly acquainted with him.

When the actors start to move, the verb they have now in the back of their mind functions as a guide for their physical actions, a buoy to steer them on their voyage to the secrets of the character's actions, emotions, and thoughts. Their intuition will help them in their search, but the results will be so concrete that they will not be solely dependent on it anymore.

How to Play an Emotion

It is, of course, possible for an actor to begin rehearsing, without much reading beforehand, and with only a vague idea of what his character's emotional state is or what his action should be; it is usually during the rehearsal process itself that he will discover the emotions and "mental dispositions" he needs. At first these will only reflect the general "mood" the character is in. But as the rehearsal process continues, the actor will become more and more precise about the emotions that are generated by the actions he plays. He can search for precise words—nouns and adjectives—to name the feelings and thoughts, and these words can help him imagine those feelings and find just the right forms of expression for them. *Pride* or *proud* is not the same as *worry* or *worried,* and *anger* is very different from *sadness.* And since the actor knows how it feels to be proud or worried, or sad, or angry, he can physically embody this condition. As soon as he can become specific with his physical and emotional choices, the actor can also consciously experiment with other emotions for his character. *As long as he keeps focusing on his actions,* he may find other, more appropriate emotions that go along with them. In this way, the actor's work will keep deepening and evolving.

For instance, if the actor playing King Lear discovers that he would like to show the authoritarian nature of Lear's behavior from the very beginning of the play, he might try to do so by accentuating Lear's arrogance ("I am not only your father; I am also the king!"). But he begins with his action, which could be to "intimidate," to "shut up" everyone. Lear might act completely unapproachable, as if he has withdrawn into the ivory tower of his power. To show this physically, the actor could speak very quickly, never allowing others to speak and never really listening or waiting for an answer. He might draw immediate conclusions or even interrupts others. With his body, the actor might display both rigidity and a hypermobility—surprising perhaps for a man of Lear's age—the physical and emotional expressions of Lear's arrogance.

But it would also be possible for the actor to play Lear's peremptory behavior as an expression of his ignorance, as if he were childish or a demented old man—the very opposite of arrogant ("I'm the king, am I not?"). Lear's action could be "searching for love and support." The physical choices the actor makes to embody this approach will look completely different. Lear might still be a man who doesn't accept any form of contradiction, but now his behavior will appear more erratic, more whimsical, perhaps even more dangerous and unpredictable.

In my production of *King Lear* (Toneelschool Amsterdam, 1997) I asked my twenty-two-year-old Lear to try out the emotional state of a boyish naïveté, showing Lear's good-heartedness and joviality. The theatrical image we used for the first scene was that of a birthday party, complete with Stevie Wonder's "Happy Birthday" and presents like a Michelin map of the UK and a minigolf set—the sort of things you give to people when they retire. These gifts surprised the king, and he was taken aback for a moment or two. But mistrustful as he had become through years of unchallenged power, he began to test his daughters. When Lear asked his daughters to profess their love, he did so in the pleasant tone one might take at such a party. So then when Cordelia spoke, Lear's first reaction to her was amazement rather than anger. Her words seemed a surprise to him. A moment later his anger rose, which seemed to be a proof of his unpredictability, his senility even, and a sign that he didn't know what to make of Cordelia's answer, rather than an expression of hurt pride and inflexibility, or of his inability to relinquish his power. But the rest of the performance showed clearly that Lear was spinning out of control, and more and more losing his mind. This is how the actor, through the way he plays the action, can demonstrate the character's mood.

Motive

Motivation, within the convention of realism, is another important element with which the actor embodies his character. Motives are mainly psychologically based. For every action and every emotion there is a motive, or a series of motives. Literally, a "motive" is a "reason to move," and is therefore inextricably bound up with the action and precedes an action. Motives are made up of the thoughts and feelings that underlie the dramatic actions of the character, and at the same time they define his actions and the feelings and thoughts that go along with them. If we examine the motives that precede an action, we find two categories: *direct motives,* which are immediately related to the actions of the characters in the play, and *indirect motives,* which are related to what happens in the play but are not directly tied to the characters' actions.

Direct Motives

Within the category of direct motives, again there are two kinds of motives.

1. Motives that can be found in the history that *precedes* the play and are activated during the play, for instance, in *Hamlet,* the death of Hamlet's father and the following marriage of his mother with his uncle Claudius, which sets in motion the tragic events of the play; and in Ibsen's *Ghosts,* Mrs. Alving's husband's debauchery, which ends with his miserable death from syphilis and motivates her to protect her son Osvald.
2. Motives that appear *within* the play but precede a character's action. Such motives can once more be divided in two categories:
   a. The action of a character, which becomes the motivation for a following action by the same character—or of an action by another character.
   b. A series of actions or events, in which different characters act—like the apparition of the ghost of Hamlet's father, which becomes the motive for Hamlet to organize a theater evening for his mother and uncle Claudius, which then becomes the ultimate motive for Claudius and Gertrude to send Hamlet away to England and to have him killed, which, in turn becomes the motive for Hamlet's final revenge. In this case, we might think of motives and actions as being a chain (re)action. But since there is no action without feeling or thought, we can also say that Hamlet's indignation and confusion are reactions to what he learns from his father's ghost and lead to his suspicion, which in turn brings him to his decision about the theater evening for his parents.

Indirect Motives

Indirect motives can be found in four contexts: the given circumstances of the play, the historical context of the play, the social and political context of the play, and the psychological makeup of the characters.

1. The given circumstances, as Stanislavski called them, are factors of birth, social class, upbringing, place and time, specific circumstances such as fashion, or the infrastructure of a country or a city, but also other factors such as the weather or the high price of salt. They are important for the understanding and the interpretation of the behavior of the characters in a play.

2. The historical context of the play can have a big influence on the behavior of the characters, for human behavior is not fixed but changes with the changing times. From a modern point of view we look at the behaviors of a bygone era in a different light than did contemporaries. Behavior is the sum total of someone's actions, including his feelings, thoughts, and motives. Interpreting the behavior of the characters of a play is therefore not only a subjective matter, but also of the chosen historical perspective. There are actually three time periods to consider in this regard:

   a. The time in which the play takes place, in which factors of historical importance play a role for the interpretation of what happens in the play; for example, in *Macbeth* and *Hamlet* the middle and late Middle Ages, respectively.

   b. The time in which the play was written, which affects the writer's view of human behavior, for instance Shakespeare's views of power, of the rights of kings, and of usurpation in Elizabethan and early Jacobean times. The actions of the characters in *Hamlet* and *Macbeth,* as Shakespeare envisioned them, were subject to Elizabethan norms and values, rather than to those of the dark eras of the Middle Ages in which these plays take place.

   c. The time in which the play is performed, and in which the director and the actors are interpreting the events of the play from their contemporary point of view. For instance in the nineteenth century the Duke of Meiningen staged *Julius Caesar* from a historically accurate point of view. In the second half of the twentieth century Hamlet appeared often in dinner jacket, for instance in Thomas Ostermeyer's production at the Berliner Schaubühne (2000).

3. The social context affects all playwrights, from the authors of Greek tragedies to those of the most modern plays. The points of view from which plays are produced are subject to the current political and social makeup of society. This is most striking in productions of historical plays, when they are reinterpreted according to the needs of contemporary society.

4. Finally, many indirect motives can be attributed to the character structure of the people in a play, or to their psychological makeup. For Stanislavski the psychology of the characters in the plays he directed was paramount, for example, the inability to act and the assumed self-indulgence of the characters in Chekhov's plays. This psychological interpretation of the character's actions became the dominant trend in twentieth-century stage direction and acting. From this perspective, one could suddenly interpret Shakespearean characters, or characters from classical plays, according to their psychological makeup.

Just like the actions, feelings, thoughts, and direct motives we discussed earlier, these "indirect motives" are subject to interpretation. They simply lie hidden more deeply under the surface and belong to the realms of psychology and sociopsychology. The four possible indirect motives influence each other and are often interrelated.

Avoiding Speculation about Motives

Often a motive arises between one action and another. The motive may be caused by another action or by something within the psychological makeup of the character. This motivational thought or feeling then leads to the action, which follows it. But for the character, the motive is often quite unconscious. In real life we usually don't know why we do certain things, and we may discover certain explanations for our behavior only after the fact. The same is true for dramatic characters. Only on rare occasions do characters know exactly what the motives are for their actions—characters like Richard III, for instance, who is downright calculating and who seems to understand his own motivations and perhaps even fears them.

It is simply impossible to play a motive separate from an action, but during the rehearsal process the actor inevitably becomes aware of the motives of his character: they help him understand the character's actions, his feelings and his thoughts. In the reading phase and in later rehearsals there is often a great deal of speculation about character motivation, and often the motivations for a character's actions may be mistaken for actions themselves—or vice versa. This can cause a lot of confusion, and it can put the actor on the wrong track for a long time. It can even make it impossible for him to find choices that will work. So directors and dramaturges need to understand the distinction between character motivations and playable actions. If they do, they can help steer the actor away from needless discussions.

Intention

The last important element with which the actor embodies his character is *intention*. Like motives, intentions are inextricably bound up with the action of the character, and like motives, they are made of feelings and thoughts that lie behind the dramatic action of the character. In addition, through the action intention and motive are interconnected. But motives (reasons to move) *precede* an action, whereas intentions *disclose the purpose* of an action. Their fulfillment can come much later (and sometimes does not occur at all—or at least not in the way intended). Intentions are geared toward what is yet to happen. For example: I am hungry (motive for action); I decide to buy a loaf of bread (action) in order to still my appetite (intention). Similarly, Hamlet's *intention* in organizing an evening of theater for his family is to expose the foul play by his uncle Claudius and his mother. This is very clear when Hamlet gives his instructions to the actors. His *motive,* on the other hand, occurs in the beginning of the play, when his father's ghost makes him suspicious. Call it a long burn.

Sometimes characters in a play discover their true intentions only during the course of events. For instance, Serebryakov in Chekhov's *Uncle Vanya* discovers that he wants to sell the estate because he can't find the peace he first came for. Sometimes intentions shift during a play, contributing to the dynamics of the developing drama. For instance,

Lear's intentions shift several times during the course of events in the play. And sometimes the characters know from the outset what their intentions are, like Richard III, for example, who kills and manipulates in order to gain and hold the ultimate power.

But just as characters are often ignorant of their motivations, so too are they often ignorant of their intentions. They are, after all, human beings. But the actor still has to be aware of them, so that he can choose his actions clearly. We must note, however, that not every action has a conscious intention. Many actions are undertaken without an eye toward their later effects, so not every action is consciously calculated, although some people do have secret agendas. Moreover, as we can see in their actions, characters are often driven by contradictory intentions.

Speculation about Intentions and a Confusion of Words

Intentions, like motives, do not exist separately from actions. They are included in the actions, become visible as action, feeling, and thought, so *it is impossible to play the intentions themselves*. It is important not to be too speculative about them, just as with motives, because that approach can lead to a lot of confusion. In realism, when we talk about intentions, we inevitably get into a discussion of the psychology of the character. But as with motives, we must keep in mind that psychology is not something we can play: it's an academic discipline that studies the human psyche.

Very often the word *intention* is used to mean "emotion," or "action with an emotion." This confusion of the distinct notions of "intention" and "emotion" grows from the fact that every intention consists of feelings and thoughts. Intentions, like motives, are emotionally charged— whether they are rational or irrational. They are the breeding ground for feelings and thoughts, but they are distinct from them. The emotional content of the motives and intentions behind an action can be very different from the emotional content of the action itself.

The actor, Stanislavski suggested, must find the intention and motivation of the action in the inner life of the character he plays, in what he thinks and feels. This inner activity of thinking and feeling will become apparent in the way the actor expresses them physically. In fact, the inner life cannot be separated from the physical action, or become an aim in itself. Rather, it must feed the visible physical action and give life to it. To portray the actions of his character truthfully, Stanislavski suggested the actor must *live through the feelings and thoughts of the character, and to do that, he must employ his own feelings and thoughts*. The physical and emotional actions of the actor become the physical and emotional actions of the character. Thus the actor *identifies* with the character: he becomes one with him.

3 The Actor as Eyewitness to Social Processes: Brecht's Approach

"Not This, but That"

Stanislavski's acting technique of psychological realism was meant to ensure that the audience would experience the dramatic situation and the characters as a kind of substitute reality with which they could identify: the more truthful, or true to life, the characters were, the more believable their actions. Whether the audience really had such an experience depended not only on this new way of acting, but also on other, more material, factors, most importantly on the architecture of the theater (see the last chapter of this book).

Brecht's epic theater was meant to be an answer to what he called the "dramatic" or "Aristotelian" theater, which allowed audiences to identify with the fate of the characters on the stage.[1] He wanted the audience, instead of being emotionally carried away, to be able to assess a situation, to think about it. Emotions, Brecht maintained, make it impossible for the audience to do that.

His concept of epic theater is based on the study of social and political reality. His acting technique is meant to enable the audience to judge the actions of the characters on the stage. This is only possible when an audience can see that there might be alternatives to the way the characters perform their actions. Brecht called this idea the principle of "not this, but that." The actor has to show, through his actions, the choices the character makes in order to achieve what he wants to achieve: my character does "this," not "that." The actor should signal to the audience which choices the character has in the given situation. These choices are not psychological, but rather social, sociological, and sociopolitical.

The Actor as Eyewitness: The "Street Scene"

In epic acting the actor *is not* his role, but instead *demonstrates* him. Rather than hiding the fact that he is acting, the epic actor purposefully *shows* that this is what he is doing, by creating a *distance* between himself and the role he is playing. The "not this, but that" principle helps him to create this distance between himself and the role he plays. This doesn't mean that emotions are excluded from his acting, but it does mean that everything in Brecht's theater is focused on the character's— socially defined—*behavior,* not on his psychological makeup. Rather than *becoming* his role, the Brechtian actor "reports," as an eyewitness, on what his character *does,* on his *actions.* Feelings and thoughts, inevitably generated in the process, are equally socially defined.

In the famous "Street Scene"[2] from *Der Messingkauf* (*The Copper Transaction*), Brecht shows how he wants to bring this behavior about. The eyewitness to an accident tells the bystanders who have come flocking how it happened. While he does so, he demonstrates the incident and the behavior of the parties involved, of the victim just as much as of the chauffeur of the car. The eyewitness is not concerned about a precise or artistic imitation of the behavior of the people involved in the incident, nor about their emotions: he is not an actor, and he is not giving a performance, but he is just an accidental passerby who explains to the bystanders what he thinks has happened. This doesn't mean that there are no emotions involved; on the contrary: in order to get his story across, he has to show how he observed the emotions of the parties involved. In doing so, he doesn't identify with the people whose actions and emotions he refers to, he just demonstrates their behavior. The circumstances force him to proceed this way; even an actor would do it this way: he is on the street, it is in real-time reality that the accident took place, and he reports about it in the here and now. The bystanders want to know what exactly happened—with all the details! They are not there to applaud his acting. That's why he doesn't transform himself into the victim or the perpetrator. Yet he is able to vividly revive the accident in a visual and physical manner. He can quote the words of the victim when he saw the car coming; he can indicate the speed of the car by movement and by making the sound of it, just as he can demonstrate with his voice how hard the victim yelled when he was hit. With his briefcase—if he is a businessman—he can point out the route the car took, and with his umbrella he can show where the victim was before the impact. He can use himself to show why the victim couldn't get away in time. He is even able to repeat this account in front of the police, probably adding more details. He is not interested in the character of the people involved in the accident, but in their actions. Yet he is very involved with them. He does not merely report what he saw, but also gives his opinion: he takes a *point of view*. It goes without saying that, in Brecht's vision, this is a social point of view: "These bastards with their fancy cars, they think they own the street, they never watch out and the poor pedestrian can suffer for it!" Or quite the opposite: "These stupid pedestrians, they think they own the street, they never watch out, and when they're hit by a car, it's the driver's fault!" He ventilates his opinion in the way he, physically, demonstrates what he has observed. He *quotes* the words of the people whose story he tells, and in his *gestures,* sounds, and movements he *quotes* their actions.

This is what Brecht wanted the actor to do. The actor quotes the words and actions of the character he plays. He demonstrates them. The form this demonstration takes might have been rehearsed in its smallest details, but his performance looks like an improvisation.

Gestus

Brecht liked to compare the actor with the Chinese painter who, after years of study, throws in one brushstroke the essence of a reed on the canvas: one reed becomes all reeds in all seasons. It shows us the reed in the winds of spring, summer, fall, and winter; it shows us how its color changes, how it springs to life, and how it dies. That is how precise and detailed acting should be. With this example we also can see how physical epic acting is supposed to be: there is movement in the painting of the reed-of-all-seasons. Epic acting is very dynamic, condensed to the essence of the action, stripped bare of all superfluous dead weight, and full of meaning. Every gesture shows the possible alternatives.

With the word *gestus* Brecht tried to encompass all the elements of epic acting at once. It is not always clear what Brecht means by the word *gestus*. Sometimes it seems to mean the *physical action;* sometimes it is the *meaning* and *significance* we can attach to a physical action, which make the gestus into a *dramatic action*. This implies feelings and thoughts, motives, intentions, and objectives.

Brecht's gestus understood this way is very much like Stanislavski's *action,* but seen from a sociopolitical point of view. In addition, the term *grundgestus* signifies something similar to Stanislavksi's superobjective: the *grundgestus* is the sociopolitical meaning and purpose of all actions in a play.

Like Stanislavski, who wants the dramatic action to be defined by a verb, it is with a verb that Brecht wants the gestus to be defined. This verb is also for Brecht the most important tool for the actor: this is what he plays. Stanislavski's approach to human behavior is psychological; Brecht's is social and political. These different approaches have their effect on the interpretation of dramatic situations, actions, and texts.

Gesture and Attitude

The gestus includes both *gesture* and *attitude,* two other words Brecht introduced for his epic acting system. Again he does not make entirely clear what he means with these words. *Gesture,* obviously, is something physical, but it doesn't just mean gesticulation or facial expression, although these physical expressions are definitely part of it. Like gestus, gesture always refers to a social content.

The meaning of *attitude* is even more difficult and unclear. "Attitude" is the English translation of the German word *haltung*. Unfortunately, the meaning in English has become narrow, and the word therefore has a negative connotation. But *haltung* in German has a positive connotation. With *haltung* we relate to our own actions, feelings, and thoughts, and to those of others; things that happen, phenomena of all kinds, from war to weather, and even how we relate to objects. *Haltung,* in this meaning of the word, is an inner state, very much comparable to the complex of Stanislavski's *feeling, thought, motive,* and *intention.*

The word *haltung,* like *attitude,* has a physical component: it also means the *physical expression* of this inner state of mind. Brecht wanted his actors to express attitudes, rather than moods (feelings). They might be inspired by a social context, but looking at it closer, we see often that they are also psychologically inspired, and that they are emotional. Mother Courage shows emotions. So do her sons and daughter. So does Galileo in *Life of Galileo Galileï.* So does Grusche in the *Caucasian Chalk Circle.* So does Shen Te in *The Good Woman of Setzuan.*

The gestus of a scene might have been deduced objectively from the text of the scene, but the interpretation of it is subjective. Perhaps we should think of gestus as the expression of sociopsychological behavior as a result of social contradictions and conflicting interests, attitude as the emotional condition of the character defined by social and political factors, and gesture as the physical expression of these together. If the gestus is the action, the gesture and the attitude, with which the actor all at once embodies the character, like the Chinese painter who throws the reed-of-all-seasons on the canvas, then it explains the highly stylized form of Brecht's epic theater.

In his *New Technique of Acting,*[3] speaking about the actor's training, Brecht uses an example from *Mother Courage and Her Children* to clarify what he means by gestus: while Courage is doing some shady business with army supplies, she *admonishes* her son to be honest in all circumstances. This is the gestus of the scene. We immediately see the (social) contradictions: she is trading in order to survive, and at the same time she tries to bring up her son. Brecht also indicates how the actress could play this gestus, even in two different ways: Helene Weigel, in the Berlin performance (1949),[4] admonished her son not to listen in on the dirty trade, because it is none of his business; Therese Giehse, in the Munich performance (1950),[5] admonished the trader to continue talking while the boy is listening. Both used very specific, but opposite, physical gestures and attitudes. Weigel tried with her gesture, hypocritically (and didactically!), to separate the dirty deal she is about to close from the upbringing of her son. Giehse, cynically, showed her son how corrupt people including she herself are, thus making it a part of his upbringing: he should know that at an early stage. Not accidently Weigel performed her *Courage* in Communist East Berlin, and Giehse hers in capitalist Munich. Their gestures included the possible alternatives for this action: both had to make decisions for the continuation of the scene.

Motives Lie Primarily outside the Theater,
Intentions within the Play

In Brecht's epic theater concept motives for the actions of the characters lie outside the theater: on the street, in history, in the workplace and the dealing rooms of the stock market and on the battlefield. They are indirect motives, which have a direct effect on the behavior of the characters in a play.

For Maxim Gorki, Gerhardt Hauptmann, Maxwell Anderson, Clifford Odets, and other playwrights of the first part of the twentieth century, the sociopolitical context often took the form of an outcry against injustice, but Brecht saw his plays—at least his later plays—as an investigation, a Marxist analysis of the workings of social injustice, the contradictions of society, and the dialectical processes of change and progress. This perspective gave him a lot of room for showing conflict, and inevitably also allowed him to hint at "solutions" for the problems he described in his plays.

Brecht signals in his plays and stage directions that he was primarily interested in the historical-materialistic motives of behavior. The psychological motives he gives for someone's behavior are mostly materialistic in nature. For instance, Galileo's actions are inspired partly by pleasure seeking and partly by cowardice: he loves good food, and he fears pain. And Anna Fierling (Mother Courage) is an opportunist, a woman who sacrifices everything—all her children—to the financial gain of her transactions, and eventually to her own survival. Perhaps, however, one could describe Anna—and play the role—as a desperate gambler, a woman who, after her last loss, cynically—and against her own best judgment—bets everything on the next deal the war may offer her. But she suffers too, probably even more than other tragic characters, because she is aware of the choices she makes. Brecht doesn't deny that Anna Fierling is a tragic victim of the war and her own behavior, but he wants to emphasize that *she doesn't learn anything*.

As we can see in these examples, indirect motives from outside the play are interrelated with direct motives from inside the play. For example, the historical context of *Galileo* interrelates with both the sociopolitical context of the time and with Galileo's psychological character-structure.

Contrary to motives for the actions of the characters, their intentions lie entirely inside the play: they want to achieve something. Anna Fierling uses the war for a living and stubbornly negotiates through it. Galileo's intentions change from "making a living" to "defending the freedom of academic research" against the moral rules of the Church, and then to "survival."

It is clear that to play a character's gestus, actors have to study, especially the realm of motives and intentions. In the epic theater, which is more rational and analytical than emotional and "natural," the actor really needs to know and understand these motives and intentions from a perspective broader than his own intelligence and intuition. Speculation about them is impossible. Moreover, speculation about motives and intentions often leads to passionate political debates among the actors. But these debates we cannot play, nor can we play a political ideology. In Brecht's epic theater the actor can only play actions. And in order to do so, the actor also has to study the physical expression of people's behavior in real life. Moreover, as in Stanislavski's psychological realism, their actions have to be truthful and believable.

Amazement and Wonder

It is true that Bertolt Brecht didn't like to see actors primarily playing feelings or evoking feelings in the audience. But it is a misunderstanding to think that Brecht wanted to emphasize rational thinking only, or that his form of theater must be cold and cerebral. An actor or director who employs the formal stylization of the epic theater to exclude feelings, simply contributes to this misunderstanding. Brecht's gestus and haltung are, in fact, *dramatic actions with feeling and thought,* informed largely by notions about society and the political meaning of the action.

Brecht encouraged his actors to approach a text with "amazement and wonder" from the first reading, and by doing so to create a distance and a distinction between the feelings of the actor and those of the character. He didn't want his actors—or the audience—to take anything for granted. In particular, he didn't want either the actors or the audience to simply accept the ways in which a society is organized or functions. He wanted them to say: "Isn't that strange?" And: "How could that happen?" "Isn't it strange that King Lear questions the loyalty of his daughters after he has decided to divide the realm under them?" And: "Why couldn't Lear be less stubborn or more forgiving?" Or: "Isn't it strange that Mother Courage goes on with her business, even after she has lost all her children in the war?" And: "How is it possible that Mother Courage does not recognize her son and can sacrifice her daughter?"

The Alienation Effect

By showing "not this, but that," the alternative to the way his character performs his actions, the actor leaves space for a different choice. This space is performed physically through gesture and attitude, and in time and space. This highly precise and calculated (not impulsive) way of acting also gives space to the audience for thoughts about alternative solutions. But this principle often made Brecht's plays didactic, pointing the way to a solution for the obvious wrong choices a character makes.

In order not too easily to identify emotionally with the characters on the stage, the audience needs to be put at a further distance. For this purpose Brecht designed the *alienation effect*. In the "Street Scene" we have seen how the actor can create a distance by not identifying with the character, but by demonstrating and quoting him. In the all-encompassing gesture of the "not this, but that," the actor can show that what happens to the character is something very special and exceptional, and what he does is something the audience has to pay attention to. What the character does in his actions must not look "normal," like everyday life, but like something that has "historic proportions." The actor must show that life as it is is not normal. Nothing in life is normal—and nothing should be taken for granted. The audience should be brought to think that the most apparent things really are strange. *Alienation*, as Brecht uses the word, means literally "estrangement," making things look strange, alien. The actor must make the most obvious things of human life and behavior look strange. This too explains the stylization of the epic theater form.

Not only does the actor do this through sharply defined gestures and movements, but the stage does it too. The stage, in Brecht's concept, is not an imitation or a copy of reality, but rather a stylized space for the actions of the play. The alienation effect is very much a theatrical device, created by the actors and by the other features of the production, and designed to prevent the audience from emotionally identifying with the characters. Brecht introduced different theatrical devices to interrupt the ongoing action of the play. In fact, every theatrical device that can be used to make things look strange, alien, can be called an "alienation effect."

He inserted songs to interrupt the action and to comment on it ironically; plays within the play, loud announcements; narrators; and written scene titles or short descriptions of the core action of the following scene and the motives of the characters, which were projected on a screen. For example, in *The Resistable Rise of Arturo Ui,* there are projected newspaper headlines referring to the historical times, such as

1929–1932. WORLDWIDE SLUMP HITS GERMANY HARD. PRUSSIAN LANDOWNERS ANGLE FOR GOVERNMENT SUBSIDY—ATTEMPTS SO FAR UNSUCCESSFUL.

Meanwhile, The Announcer calls, like a newspaper boy: "New Developments in Dock Subsidy Scandal," and "Sensation at Warehouse Fire Trial," referring to the play. The effect was that scenes were like illustrations from a comic book.

By presenting the audience with a series of events that are interconnected but can be appreciated each by its own merits, instead of seeming to be an uninterrupted and unavoidable—tragic—flow of dramatic and fatal events, Brecht built upon the new tradition of the *montage,* which had recently been invented by the Dadaists, and further developed for the stage by Piscator. Placed side by side, these disconnected scenes created a consistent narrative of a new kind: one big story constructed or composed of a series of smaller stories.

The Chinese Actor

Brecht found a beautiful example of the type of acting he dreamed of in the Chinese theater, which he had a chance to observe during a visit to

Moscow. The Chinese actor "makes public that he knows that he is being watched by an audience." The actor has eye contact with the audience. He is, while he is acting, able to "observe himself," to "watch his own movements and gestures," and communicate this self-awareness to his audience. This means that he not only knows what he does when he acts, but also communicates to his audience that he knows it. This is like the circus clown who has permanent eye contact with the audience about the gag that he fails to accomplish . . . until he does accomplish it, to his own exhilaration and that of the audience, whom he has made into a witness of his efforts. For everything he does, the Chinese actor checks the tools he uses to create his character, in the same way the cook checks the knife with his thumb before he cuts the roast beef, or the tennis player plucks the strings of his racket and examines the ball before he serves. By this way of performing alone, the Chinese actor includes the act of performance in his show, and thus quotes the character he plays, rather than completely becoming him. The audience sees the actor, rather than identifying with the character he plays. His craft is based on physical action. The tools he uses are simple props and elaborate costumes and masks. The actor always stays visible while he acts; the audience observes him as an *actor at work*.

Taking the Chinese actor as an example, Brecht, without realizing it, refers to the *presence of the actor*. He wanted his actors, like the Chinese actor, to show not only the gestus of their characters, but also the *gestus of the acting itself*. Showing the gestus of the acting would ensure that the actor was, indeed, a true eyewitness to the character's actions. Brecht meant this display to be the most essential element of the epic acting style.

Part II

Acting in Real Time

4   The Technique

Presence of the Actor

The identity of an individual is defined to a high degree by what she does, and what she does is influenced by character structure, temperament, and all mental characteristics. External events—political and social history, the time period, factors like class and education—all affect how her internal characteristics manifest themselves.

From the outside, what we notice first about a character is her physical appearance. Then, looking more deeply, we identify all the idiosyncratic mental characteristics that distinguish her from others. Together with her actions, these elements comprise the character's "behavior."

The actor himself also has such characteristics, just like any other human being. The audience can recognize him by his physical shape and facial expressions, but his other qualities contribute more to his real identity.

As an actor, he uses his own personal qualities to play his roles. The very special thing about this is that he uses his own characteristics to embody another person, a person who has an identity of his own, with all his own idiosyncratic qualities and characteristics. The audience must be able to recognize this character's identity as believable and truthful. To make the character truthful, the actor must first be truthful to himself, and for that he must know himself as an instrument, just as thoroughly as a musician knows his instrument. He must also command sufficient acting technique to play upon this self-instrument. And just like the musician, he plays not only the notes—he also puts his soul in the music.

This is as true for the actor who performs within the tradition of realism as it is for the actor who performs in real time. The difference is that, due to the rules of the convention, the actor in realistic theater is forced to act as if he himself is virtually "absent," whereas the real-time actor is *present as himself.*

Double Function of the Actor

The real-time actor is not a storyteller in the traditional sense of the word, nor is he a stand-up comedian. Real-time theater is not storytelling theater, which is a term used for a specific genre of theater, nor is it a form of cabaret.

However, the real-time actor *does* tell the story of the play: by playing it, by acting out his role(s), *and* by being present on the stage as himself. We can call the real-time actor a narrator of plays, dramatic situations, and characters. At one moment the actor is the pure "narrator of the play" by being present as himself; at the next, he is the "narrator who plays a role." In real-time theater there are always two levels of action. That is the double function of the actor.

His first "through-line of action" is the acting itself—his work as an actor. Brecht would call it the "gestus of the acting itself." Through pure theater actions he *stages* himself in the actions of his character. This second level of action is most of the time not ongoing through the whole play, but is interrupted by actions of other characters and is therefore fragmented. The real-time actor steps into his role and out again, and watches the action of the play as it unfolds. He can even "watch" himself while he is acting his role. This is *what* the real-time actor does: Stanislavski's first *W, who,* coincides with the second *W, what.* After all: we are what we do.

And *why*—the fifth *W*—does he do this? That's very simple: because it is his profession or his avocation, because he is passionate about it, because he enjoys it, and because the play demands it from him.

And *what for*—the sixth *W*—for *what purpose* does he do this? So that he can tell the audience something that he wants to share, or that he can entertain the audience, and give them a beautiful or meaning-ful experience.

This doesn't mean that the real-time actor doesn't have to do his homework on the character he embodies. He still has to answer the questions posed by the four-plus-two *W*'s for the character he plays.

The central task of the real-time actor is to maintain the separation of his two functions, so that the audience can perceive both beings at once. As narrator of the play, the actor is seen by the audience as him-self: the actor. As the narrator who plays a role, he is seen simultane-ously as the actor *and* as the character he plays. The real-time actor is a *transparent* actor, an actor who remains visible to the audience *through* the character he is playing.

Feelings and Thoughts of the Character / Feelings and Thoughts of the Actor

When he is acting, an actor is *using* his body and mind, thoughts and feelings as an instrument to give shape to his character's physical ac-tions, thoughts, and feelings.

But because the actor's thoughts and feelings are not the same as those of the character, the actor is not sad when his character is sad—in fact, tonight he may feel quite happy, while his character feels ex-tremely sad. And tomorrow he may feel differently.

In both the realistic and the epic theater, the actor himself seems ab-sent. Behind the fourth wall,[1] it is hard for him to signal to the audience that the feelings and thoughts he produces are not his feelings and thoughts, but only those of his character.

In real-time theater, however, rather than feeling sad himself, the ac-tor makes performative choices to play the sadness of his character. By using his presence on stage to create a distance and a distinction be-tween himself and his character, he signals that he "only" gives form to the thoughts and feelings of the character he is playing. The act of "per-forming" is itself a purposeful activity, involving thoughts and feelings of himself. The actor's feelings and thoughts can shine right through the character's sadness. In *Allein das Meer / The Same Sea* (my stage adap-tation of the novel by Amos Oz, Neues Theater, Halle a.d. Saale, Ger-many, 2005–6), the actress who played Nadia told the story of her dying: the pain, the confusion, the slow process of losing her grip, of drift-ing away, but she did this in a very calm manner, with wonder, curios-ity, and sometimes even slight amusement: not acting as if she were feeling the pain of dying herself, but investigating compassionately Na-dia's pain. She gave words to Nadia's observations and the sensations that went through her. As she told the heart-wrenching story of Nadia's death to the audience, she was simply sitting in a chair, looking at the audience, eyes wide open, sharing with them Nadia's suffering, usually with a slight smile on her face. The other actors watched her from a dis-tance. Then she got up from her chair as the *actress who played Nadia,* walked over to join them, on the way making a halt to watch a stream of white sand flowing down the ceiling. Nadia's dying became in this way a process for everyone to witness. The audience was often sad, but the actress could feel good about herself.

All actors experience this duality of thought and feeling, but in the realistic and the epic theater, they must hide the thoughts and emo-tions they are experiencing as actors—for when these thoughts and emotions are allowed to coexist, their joy can seem to be an undesired comment on the sadness. In real-time theater the actor creates, through his presence, a kind of *transparency of means,* which he applies to per-form the actions of his character. One important element of the tech-nique of real-time acting is to create *the time and the space* the actor needs in order to show how he plays the actions of the character. This leaves the real-time actor with freer access to his instrument than has the actor who must hide himself within the character. It also allows him the freedom to show the audience which feelings and thoughts are his and which are those of the character.

No Need to Justify Oneself

Within the realistic convention, where the proscenium arch separates the actors from the audience, the actor may feel a strong need to *justify* his presence on the stage. He needs to know who he-as-the-character is, where he comes from, where he is going, and why he does what he does. Otherwise he feels he cannot play—or even be present—as the character. He may even feel that he, the actor, does not exist if he doesn't understand the motivations for his character's actions. That all may be true, but the motivation of the character's actions must not be confused with the actor's justification for being on stage.

Brecht invented "alienation effects" to escape the traps of realism. But in both conventions, the actor must justify his presence on the stage on the basis of the dramatic situation of the play. The identity of the actor and the character remain enmeshed.

In real-time theater, however, the actor "knows" the motives of the character's actions, without having to identify with them. The particular actions of a character must still be motivated, but, as we have seen, the actor is also performing the "gestus of the acting itself." He shows that he knows things the character does not know. The real-time actor says to his audience: "This is me, the actor, and this is my character," just as a modern puppet player allows both himself and his puppet to share the stage. Disengaging from the character, the actor says: "Look, now my character is doing this, and now he is doing that." Thus he *consciously* allows the audience to witness, what his character is doing *unconsciously*.

For the real-time actor, there is no other reality than the stage, no other time than the time on the clock, no other activity than his act of creating a role. He is not only able to share with the audience the actions, thoughts and feelings of the character he plays, he also signals how he gives these a theatrical form.

In real-time theater, the actions and feelings and thoughts of the characters are ultimately "motivated" and "justified" by the actors who connect the actions of the characters to each other: they become *necessary,* instead of *inevitable,* only because the actors make them happen.

Therefore, the presence of the actor is justified and motivated by the acting itself, that is, by the simple fact that *he has a story to tell to the audience. It is not the dramatic situation that justifies his presence, but the reality of the stage.* There is no confusion about who he is: he is, first and foremost, the actor-who-plays-the-role. This essential reality constitutes the starting point of a whole new aesthetic for the theater.

The Actor Makes His Presence Known

In real-time theater the actor acknowledges his distance from the character *by making his own presence visible.* It is he himself who sees the audience, who hears it, feels it, smells it and, perhaps, even touches it. And the audience knows it. In other words, he and the audience communicate directly with each other.

For the actor there are many ways to make his presence known. One of them is a very simple device, which I used in several productions. In Brecht's *Fear and Misery in the Third Reich* (Theater Academy, Maastricht 1981), in *Kassandra* (my adaptation of the novel by Christa Wolf, Southern Comfort, 1988), and in *Mephisto (2)*[2] (my adaptation of the novel by Klaus Mann, Hummelinck Stuurman, 2006), the actors opened the play by telling the audience which roles they would be playing. In this way an actor can show to the audience that he is the actor, and that he will merely be playing upon his acting instrument to create his role. For the audience, in this moment, the actor becomes one of them.

It's a simple device, a good way to begin, and very much the same way Shakespeare ends some comedies, like *Twelfth Night* and *All's Well That Ends Well,* or Brecht begins and ends some plays, like *The Exception and the Rule* and *The Resistable Rise of Arturo Ui.* It gives the audience immediate access to the actor and to the character the actor plays: it demystifies the character rather than glorifying him. It permits his behavior to be criticized and scrutinized rather than making it inscrutable. It makes it a subject for discussion, placing the actor, his role, and the audience all in dialogue with each other. And while these choices distance the actor from his role, they also place him in the same reality as the audience. This allows the audience to feel closer to the character in a new way.

Thus *distance creates proximity.* This is a new paradox, but it is a paradox that is workable and a source of pleasure for both the actor and the audience.

Action of the Acting Itself

Here are a few applications and effects of the actor's presence as himself:

1. The character is pursuing the dramatic action as it is written in the play, but because of the *action of the acting itself* there is a noticeable difference between the dynamic of the actor and that of the character: as the actor he can stand still and keep silent while he is

watching; the next moment, as the character, he can run, jump up and down, be involved in an argument or a fight, sing a song.

2. The actor transforms publicly, in front of the audience, from *being* himself into *playing* his role. In this way, the actor gives the word *transformation* a very practical meaning: here transformation means the way in which the actor begins the action of playing his character—in full view of the audience. This is quite different from the realistic theater actor who, out of view of the audience, attempts to *change into* the character he plays, a character—imaginary or not—who preexists in the text of the play and whom he attempts to imitate, as truthfully as he can.

   The real-time actor can accomplish what Brecht desired in epic theater: that the audience be able to pay attention to *how* each character behaves. For the character's behavior now is visible in *how* the actor takes on the character and *how* he develops him each time he is "on." The old unspoken truth that "the actor is not the role, but plays the role" takes on a new, more tangible reality: the audience is no longer tempted to identify the actor with the role he is playing; and the actor is no longer in danger of losing his identity in the character.

3. By *staging* himself into the role, the actor not only starts, but also stops playing the role when his scene is over. As a consequence, he *doesn't need to make an entrance or an exit, to begin or end a scene.*

4. The actor can take on (many) different roles and, if necessary, change his costume.

5. Instead of waiting in the wings for his next cue, or drinking coffee, playing cards, or watching TV in the green room, the actor, through his permanent presence, will be personally engaged with the story of the whole play, and the role he plays in it. On top of that, he isn't confined to thinking only about his own role: he can also be concerned with all the other characters in the play. Their actions are a part of his story, and he is part of their story. And he is there when he is needed.

6. The actor's *preparation* for the role doesn't take place privately, "in the wings," but publicly and in relation to the play as it unfolds before his very eyes. This can be a great help and support for the actor: he knows he is not alone out there. The story that is being told gives him his cues and prepares him for his next "entrance."

He has a better chance to develop his part, through his continuous presence.

7. The actor's new relationship to the play also changes his relationship to the stage itself. It is no longer an imaginary location, but a concrete, real place where the actors play their play.

8. Through his presence the actor sets and keeps the play in motion. It is he who makes it happen; the play doesn't happen to him, as by magic. The dynamics of the performance are entirely in his hands, and that fact is not hidden for the audience.

Two Realities

The actor's functions as narrator of the play and narrator of the role can be performed in alternating fashion or simultaneously. If alternating, the actor as narrator of the play is sometimes playing his role and sometimes just present, watching. This may seem to be a very simple principle, but it isn't. In fact, in practice, it appears to be one of the most difficult things for an actor to do: not acting. If the functions are simultaneous, the actor as the narrator of the role becomes the *creator* of the character. As its creator, he can show the means he uses to embody the character: his own instrument, and all the tools of the theater.

Some examples of each approach may be useful here.

Alternating. In Ariane Mnouchkine's play *Mephisto (1)*[3] (her adaptation of the Klaus Mann novel), theater director Magnus Gottschalk and his wife, the Jewish actress Miriam Horowitz, decide during their last scene together to kill themselves by jumping from a railway bridge when a train is approaching. The first time I directed this play (Theater Academy Maastricht, 1983), I myself played Gottschalk. After their last talk, I disengaged myself from the actress who played Miriam, walked downstage to the sound equipment, pushed the button to play the sound of an approaching train, walked back, joined my partner, and let the sound of the thundering train overtake us as we stood there hand in hand.

Thus, I had staged our suicide, or more precisely, I had staged the suicide of the characters we were playing. I did this as myself, in my function as actor. The moment that I stepped out of my role I became

the pure narrator-of-the-play and I "watched" the action of my character. At the same moment, my partner also stepped out of her role and
watched me handle the sound system. As the character, I didn't really
do anything at all. Yet as the actor, I was the perpetrator of this death,
because it was I who caused the frightening sound of the thundering
train that rushed over the stage. This had an enormous impact on the
audience.

The action of the pure narrator-of-the-play was more than just
watching, but by staging this action myself, I—the actor—had to help
the characters' suicide, and in so doing I added a theatrical image to the
dramatic action. This staging was an image for the intentionality of suicide, because anybody who wants to kill himself must do so deliberately: he has to make a plan and he has to organize the whole terrible
and ultimate thing. So in a way, he must really "step out of himself."
Performing this moment was the first time that I personally experienced the power of being present on stage as oneself, and how difficult
it can be: when I stepped out of the relative protection of my role for the
first time, I could feel my knees wobbling.

Similarly, in Anton Chekhov's *Ivanov (1)* (Theater School Amsterdam, 1995) the actor who played Ivanov interrupted his scene with
Sasha in act 2 in order to lower the lights for his romantic declaration of
love. This again was a pure theater action of the pure narrator-of-the-
play, which added something to the dramatic action of the scene: with
humor and irony the actor created an image for secrecy, intimacy, and
Ivanov's sentimentality.

Finally, an actor who is merely watching the other actors play can
give extra meaning to the dramatic action that is unfolding before him.
In *Black Box* (my adaptation of the novel by the Israeli author Amos Oz,
Southern Comfort / Hummelinck & Stuurman, 1999) the characters Manfred Sackheim, Alexander Gideon, and Michael Sommo were negotiat-
ing about the sale of some real estate from the family's possessions. But
as they negotiated, all the actors in the company were present on stage;
the whole group sitting with their backs to the audience, the men with
their yarmulkes and the only woman with a shawl draped around her
head. These actors, without having to act anything, created the image
of a Jewish temple just by watching. And although all they did was
watch—though the woman, Ilana, sometimes dropped in and out of
the action—their presence added a feeling of embarrassment for the

characters in this violent dispute, especially when it finally was fought out between Sackheim and Gideon, excluding Sommo from the deal they were making over his head.

Simultaneous. In *King Lear* (Theater School, Amsterdam, 1997), when the character Gloucester has his eyes put out, the actor who played Gloucester grabbed for the sponge that he had put under his chair before the scene started. As the character, he used the sponge to ease the terrible pain, while as the actor, he pressed it against his eye to squeeze out the stage blood that then ran down his face—though because he was screaming of pain, this action was not at all funny. After this moment, he put the sponge calmly away in order to undergo the second part of his torture, thus becoming, once more, the *pure narrator-of-the-role.*

In Brecht's *Man Is Man (2)* (Tisch School of the Arts, New York, 2007), the actor who played Sergeant Fairchild held a little puppet of a soldier, whose penis was attached to a string. The actor held the string, while he went through the agonizing process of deciding to castrate himself. Another actor filmed this process in a close-up that was projected on a screen. Then, when he finally pulled off the miniature penis, he fell with a loud scream of pain against the wall behind him and then onto the floor. The other actor turned the camera off and put it away.

Making a "Proposal"

What Brecht wanted to achieve by the alienation effect, real-time theater can achieve with the sheer presence of the actor. Using the distance between himself and the character, the actor can demonstrate the distinction between the actions of his character and what he, the actor, is thinking and feeling about those actions. The actor playing Lear, for instance, can show that the king's arrogance is a *choice* that he, the actor, made for him. In this way, perhaps Lear's arrogance can be viewed with compassion or pity. Or in the suicide scene in *Mephisto (1),* we, the actors, could show that we were shocked by the calm determination with which Miriam and Gottschalk faced suicide. Such actors' choices can, in turn, help the audience experience Lear's arrogance, or Miriam's and Gottschalk's desperate resignation as *possible behavior* rather than as *fated, inevitable events* or *accomplished facts.* They are options one might want to discuss, *proposals,* as Brecht would say. In this way, real-time theater can achieve exactly what Brecht wanted his epic theater to achieve: to stimulate thinking and debate in the audience.

Members of the audience watching my production of *Ivanov (1)* sometimes became quite angry at Ivanov's moral indignation, so much so that they felt the urge to protest against the overt "honesty" with which Ivanov defended his actions, for they could see how hypocritical it was. And in *The Three Sisters* (with professional actors and students of the Actors and Directors Department, Theater School Amsterdam, 2001), more than once the audience felt the need to answer Versjinin, as the actor seemed to be inviting them to debate the character's philosophical musings.

Conditions for the Presence of the Actor

In order to be present—and to make his presence known to the audience—an actor must do several things. It all begins with his *will* to be there and his desire to tell the story of the play—his *commitment, enthusiasm, conviction, pleasure, eagerness,* and *passion.* Then he has to overcome his self-consciousness over being observed by the audience, and to use his awareness of his presence on the stage to mobilize his powers of observation (with his eyes and ears, with his other senses, and with his intuition).

The ability to observe is something that can be developed and trained. But the other states of mind—commitment, enthusiasm, and so on—are primarily personal qualities. They are not tasks that a director can elicit by giving directions, or skills that an acting teacher can train with specific exercises. Instead they are energies that reveal themselves of their own accord if the director/teacher is able to create an open, trusting, creative, and encouraging workspace, and if the actor is ready to

- Give up the relative safety that is usually offered to him within the conventions of realism and the proscenium arch stage.
- Overcome his fear of exposing himself if he does not hide behind the mask of a role.
- Take the risks of entering terra incognita.

The Actor as Host, the Audience as Guests

In real-time theater the actors can be present when the audience enters the theater. With their presence they welcome the audience, which does not need to wait for the actors to appear. The actors are the hosts, and the members of the audience are their guests. This change from what normally happens in conventional theater is not a directorial trick or artistic novelty to be used once or twice and replaced by another clever device. On the contrary, this arrangement is one of the essential characteristics of real-time theater, just as in the traditional theater, for hundreds of years now, actors have come on from the wings or entered in the dark.

The slight excitement before a performance starts is now something that both the actors and the audience share and can sense at once. The actors are a little tense and the audience is a little nervous, but the informality of this situation is reassuring to both parties.

With this arrangement, it is no longer necessary for the stage to go to black before the performance starts, and this is also reassuring, both for the actors and for the audience. Since the actors are already present on the stage, they don't need a blackout to take their positions on stage as the characters they play; real-time actors can move in full light. They don't need the mystery of darkness to transform themselves into their characters. They begin to play as soon as the doors close, the audience is seated, and the lights and houselights have changed for the performance. The actors and the audience both see these changes, and they share the experience of entering the performance. These changes may seem small, but they are invaluable artistic and psychological factors that contribute to the effect of real-time theater.

When and Where Does the Play Take Place?
Now and Here!

Being "present" means being *here* on the stage, and *now*, in this very moment, the time of the performance itself—from the moment the audience enters the theater until the end of the show. This means that the separation between the "real time" of the audience and the "imaginary time" of the play is eliminated. It also implies that the whole of the performance takes place in *real time*, which is the same for the audience as for the actors.

As a consequence of this *the acting itself becomes real*, while *what is acted* (i.e., the play) can remain an *illusion*. In this way, actors and audience are both freed from the need to pretend something they both know is not true. In the undivided present moment, real-time theater presents an illusionary time without denying the "real time" on the clock. This creates another bond between audience and actors and promotes their direct communication.

The Real-Time Actor Is Like a Musician

Many actors feel insecure on stage and are consumed with stage fright. This is very understandable: they are "naked" out there on the stage, and vulnerable. The realistic theater provides a seeming protection from this vulnerability by allowing the actor to hide himself behind the role he plays. But the confusion this brings about actually enhances his insecurity: in the realistic theater the identity of the character takes precedence over the actor's own identity. The result of this is that the actor can feel that, on stage, he has a double identity, one of which he must hide or deny.

The real-time actor isn't troubled by this double identity: *he uses his own identity to disclose the identity of the character he plays*. He doesn't have to claim that "I am whom I play," or that "I always play a role when I'm on stage." He doesn't have to leave his own identity behind in the dressing room; he takes it with him onto the stage.

It certainly takes courage and confidence for an actor to do this. But once he has overcome his initial fears, he will find that "being with the audience" can be a very reassuring thing. The real-time actor is making a full disclosure to the audience—an honest pact that makes him more comfortable on stage and allows him to take greater risks. There's no place for vanity and arrogance here: such personal traits would be too obvious, and could even become embarrassing. The honest pact with the audience allows the real-time actor to take more risks, be more courageous, and ultimately be more "naked" and transparent on stage. It allows him to focus more fully on creating his role, and it allows the audience to recognize the actor's creative work in this effort, and to love him for it.

Musicians—soloists and ensemble players alike—are always present on stage as themselves, when they play and when they don't play. When they don't play, they watch and listen closely to the other musicians, and they are ready to jump in when it is their turn. When they do play, they pay attention to the sheets of music on their stand, to the conductor, and to each other. If you look at how (jazz) musicians watch each other, playing and not playing, you will often observe the beautiful moments when their eyes and body language show how much they appreciate what another musician just has done, or how much they like the harmony they just played together. The real-time actor inhabits the stage in this same way. The musician is his example.

Instruments of the Actor 1: Imagination

With his imagination the actor can see the character before his inner eye, and in this way get closer to the character and begin to understand him: imagination is *seeing with the inner eye,* and *hearing with the inner ear.* Observation, memory, and experience help the actor to develop his imagination. The actor has to be able to picture with his inner eye what his character is doing (his action), what his motives are, and what intentions, feelings, and thoughts inspire those motives. All these imaginary elements arise within the actor during the rehearsal process, and need to be repeated during the performance: if the actor "sees" the action of his character, the audience sees it too. Imagination is not a passive source, like a picture in a book; it is a driving force for rehearsal and performance alike.

Imagination is not the same as fantasy. Fantasy can be stimulated by what we see or observe, or experience, so it may be aroused by the text of a play as well. Fantasy doesn't have boundaries; it is not reigned in by concrete facts, or certain givens of time and space. Fantasy is completely free. But in a play, we are dealing with concrete facts of action, and things that happen in time and space. So, even if it begins with fantasy, we need to use our *imagination* to be able to "picture" what really happens in the play, and to give it form.

In the convention of naturalism and psychological realism, the starting point for the imagination is the givens in the text of a play. In realistic plays we usually find extensive descriptions of the external circumstances and the disposition of the characters. Bernard Shaw, for example, became famous for his prefaces, which were sometimes longer than the plays themselves.[4] These stage directions, which are meant to inform us about the psychological makeup of the characters and about how they look and behave, function alongside the text itself as a sort of model or *mold* after which the actor can *cast* his character. If, according to the stage directions, a character laughs or yawns, the actor, according to the "rules" of psychological realism, will find that gesture by imagining how his character would laugh or yawn. The actor identifies with the character he portrays, inhabits that character's body and soul, and disappears within him. With the help of examples from reality, the actor forms a picture in his mind of the psychological and physical makeup of his character, which he then tries to copy or imitate. If the actor has to play an old man, for example, he will study the movement patterns of old men: he may stoop, or shuffle step by step, talk slowly, with a crack in his voice, and little by little transform himself into an old man. Costumes, props, and set help him to do this, and make it easier for him to enter the historical reality of the play. In the tradition of realism, the actor must closely fit in the "mold" in order to play the part. If he is lucky, he can create this mold himself. But usually this is already done for him: an older actor whose temperament, physicality, and charisma correspond with kingliness will probably be cast to play King Lear.

The convention of the epic theater also follows this procedure, except that the plays written in this style are much more parsimonious, without such detailed descriptions of the external and internal circumstances or the characters. The inspiration for the actor's imagination in the epic theater comes primarily from the social and political circumstances of the play. The epic actor must study models from the social and political situation and the context of the character's social status, aiming to distill his perceptions into a single "gesture." Often such gestures are highly stylized—enlarged, sometimes with the help of masks or grotesque costumes—or minimized to a single movement with the hand, in order to express the essence of the action in the play.

The actor in epic theater often becomes more extreme in his acting choices than the realistic actor might. He needs highly developed physical and vocal skills. The actor who plays an old man in the epic theater convention will not emphasize the man's age, but rather the social and political authority that he derives from his age. What he does in this "function" determines his "gestures." To enact a character like Lear, the epic theater would probably emphasize the unpredictability of his worn-out power, his social isolation, and finally his madness, as Kurosawa[5] did in *Ran,* his film version of the play.

In real-time theater the actor needs his imagination not only to picture what the characters in a play are doing, but also to find a theatrical form for his character's actions. He searches for *theatrical images* for the dramatic action and the events in a play, not just for portrayals or for the imitation of the dramatic situation. These theatrical images are meant to *illuminate,* not to illustrate, what happens in the play. So the actor's imagination is trained not only on the content, but also on the form, and his creativity influences the "directorial" choices of the production. Physicalization and visualization are essential in this approach.

Focusing mainly on the dramatic action, actors don't put their bodies and voices at the disposal of their characters in their efforts to *portray* them; instead they use their acting instruments for both the creation of their characters and the construction of theatrical images. This means, for instance, that a production of *King Lear* doesn't necessarily require a realistic representation of his castle or of the battlefield: the stage can be bare or filled with tin soldiers. Alongside the stage-space itself, lighting, and set design, the actors create theatrical images to clarify the dramatic actions. These images need not "symbolize" anything; they can stand on their own and tell the story of the play in their own way; they add something to the play that we usually don't find in stage directions; they allow new perspectives and interpretations of the play.

The actors use their own means of expression: their bodies and voices—rather than those of their characters—to perform their interpretation of the text. They employ their own acting instruments and energy to create images with which to tell not only *the* story of the play, but also *their* story of the play and how they relate to it.

Theatrical Images, Not Illustrations

Arthur Schnitzler's play *The Green Cockatoo*[6] takes place in a basement café during the hectic days in Paris just before the French Revolution, but in my abbreviated version of the play, which was combined with Jean Genet's *The Balcony* (Genet/Schnitzler, *The Balcony with the Green Cockatoo;* Theater v/h Oosten, Arnhem, 1989),[7] the actors created a theatrical image by filling the proscenium with a chaotic line of chairs of many periods—including Louis XVI chairs. Among these chairs, the actors appeared in modern dress. The characters were the-actors-who-perform-a-revolution and gentry-who-watch-the-grueling-spectacle-of-their-own-downfall. The actors in this production didn't play the hysteria of the revolution-actors or the horror of the gentry-audience, nor did they portray the confusion that follows upon the outbreak of a real revolution. Instead, they showed a careful astonishment, a slight amusement, and an almost scientific curiosity while in the meantime they dressed up in oversized costumes for *The Balcony,* which they were going to play next. This setup changed the dynamic of the play completely, and opened an unexpected view on the phenomenon of revolution: it disclosed the social mechanisms that manipulate the public's perception. Our choice showed this to be the central issue in both plays.

The theatrical image for the action of the play—actors dressing up, standing amid a row of chairs that they would use later—was not directly connected with the dramatic situation of the play. It stood on its own to show how reality can be manipulated. Without attempting to "portray" the characters, or even hinting at a representation of the depicted situation of the play, the actors created an entirely new image to reveal what happens in the play, which image could *illuminate* the play's meaning as we saw it.

In the scene of *Black Box* that I mentioned earlier (the negotiations between Manfred Sackheim, Alexander Gideon and Michael Sommo) the idea for the temple arose by memory and association. The actors themselves used just a few chairs in a row to create an *image,* which gave the scene a framework. This was a very concrete image, but not an imitation of the real reality: men and women don't sit together in a Jewish temple, and they were ostensibly the actors, not people who attended a service.

In the same play, while Alex and Ilana played their final dialogue, all the other actors brought their chairs and gathered on the small wooden platform, which sat in the middle of the stage. They simply watched respectfully while Alex and Ilana spoke, but by being there together, they created the image of a close family, in spite of their differences. Audiences sometimes interpreted this as an image for the country of Israel.

In *Allein das Meer / The Same Sea* the actors, sitting closely around Nadia, listened to her telling the story of her first marriage in Bulgaria. In the beginning they stood together looking at Albert, mourning over the death of his wife Nadia. Later we saw the same group when she died. In all three moments, they were not playing roles. They were just there on stage as themselves, listening and watching, but they created images of family, mourning crowds, and spectators.

There are also more abstract, expressionistic or purely physical images. In *The Balcony with the Green Cockatoo* we used a repeated action to create the image of defeat. In the scene in which Chantal, one of the prostitutes in the brothel, is killed and thus becomes the symbolic hero of the revolution, the Police Commissioner and the other Dignitaries were assembled on the balcony of the brothel (a table turned on its side by the actors) looking out over the stage and into the audience. The actress playing Chantal came running out of the corner from the theater and dropped on the floor. The actress got then up, walked quietly back, as herself, and repeated this heroic gesture of death twice in exactly the same way, but every time physically more strained and finally exhausted. Her run as Chantal, together with her walking back as herself, was like a dance. At first the Dignitaries reacted nervously, but at the end of Chantal's third run they got their composure back: the victory was theirs. By repeating this physical action, the Dignitaries got a chance to overcome their insecurity.

Usually theatrical images originate from the dramatic action: what happens in a scene gives us the cue for the theatrical image. Sometimes they can also originate outside the dramatic action to be added as a pure theater-action or as a part of the stage or of the design of the space. When there is enough "space between the lines of the text," there is room for such images. The process can also work in the reverse fashion: theatrical images can create a "space between the lines of the text." Theatrical images often originate within the transformation between actor and character. The suicide scene in *Mephisto* (*1*) is a good example of an image that developed directly out of this actor-character gap.

In *Black Box* the actor who played Boaz moved several chairs from upstage to downstage while he argued with his stepfather, Michel, who stood on the opposite side of a small wooden floor. The wooden floor separated them—both physically and emotionally—but the chairs had nothing to do with the dramatic action. On the practical level, the chair movement served simply to change the arrangement of the stage, so that the chairs would be in position for the next scene. But the actor who played Boaz moved the chairs with great energy and precision, helping him show that Boaz had to restrain his rebellious anger against his stepfather; thus this pure theater-action added very strongly to the dramatic action but did so without any symbolic significance. Afterward, many people asked us what this action "meant." We could only say, "That's up to you. He's moving the chairs." The image of the chairs originated outside the dramatic action; it took place at the same time.

Often directors are tempted to *substitute* an image for the dramatic action, attempting to *illustrate* or *symbolize* the dramatic action rather than illuminate it. I myself fell into this trap with *The Three Sisters*. In Chekhov's play, the character Chebutykin throws a clock and breaks it. We had several clocks on the piano, but we found throwing them down too literal, so we had the actor push a button releasing a curtain, which came falling down. It was a beautiful and purely theatrical image, but, as it turned out, it merely symbolized and illustrated the dramatic action rather than illuminating it. We should have taken advantage of the space between the text, have the curtain coming down as a pure theater action, not as an emotional impulse of the character Chebutikin. Sometimes it is hard not to paint red roses red, and often one does not realize that this is what one has done until much later.

In *Black Box* again, the actors who played Alex and Ilana strolled three times from upstage to downstage and back again. At this point in the play, the ex-couple could relax about their past relationship and could talk about it, the way one does when strolling in a park. But they did not actually walk *as if* they were strolling through a park. Their strolling did not refer to a park in any way; it was purely theatrical, and, in a teasing way, it lent the conversation the casualness it needed. The image signalized that, now that they had acknowledged that Boaz was their son, a heavy burden had fallen from their shoulders. Thus the walk was an image for the dramatic action, without being an illustration of it.

Dying on stage is one of the most difficult dramatic actions to perform. Since one cannot really die on stage, it is hard to be truthful, no matter how you do it. It is crystal clear that one must find an image for it: dying requires some sort of substitution. In realism, actors fall down, rattle, scream with pain, groan, and heave, forms of expression that imitate and substitute for the reality of dying. In epic theater dying is more stylized, but in both conventions, the victims usually lie down. In real-time theater such images seem terribly literal or even ridiculous because they never can be truthful enough. In my production of *King Lear,* the names of the characters were written down in a long list in elegant letters. During the course of the play, many of the characters die, so anytime a character died, the actor simply stopped acting, stepped out of his role, and deleted his name from the list with a black marker. This was an image of dying without any physical convulsion, or any untruthfulness. The actions of ceasing-to-act, walking to the list of names (which became a death list), and deleting the names were physical actions that the actor performed—pure theater-actions—which lent a grim dimension to the dramatic action.

And one last example: in my production of *The Exception and the Rule* by Brecht (The On(c)e and Only Theater Group, Berlin/Frankfurt, 1976), we had all characters played by clowns. When the coolie was shot, he rose from his own death to be carried away in a frantic funeral procession. Then he returned to play the part of his own widow in the trial against the merchant who had killed him. Richard Lester does a similar thing in his film *Oh, What a Lovely War,* in which the soldiers who die get up again and march on with blue faces.

Montage and (De)construction: The Actor at Work

The action of the actor-as-narrator-of-the-play as the framework for the action of the character fundamentally alters the function and the nature of the theater. The action of a character in a play is often interrupted and fragmented. In the realistic and epic theater conventions the actor does not play an ongoing, uninterrupted performance, although his preparation is geared toward what Stanislavski calls the "through-line of action." But the real-time actor's presence is permanent and ongoing, from beginning till the end. His performance is a kind of *montage* of the separate parts of the play: he puts the play together.

As he creates this montage, the real-time actor is always *actively acting,* instead of passively undergoing the dramatic events of the play. He is thus *constructing* not only his performance, but also the play itself, and in so doing, he adds to the dynamic of the play the dynamic of this activity of construction: *he moves the play on.*

If he can construct, the actor can also *deconstruct,* taking the play apart and putting it together again in a different form, adding other material to it, interspersing it with the use of other media. The Wooster Group[8] of New York, for instance, radically *deconstructs* the material they perform.

This (de)construction is not a spontaneous action of the actors—it must be well prepared in the creation of the scenario, in the script, and during the rehearsal process. But it is made visible in the stage action of real-time theater actors: it happens before the very eyes of the audience. This has become one of the most important features of real-time theater.

The actor in the realistic theater or the epic theater presents the fully realized character to the audience. The actor in real-time theater shares with the audience the action of creating his character.

Because the audience sees all these elements of creative activity, they gain access to what it is the actor actually does on stage. Thus the actor gives the audience insight into the process by which conflict arises. The audience can witness how the characters then deal with it. One might even say that the audience in real-time theater is in the same position as the audience of a puppet show: they are party to the "construction" of the performance.

In other words: the audience sees the *actor at work.* In the way he stages himself, arranges the stage, and uses props, his acting becomes *clear, observable,* and *transparent.* In my productions of Brecht's *Man Is Man* (Drama Department of the Tisch School of the Arts of NYU / The Elephant Brigade, New York, 2007) and of *Der Mann der . . . / The Man Who . . .* (Neues Theater Halle, Germany, 2007), the actors used video cameras to film small objects to be projected live on screens: as they did this, the actors couldn't play roles or be anything else than actors-who-handled-a-camera.

As a result of the montage and the (de)construction technique in real-time theater, the purpose and intention of an action can be the action itself. This does not mean that in real-time theater one must be cynical or presume that life is without meaning; it suggests rather that, perhaps, the purpose of life is life itself, and that we really never see life as a whole with its hidden motives and intentions. Usually, all we see are isolated incidents that sooner or later we may be able to connect with each other, and understand the deeper meaning of. In real-time theater, this task of connection is left entirely to the audience.

The Space between the Lines of the Text

One of the things the actor might discover in the montage process is that there is often space "between" the lines of the text. The space we are talking about is between the words, a space in which the character makes a *decision* to change his course of action, or a space in which the character considers his next step, or a space in which the character allows himself to look for a reaction from other characters, which, if it comes, may bring him to the next part of the action. Some authors indicate such spaces by stage directions like *silence* or *pause,* but Shakespeare, for instance, doesn't do that. In act 4 of *King Lear,* when Lear meets Gloucester in the field, at first Lear does not know who Gloucester is. The king has lost his mind, and he is desperately confused. Gloucester, who lost his eyesight, thinks he recognizes Lear's voice, but it takes Lear a long time to "recognize" Gloucester. In my production of the play, we discovered that it was possible that Lear's failure to recognize his old friend was intentional, that he isn't as raving mad as he behaves, and that, by acting as a madman, he is finding a way to look Gloucester in the eyes. In rehearsal the actor used the verb: "*delay* (the moment of confrontation)" or "*prepare* yourself" (for this inevitable moment). The actor had the whole, empty theater space at his disposal for these actions. Physically doing "crazy things" with it, we found that the elaborate text could be performed as a series of associations and grandiose *images,* which allowed us to see what Lear feels and thinks about Gloucester. Lear seems to know everything that happened to him, and he feels terribly guilty about it. In the space between the lines of the text, the actor found plenty of space and time to change Lear's course of action, to think of a new association, or a new turn, and to look for Gloucester's reaction until he found the time ripe to look him in the eyes: "I know thee well enough, thy name is Gloucester." In the space between the lines of the text, the actor had the opportunity to find space and time to stage himself into physical and theatrical images for the subtext of the play. He even could repeat an image. In real-time theater the space between the text gives space to the actor himself.

Instruments of the Actor 2: Body and Voice

The actor's main instruments are his body and his voice. No matter in what style or theater convention he performs, his body and voice must be trained. His body has to move, to walk, to run, to fall, to sit, to dance, to lie down, to gesticulate, and simply to stand. And his voice has to talk, to sing, to scream, to cry, to laugh, and to whisper. It is through the ways in which he uses his body and his voice that the actor can express his feelings, thoughts, and sensory reactions. Like a musician who adds feeling to the way he plays his instrument, the actor fills his voice with feeling. And just as the musician must know all the qualities of his instrument in order to play it optimally, the actor must train and employ his physical awareness to play upon his acting instrument. To express his character's feelings—and his own—he must be able to employ subtle inflections of the voice, as precisely as he uses the movements of his body.

The real-time actor speaks in his own voice; he moves in his own idiosyncratic way, not attempting to imitate the imagined voice and movement of the character. The age and type of the actor, even the gender and skin color, are usually not very relevant for the role he plays. A young actor can play an older character because he doesn't have to go out of his way to "become" an old man; the actor doesn't have to stoop or shuffle or be eighty years old to play King Lear. He also doesn't have to wear a king's robe to indicate that he is playing the king. It is obvious enough through the text and through his actions. He need not even be a man; Lear can be played by a woman, just as the actor playing Othello doesn't have to be black, or the one portraying Richard III walk with a limp and have a hunchback. All these external *imitative* forms of appearance are employed to lend more "truthfulness" to the character, but in fact, they are only illustrations of the qualities of the character, and not necessary in real-time theater.

When directors attempt, while sticking within the strict rules of realism, to make this way of telling the story the central focus of their directorial choices, big problems can arise—both for the actors and for the audience: the actor, who is used to justifying his actions on the basis of the dramatic situation of the play, can find it difficult to base them on the reality of the theater situation. And the audience can have difficulty resisting the temptation of identifying with the characters on the stage. Since realism and naturalism demand great verisimilitude, the audience wants to believe in the actual truth of what it is seeing and hearing, so the audience will have a hard time seeing Lear as a woman. To counteract this temptation, Brecht created what he called *alienation effects,* to undermine the illusion of reality that the realistic stage attempts to accomplish. But also in epic theater the actor justifies his actions on the basis of the dramatic situation, not on the demands of the theatrical form it takes. The paradoxical result has been that even in nonproscenium, flat-floor theaters, actors erect virtual fourth walls and play "realistically."

In my production of *King Lear,* the actor playing Lear was twenty-two—he had a young voice, and for him it wasn't a problem to run around naked with Edgar when they met each other on the heather: playing mad with "mad" Edgar. With an old man that wouldn't have been possible. In my production of *Black Box,* the actor playing the Orthodox Jew, Michael, was actually a Muslim of Egyptian descent, whose Arabic name itself helped the audience to make the distinction between the actor and his role, which in this case was pretty striking. In the *Cherry Orchard* (Theater School / Directors Department, directed by four students under my supervision, Amsterdam 1997) a man played Andreyevna and a woman played her brother Gaiev. The actor playing Andreyevna wore an elegant white suit and had something decadent about him, but he never played at being a woman; the actress playing Gaiev wore a brown suit, but she never hid her femininity. They used their own voices. Because of the change of gender, the eccentricity of the characters became effortless, natural and somehow very moving. Such choices do not place the real-time actor at the disposal of the character (as in realism) or of the form (as he might in epic theater). Instead, they allow him to put himself at the disposal of the story he has to tell about the character and the play, and create a form for him.

Instruments of the Actor 3: The Mind, the Heart, and the Senses

Thoughts belong to the mind, feelings to the heart, and sensations to the senses. Heart, mind, and senses are used here metaphorically: they are immaterial and difficult to define, but all the same, they are located in the body. Therefore we could say that, for the actor, they are the *inner instruments* upon which he plays.

Of the three, the senses, though the most physical, can also be the most elusive. Take for instance the sensation of physical pain, which is difficult to describe: although it is a physical sensation, pain is experienced not only as a physical but also as an emotional phenomenon. And, emotional pain is often experienced as physical pain. Pain is something we *feel*, and we feel it only for the moment when it occurs. We usually experience the physical intrusion as something other than the pain it causes. The memory of physical pain itself hardly exists, at least not in the way we have visual memories. We may remember that we *had* pain, or how we *expressed* the pain, but not the pain itself. Sometimes we may even find it difficult to locate the place in our bodies where we felt the pain. So, generally speaking, our physical memory is not so well developed. But we can *imagine* pain and even, through our imagination feel it. And there is the phenomenon of phantom pain.

Emotions like sadness, on the other hand, although purely mental, can be felt as physical pains: tightness in the chest, for instance, or a cramp in the stomach contains our heartache or our agony. Such purely emotional feelings seem to have a location in the body and can be remembered, recalled, and reexperienced. We use images for them: when we are proud, we say our "chest swells with pride," and when we are nervous, we speak of having "butterflies in our stomach." And shame can make us blush.

Stanislavski devised a method for the training of the "emotional memory" in which actors attempt to reconstruct their own feelings. They then employ these remembered feelings to enact the emotions of the characters they are playing. This method was further developed by Lee Strasberg in the Actors Studio,[9] although Stanislavski himself later repudiated the method and instead encouraged the actors to use their imagination, rather than their emotional memories. Although it contributes to his confusion about his identity, in psychological realism this method can be useful because it enables the actor to substitute his own feelings for those of the character. It became one of the cornerstones of modern psychological-realistic acting.

In real-time theater, the actor does not necessarily have to remember feelings of his own in order to play the feelings of his character. Instead, he can *imagine* such feelings and search for forms and images with which to enact them. Since feelings and sensations are within the body, the actor with a developed physical awareness is able to locate them and find a way to express them. To do this, the actor must listen with his "inner ear" to his own heart and mind. Opening up to them, he can allow them to play upon the inner instruments of his mind and his senses. In order to express the thoughts and emotions of his character, and to visualize the emotional and intellectual meaning of the story he is telling, the real-time actor "constructs" the theatrical images he uses. This construction of images is a conscious and concrete physical action in "real time." At the same time he *is* in the image, physically and mentally.

Instruments of the Actor 4: Language

Words themselves can also be considered an instrument, not only of the mind, but also of the body, for they are simultaneously mental and physical phenomena. The words we speak live in our body and mind; our brain brings order in them, making language a part of our organism. When we are "looking for the right word," we take a trip through the archives of our mind. But when our feelings are overwhelming, we say, "I have no words for what I'm feeling." We replace words by tears or sounds or we shrug our shoulders for lack of words, and these gestures are all physical expressions of what we feel.

The language we speak is itself the vehicle of our thoughts and feelings; the voice is the vehicle of language. The language the actor speaks on the stage is often not his own language. To make it sound truthful, he has to *make it into* his own language. Language expresses thoughts and feelings. Therefore the actor must *understand* the thoughts and *imagine* the feelings of the character. Playing the action and using his instrument, he can "think" the thoughts of the character, and "feel" his feelings, without confusing them with his own thoughts and feelings. With his voice (color, volume, pitch) he can express the meaning of the words and the emotions of the character as he interprets them.

Fine-Tuning the Instruments 1: What Does the Actor See?

What does the actor see when he is on stage? The answer is: the stage. In the old days, if there was a set on the stage representing a living room, the actor saw that it was made of cardboard, that it was not real. Yet within the convention of (naturalistic and psychological) realism, the actor had to act *as if* it were real. He had to see something that, in reality, he didn't see at all. He had to pretend something was real that didn't exist as such.

Nowadays the cardboard walls may be replaced by wood and steel and glass, and the furniture will be real. But the world that these real materials and objects represent is still not real because, for instance, a living room depends on lights that are always a fraction of a second too late or too early, even in our computerized age. In this space, the actor has to act as if it were the most normal thing in the world to find himself suddenly in a living room, even though everything around him tells him that this is not actually so. In fact he must ignore the real reality. And we, in the audience, see him ignoring what he really sees, especially when he stares into the void, often above and beyond our heads, pretending he's looking out of the window.

Of course, the actor must forgive himself for this innocent form of deceit, especially since the audience forgives him too, and nobody is hurt or damaged by the deceit. But under these circumstances, the actor's acting also becomes a kind of innocent deceit. In order to take himself seriously, he may be tempted to create mysterious explanations for this strange phenomenon. He may even begin to believe in "the secret of the actor," magical powers that allow him to take an imitated reality for the real reality, powers that make him somehow different from other mortals. I think it was Laurence Olivier who said: "Acting is a superior form of lying." He got away with that, and he became world famous for it.

In real-time theater the actor sees what he really sees, without the need to pretend otherwise, or to attribute what he sees to "substitution" or symbolism. He sees what is actually there: the other actors, the stage and everything on it, the auditorium and the audience. The illusionary world of the play gives way to the material reality of the stage itself.[10]

The actor sees his fellow actors. If, while he is acting, the actor really looks around, he sees not only the stage and everything that is on it, but also his fellow actors. They, like him, are playing roles or are simply being present as themselves, and watch. But often actors don't really *see* their scene partners while they're performing; instead they are so completely engrossed in their roles that they never actually make eye contact with their partners, but merely act *as if* they see the other characters. Sometimes it is quite obvious that such an actor sees neither the character nor the actor who is playing the character. Instead, he is looking through the other actor, or over and beyond him, staring in the direction of his scene partner without really taking him in. In such a moment, if the actor is not speaking or moving, he is usually "in his head," busy thinking about his next line, anticipating it and waiting for his cue. This happens often in realistic theater, where the acting is so introspective that the audience may not even notice. But if the actor is not aware and is not trained in other methods, he may fall into this habit in other forms or conventions of theater as well. If this happens in real-time theater, you can bet the audience will notice!

In real-time theater the actors can see each other as themselves: actors who play roles. Just as they see that the audience is watching them, real-time actors see each other, in the midst of playing, both as actors and as characters. As a character, the actor pays attention to the dramatic situation of the scene and sees the character his scene partner is playing. At the same time, as himself, he sees his scene partner playing the character and sees him on stage as a fellow actor.

There is a slight difference between looking and seeing. *Seeing* is more passive. We see what meets the eye. Simply seeing each other as actors, observing each other at work, establishes the contact between the actors. *Looking* is more active; it is intentional. Looking at each other as characters establishes the action that goes on.

Within a scene, both seeing and looking happen simultaneously. The actor finds the right balance between the two only when he has made eye contact with his partner(s), when he is completely at ease—with himself and with the situation—and when he knows precisely what he's doing. When the actor controls the gestures and forms he is using to enact the dramatic action, he is free to choose when to look at his scene partner. He doesn't have to look at him all the time, as is the "rule" in realistic theater. After having established eye contact between himself and his partner, he can look away without stepping out of the dramatic situation, and keep up the contact with him. He can even create moments of rest, in which he can see his partner, the other actors, the audience, and be himself for a moment or two. And he can vary how often and in what ways he does so. Actors should not rehearse this break, but leave it to the moment of performance.

The actor in real-time theater is not introspective. His presence as actor, which is established as soon as he makes real eye contact, heightens both his commitment to the story he enacts and his *alertness* on stage. During every performance, he can see and acknowledge every detail and every variation and react to it. Every night he and his partners may speak their lines in a slightly different way, or with a slightly new intonation, or with a new pause between words that changes the rhythm; they can discover something new in their characters and give their interpretations new twists or add new layers of meaning; they can move differently, change the blocking or work with a different energy, depending on the mood of the day; and they can react to what actually happens in the moment, and even can repair mistakes (see section "Nothing can go wrong" below), for actors are not automatons, especially not in real-time theater.

Once the actor is able to be present in this way, once he can stay present in his eyes, giving real attention to his scene partners and fellow actors, and staying aware of the situation both on the stage and in the audience (see section "Seeing and being seen" below), *the acting itself becomes what is real, not what is acted.* Once the acting itself is real, the most important conditions of truthfulness, living dialogue and believable interaction between the actors, are fulfilled.

The observing, nonplaying actor also contributes to this situation. While the actors in real-time theater, as pure narrators-of-the-play, watch the action and remain outside the dramatic situation, they do not pretend that they are witnessing an illusion of reality in which they have to believe, nor do they pretend to be watching. They don't play that they're watching, they *really* watch, in the same way the audience watches. They see what the audience sees: their fellow actors, and the

roles those actors are playing. And they do this with the same commitment, interest, and curiosity as when they themselves are playing—and
with the same pleasure. Their interest and curiosity make them a sort of
ideal audience: attentive and ready to be surprised. And the pleasure
they evince in watching can be contagious, spreading to the audience
itself. This watching is not at all easy: it means that the actor doesn't do
anything but that and has to give up the idea that when on stage, he
needs to act.

The watching actor always adds something to the performance. This
important feature of real-time theater can even change the interpretation of a scene. For instance, in many plays, an "offstage" character may
be the subject of an interaction between other characters. Naturally, the
actor who plays the character whom others are discussing will be interested in what is being said about him, and he can use his presence to
make it clear that he is aware of what is going on. Moreover, the "onstage" actors are aware that they are being observed. In *Black Box,* for example, when Alex and Manfred were fighting over Michel, the actor
who played Michel happened to be sitting on a chair right between
them. It was impossible for them to ignore him. But there was no need
for him to leave his position; that would have been an unnecessary exit.
So they acknowledged him and used him in their fight, while the actor
who played Michel observed them with the greatest interest. The result
was that there was an interaction between the three of them as actors,
which altered the way the characters Alex and Manfred talked about
Michel. Manfred's criticisms of Michel, which might otherwise have
seemed like a rant or malicious gossip, became more like a personal in-
sult. And, of course, this affected the actor playing Michel: he was
amused.

Seeing and being seen: the actor sees the audience. In real-time theater,
the performance area itself is not the only space that the actor sees. He
sees the auditorium too. When realistic theater is performed behind the
proscenium arch the actor knows that the orchestra and the balconies
are there, but he usually can't see them very well: he is focused on what
happens on the stage, and the lights blind his eyes.

Real-time theater overcomes the impediments of the proscenium
arch, or at least tries to. Without proscenium arch and blinding lights,
the real-time actor can see the space as a whole, including the audito-

rium. He can see the architecture of the theater and the audience as they see him. As he sees the stage, the other actors, the whole space and the audience, the actor also shows that he is *acknowledging what he sees*.

The audience can perceive immediately whether an actor is ignoring them or really seeing and acknowledging them. They can tell if he is taking them in or is just looking through them, or over their heads into the void, at a nonexisting, distant horizon. This also works the other way around—though that seems to be more obvious: the actors can perceive that the audience sees them. This mutual eye contact with the audience is the beginning of *direct communication: the actor allows the audience to look through his eyes into the soul of the character he plays*.

It is one of the most simple—and at the same time one of the most difficult—things for an actor to do, and it takes practice. Once an actor can do this easily, he will feel how *free* he can be on stage, how much he can trust himself to do whatever he has to do. It can be an extraordinarily gratifying experience, and a real boost in self-respect for the actor.

One of the older actors in my production of *Big and Little* panicked during our Tokyo performance when, for the first time, he was confronted with the audience in this new way. He was completely shaken, forgot his text, and hardly could stay on his feet. "I can see them, and they can see me!" he cried desperately, although all his life he had been on the stage and had performed in front of thousands of audiences. It took a few performances and a lot of courage for him to overcome his initial fear, accustom himself to this new situation, and relax into being seen by the audience. As soon as he did, his acting soared.

But it is not only the actor who must accustom himself to this new sense of seeing: the audience must also get used to the fact that the actor sees them. This is true not only in Japan, where there are cultural barriers to making direct eye contact, but everywhere where the separation between stage and auditorium is accepted as normal.

The audience is your friend. In fact, it takes a lot of guts to really see the audience as they sit there on their chairs in the auditorium. You have to straighten up, take a deep breath, and give yourself the time you need. Before the performance begins, you must walk onto the stage, stand still, ground yourself, relax, look around, see the auditorium, and see the space where you are going to tell the story of tonight's play. The stage lights are on; the houselights are on. When the audience enters, it is a thrilling moment, and you feel a burst of adrenaline. Both you and they sense the nervousness and excitement. But don't forget: you are the host; the audience members are your guests. You see them enter, you make eye contact with them, and you see that they see you. Sometimes you may even be able to greet someone you know, or have a little chat. This first contact is very reassuring, encouraging, and liberating. It gives you a chance to get your nerves under control. In the German production of *The Same Sea* (Neues Theater, Halle, 2005–6), during the performances of the play at the Theatertreffen in Berlin, some members of the audience, upon entering the performance space, approached the huge tea table that was part of the set. The actors helped them to a cup of tea, had a chat, and suddenly a relaxed atmosphere was created even before the performance started.

In this situation there is nothing you can take for granted, there is no room for "routine"; in fact, there is no routine: at every performance the situation is entirely new. The audience looks at you—every night a different audience—full of expectations. They came to see you, they arranged a babysitter and spent a lot of money. Now they are looking forward to what you are going to show them, you can see it in their faces; they are ready for it, ready for you. The audience is not a ferocious hostile beast that is ready to devour you. The audience is your friend, and that is a good thing for an actor to realize . . . over and over again.

These moments before you begin the performance are precious; they can give you the peace of mind you need for playing your role and the time to prepare yourself. Now you're ready. You can focus and begin.

Seeing and looking during the performance. By making eye contact with the audience, the actor becomes the narrator of the play, and from the moment he does so, he must live up to this function he has created for himself. He cannot drop it for the rest of the performance, withdrawing into the world of the play and his role. The real-time actor *shares with the audience* what his character is doing, feeling, and thinking. It is important, that this audience contact occurs without extra emphasis. It must occur naturally, easily, and without abrupt movements, which would call attention to the moment of seeing. This contact with the audience must be completely a matter of course; it is not an *aside*.

It also is important that the actor allows his eyes to take in a large part of the audience, taking his time to let them all feel that he is with them, and that he doesn't single out individual members of the audience or get stuck looking at one person for too long. Doing so might make that person uneasy and create the mistaken impression that the actor wants to involve him in his acting. Sometimes, however, an actor's eyes may catch those of an audience member for a moment. These moments of recognition are exquisite and exciting. With practice the actor can learn not to let such a moment distract him. Practice teaches him how to use such precious moments for his acting. In this way, the real-time actor can allow an audience member to become his partner—not his accomplice—without stepping out of his role.

We should note, however, that it is not necessary that the actor look at the audience constantly. He must stay connected with his scene-partner(s) as well. Besides, such continuous audience contact would lead to a stiff, "frontal" kind of acting, just the opposite of what one is aiming at: the sort of connection with the audience which liberates the actor.

Once this convention is established, and the audience has become used to it, the real-time actor is free to open up to the audience at any moment. In fact, it is best that these moments are not directed or scripted but left up to each actor to improvise and choose. This sharpens the actor's alertness, and allows him to react to whatever happens in the theater. During the course of a performance run, the actor may, of course, discover moments at which eye contact with the audience is particularly effective, but this technique is most telling if the actor leaves the choice up to his intuition, rediscovering such moments at every performance.

The narrators of the play are insiders. As the narrators of the play, real-time actors are equal to the audience, and the audience to them. Watching the play just as the audience does, they become a part of the audience. Like the audience, when they experience something, they have thoughts and opinions about what they have seen.

But there is a critical difference: An actor who watches his fellow actors perform watches with foreknowledge. His reaction to what he sees will therefore be different from the reactions of the audience that is witnessing the play for the first time. He reacts as an *insider,* someone who knows the whole story. So when something happens on stage that always makes the audience laugh, it may provoke nothing more than a smile for the actor who is watching with foreknowledge. He has heard the joke before, so he may simply be amused by the reaction of the audience or by the way another actor is dealing with this reaction. But when one of the actors does something new and unexpected, the witnessing actor will definitely react.

So in a sense the actors in real-time theater are always ahead of their audience. They can use this situation to their advantage, expressing their involvement with the story they're playing, allowing themselves to react when something unexpected happens. Doing so heightens the alertness of the actors, creating another interaction among the actors and giving the performance an extra dimension. In such moments, it is clear that what is happening is quite real, here and now. At the same time, this sort of improvisation adds to the actors' control of the performance and of the characters they are playing. And these moments of real-time improvisation tend to draw the audience into the performance. One of the biggest compliments the actor in real-time theater can receive is that people in the audience feel that they participate in the performance.

Comment—no comment. The fact that the actors have special foreknowledge of the play must not tempt them into having private exchanges among themselves—comments or looks that the audience cannot possibly understand and that are irrelevant to the play. This sort of commenting reaction from the "in crowd" is unfair to the audience, excluding them from the action, transforming the actors into a sort of secret society having fun on its own, and ultimately jeopardizes the play and the performance.

It is also not useful for the actors to comment on the play itself in an *aside,* as characters often do in classical comedy. In an aside, the actor, remaining in character, steps out of the dramatic situation and shares a secret with the audience, something his scene-partner is not yet aware of or must not overhear. In this situation, both the actor who gives an aside, and the others on stage who must not hear it, act as if the aside were not happening, as if time stands still. The actor who speaks the aside remains in his role, but he has a sort of alibi for going downstage and whispering to the audience. The aside often allows the audience to have fun at the expense of another character and it may draw them into an unspoken alliance with the character, who addresses them. But the other actors—those who are on stage and must pretend not to hear the aside, usually continue miming their action, or their conversation—which always feels untruthful and a little awkward. This is a good example of how much the actors, within the constraints of realism, need justifications for their presence on stage. Within the conventions of classical theater, the illusion is maintained; the aside does not harm the dramatic action because everyone accepts the convention, however silly it may seem.

In real-time theater, however, the pretence of the aside is not necessary. The actor who speaks what otherwise would be an aside, simply addresses the audience while continuing with his action. Meanwhile the other actors stop acting to listen and watch. If he were to actually comment in an aside, his words might seem to be a comment on the other actors or on the situation itself, or even the whole play. Such an aside might undermine the other actors or even the whole production. It could also be slightly embarrassing for the audience, because it would make them accomplices.

The real-time actor doesn't need accomplices: he is not involved in a fight with his fellow actors. He and they are working together to reveal the play's dramatic conflict to the audience, and the actor has *no comment* on what is being played. Everything he thinks about the play and the characters, his opinion and his point of view, are expressed in the theatrical form.

In Molière's *Tartuffe,* Orgon hides himself under the table to overhear Tartuffe approaching his wife Elmire with adulterous propositions. The audience knows that Orgon is sitting there, probably trembling with nervousness, and in spite of his stubborn narrow-mindedness, they usually are on his side because they are against Tartuffe. In my production of the play (Het Vervolg, Maastricht 1985), Orgon was visible to the audience, so they could see how painful it is for him to discover that Tartuffe is an imposter. Although he had plenty of opportunity to do so, he didn't play his part of the scene as an aside. Instead he sat quietly, slightly amazed, listening to Elvire and Tartuffe. At the same time, the actors who played Tartuffe and Elvire didn't pretend that they had not seen Orgon. The result was that the scene became a provocation, a conscious action on the part of the actors playing Tartuffe and Elvire to expose Orgon's weakness and credulity, which made him stronger. Because the actress playing Elvire also did not indulge in asides, her character became very strong, too, without having to denounce Orgon. And the actor who played Tartuffe could show that he was trying to see how far he as Tartuffe could go in manipulating Orgon. Thus, working together, the actors showed the audience how the mechanism of the scene itself, and Tartuffe's betrayal, worked.

Many plays within the convention of realism contain purely narrative moments, which we call "monologues." In fact, such plays are often filled with stories that characters tell each other—and not just in messenger speeches. In *Three Sisters* and in *Uncle Vanya,* for example, Versjinin and Astrov use long soliloquies to unfold their visions for the future of the world. In these plays, the characters tell their stories to the other characters. But the real-time actor can easily involve the audience in them. Moreover, in order to reveal the intensely dramatic nature of soliloquies, the real-time theater can transform such speeches, like those in Shakespeare's plays, into dialogues with oneself, dialogues that the actor shares with the audience. Hamlet's "To be or not to be," for instance, can be played as a sort of aside, but in a real-time production, it need not be recited as merely a philosophical musing performed by one actor alone on stage. Instead it can be shared, as a progression of active thoughts and contemplations with the other actors on stage, and with the audience. It can be revealed as a series of proposals and options that the actor is asking us to consider. Similarly, in the balcony scene, Romeo might need friends to support him, but the truth is that nobody outside the play can help him. And everybody in the audience knows this. Played as an "aside" as in classical comedy, Romeo might try to engage the audience, he might win their sympathy or their need to warn him, but nobody will ever get up to talk him out of his ominous plans. In the convention of real-time theater, on the other hand, the actor can make it clear that Romeo is in dialogue with himself, rather than with the audience. The actor can interrupt himself at any given moment in the monologue, returning to himself for a small break—drink a sip of water, change position—then resume the action. In this way the actor can share Romeo's conflict of the heart with the audience, and the audience will understand the dilemma, rather than taking his side. What the actor and the audience share is their sympathy for Romeo, or their understanding, or their concern, or their pity. The monologue can be delivered with wonder and compassion. What this would bring about is a sense of foreboding of what will happen, shared between the actor and the audience, which could have a similar impact as when in Zefferelli's film version of the play the monk on his donkey hurrying back to Mantua, meets Romeo on his horse hurrying to Verona. The audience knows what Romeo doesn't know: if only they had stopped and talked with each other . . .

Fine-Tuning the Instruments 2: What Does the Actor Hear?

Hearing and listening can serve the actor in much the same way as seeing and looking. The ear is the actor's second most important sense. In real-time theater it is an essential tool for the communication between the actors. It will not work for the actor merely to act "as if" he were listening to his fellow actors. Real listening and real hearing enhance the presence of the actor, and they enable him to react to everything that happens on stage, and to what occurs in the auditorium.

As with seeing and looking, there is also a difference between hearing and listening. Listening is an active deliberate act. Hearing is passive, something that happens to us: we pick up sounds with our ears. But there is one important difference between looking and listening: the actor cannot make the act of listening visible with his ears: *so he must listen with his eyes.* His eyes will reveal to his scene partner whether he is really listening or just pretending to do so. Not only the actor's eyes make his listening visible, his other physical reactions can do that too. Moreover, in real-time theater, not only the other actors, but also the audience perceives this quality of listening.

Often during a performance, there are sounds that come from the auditorium. In real-time theater the actors cannot ignore these sounds. On the other hand, they must not make a big point of hearing such noises, which might make a coughing audience member feel even worse than he already does. It is, however, certainly possible for an actor to acknowledge what he has heard, by pausing for a second or two when the sounds from the auditorium make him inaudible.

For example, he need not keep talking when the audience is laughing just to maintain the illusion of the play, just to maintain the truthfulness of the situation. Instead, he can just stop playing for a brief moment, stepping out of his role, acknowledging the reaction and enjoy it, without making it into a grand moment as in boulevard comedy and the opera. And if airplanes fly over during an open-air performance, or if the sirens of the fire brigade racing down the street outside are particularly obtrusive and make one inaudible, the actor need not pretend he doesn't hear what everybody else is hearing, bravely continuing with his Hamlet monologue, while everybody is thinking of something else.[11]

Consequences of Active Seeing/Looking and Hearing/Listening

Active seeing and looking and active hearing and listening are the most important foundations for the technique of real-time acting. They generate specific practical elements, which can be trained and developed:

1. Active rest
2. Relaxation and inner tranquility
3. Contact with the floor, the ground: grounding
4. Contact with yourself: connection
5. Focus and concentration
6. Alertness
7. Presence: being in the moment, in the present time, here and now[12]

These elements of the technique give the actor *self-confidence* and *trust,* which he needs to be present on the stage as himself (it is impossible to talk an actor into confidence, nor can it be trained as such, but it can emerge through concrete exercises and practical applications of the basic and specific elements mentioned above); *pleasure* and *enthusiasm,* with which he will play his role and tell his story; the *ability to observe* what is going on around him, in the reality of the stage and the auditorium, as well as in the play; the *opportunity to react* fully to anything that happens unexpectedly, both onstage and off, inside and outside the dramatic situation; and finally *easy access* to all the material that he has collected in himself during his training and during the rehearsals: the physical and mental faculties with which he plays, the text he has learned and knows by heart, the many little agreements that have been made for the theatrical form of the action of the character he is embodying, such as the music, the blocking, the choreography, the movement.

Active rest. Actors often feel caught by the constraints within which they must work. Within realism, an actor may feel trapped within the form and the strict boundaries of the illusionary "as if" world inside of which he must pretend to exist, and he may feel stuck in the harness of his role. To free himself of the constrictions of his body—and from the formal rules of theater conventions—it is not enough for the actor to be aware of the problem; he must also find a practice capable of overcoming this impediment. Active rest helps the actor in real-time theater not to feel stuck, or trapped within in his own body.

Connection and trust. Being connected is a very important step toward becoming a real-time actor. Being connected means that the actor has free access to his own body and mind with everything that belongs to them: his thoughts, feelings, senses, and imagination. Being connected means that the actor is able to employ, in full consciousness, his own thoughts and feelings, to express how his character thinks and feels, and to use his own physical, emotional, and intellectual instruments to give a theatrical form to the actions of his character, just as a musician consciously plays upon his instrument. Being connected allows the actor to focus on the theatrical forms and images with which he expresses those actions. He is not alienated from himself. He lends his own voice to the words of his character, rather than using a "borrowed" voice. And he uses his own body to develop the physical movements of his character, rather than contorting his body to "imitate" the supposed movements of his character, allowing the character to emerge quite naturally. This is how the real-time actor "builds" a character who is authentic and idiosyncratic. This is how he achieves real truthfulness and credibility.

To achieve this "natural" state, the actor must first and foremost focus on the action of the character he plays. Some actors create their character working from the inside out: from their understanding of the character's actions toward his expression of them in vocal and gestural forms. Other actors work from the outside in: from a physical or vocal form toward their understanding of the character's actions. In either case, it is essential for the actor to stay connected with himself As long as he does that, he can avoid mere imitation. None of this happens automatically: It requires a great deal of hard work. Many actors, especially actors who were trained in the methods of realism when they were young, must "unlearn" the habits and rules of that convention.

Focus and concentration. The actor never does something "in general"; he acts with precision. The focus of his attention is directed toward what happens in the play, and toward what he—through the character he plays—makes happen. The concentration that is needed for this should not be forced; it originates from, and is mentally stimulated by, the actor's genuine interest in what happens. Being grounded and relaxed helps the actor to concentrate.

Concentration is "gathered" energy. This energy exists in our bodies, and it can be directed toward the objects of our attention: people, actions, and whole events. A concentration exercise cannot work if you are not interested in what you're supposed to be concentrating on. This presupposes the personal *commitment* of the actor to what he does. If he doesn't feel *enthusiasm* for the subject matter of the play, or if he doesn't enjoy what he is doing while playing his role, it will be hard for him to concentrate.

The real-time actor has four different focus points, some of which can be employed simultaneously. His focus of attention is upon the acting itself and the reality of the stage environment; the action of the character he is playing; the story of the play and the roles of the other actors; and, last but not least, the audience, with whom he is in regular eye contact, and with whom he shares the course of events of the play.

The real-time actor is also engaged in *how* he and his colleagues tell the story of the play, in *how* they act. In performance, this changes every day. Today is not yesterday, every performance is unique: *for the audience, the story of the play is new, and for the actor, the audience is new every night.* In real-time theater, the actor's double interest—in *what* he is doing and in *how* he and his colleagues are playing—must be *real, honest, and cannot be simulated.* The reality of the theater situation itself demands this of him. In real-time theater, where the reality of the stage situation is visible for all to see, the audience will notice the slightest untruthfulness on the part of the actor.

With his concentration, the real-time actor can zoom in on whatever demands most of his attention at any time. This continually fluctuating concentration of attention springs from his focus on the acting itself, but it also receives feedback from the acting, from both *what* he is playing and *how* he chooses to play. In fact there is a perpetual interaction between these two focus points. The focus on the action of his character and on the actions of his partners' characters prevents the actor from getting caught up in the memorized text, the blocking, and other technical issues. Thus he can rise above the character he plays and take him in hand. Of course, during early rehearsals, his attention may be focused on the text and blocking, but as the process continues, he concentrates more and more upon the action of the characters, and less and less upon the blocking and the text, until finally, these elements retreat into the background of his awareness. The givens of the text, the blocking and all the other elements that define his acting, get stored in the computer of his mind, of what I like to call the *second consciousness* of the actor. Once he knows his text by heart, he must be able to react by reflex to what happens. If one woke him up in the middle of the night, he would react automatically to his cue. It is important that the actor starts to trust this mechanism. It opens the way for his *first consciousness* to focus on what is really important for him: the actions of his character.

If he really looks at what he sees, and really listens to what he hears, the conditions for the actor's presence are established. These most important sensory qualities enable him to focus on the actions of his character, not from the character's standpoint, but from the standpoint of the actor himself.

Here too, we can see the usefulness of the consciously created distance between the actor and the character in real-time theater. Within this distance, the actor will begin to discover the space between the lines of the text, and the other elements of his acting. He will begin to feel this "space in between," in which he, continuously shifting his focus, can be himself, move freely, and stage himself in the next moment, make new discoveries for the role he plays, and add new choices during performance as easily as if it were an improvisation. A role is never finished, after all, and in real-time theater, the staging is never finished: it's a work in progress.

This space in between gives the actor in real-time theater freedom to move and to react spontaneously to any situation. For example in *Man Is Man* (Drama Department of the Tisch School of the Arts, NYU, 2007), the actors used this space continuously. At the end of the show, the soldiers were fighting a tank battle, but sometimes the toy tanks didn't follow the directions of the remote controls handled by the actors. When they needed to, the actors would simply put the tanks back on the right track, even when, at the same moment, they were playing their roles, and speaking their text, which had nothing to do with the tank problem. This was truly improvisational and always different. And it was only possible with this sort of concentration and this shifting focus, from the dramatic action to the theatrical situation and vice versa.

Within this freedom, the actor cannot just "be," he can also be *with* his fellow actors. As his focus shifts back and forth between himself and his acting partners, and between himself and the real stage situation, each moment of dialogue becomes a real discussion, talk, or conversation, and each image becomes a truly theatrical moment. In this moment, the actors begin to play together. Playing together is one thing, and is pretty essential for acting, but playing together with the shared goal of telling the story of a whole play is something entirely different. This is where an ensemble can start to grow, when everyone's focus is on the same thing: on the story of the play, on moving the story forward.

While he is acting, the actor keeps an eye open for everything that is really there, and everything that is really happening around him. The separation between the real-time actor and his role enables him to direct the focus of his attention to his fellow actors—even when they themselves are not acting but just watching—or to the audience. Unless the lights blind him (which is extremely difficult to avoid within the proscenium arch theater), he can also see how the audience is reacting to what he is doing. This can be stimulating for the actor and promote his alertness. It also can be dangerous, because the actor may be tempted to draw support from the audience for his character's actions. But he is sharing with the audience what his character is doing, thinking, and feeling, making the audience a witness of these actions, not an accomplice. The real-time actor must understand that he doesn't need allies for his character. The character can speak for himself. He must also be patient: there are always audience members who seem to fall asleep, and it is easy for an actor to feel intimidated by this, because he may think it is his fault. But the actor must ignore the sleeper, be strong, and trust himself.

The real-time actor is able to divide his attention between his acting and the audience, and in this way to share with them what happens to his character. The actor's attention doesn't have to be permanently directed toward his fellow actors, his eyes always fixed on them, as long as his attention is focused on the dramatic action of the character and those of his acting partners. This gives him considerable freedom. For instance, he can maintain his focus on the action of his partner's character, and momentarily shift his attention to the audience without stepping completely out of his role or deserting his scene partner, as he might have to do in an aside. So, for instance, he is able to observe a latecomer entering the audience. In response, he might smile or even gesture the late guest or show him a seat, without having to interrupt the progress of his action at all. Because of his simultaneous presence as himself, this is a completely legitimate action, and it won't interfere with his acting. It will be fully accepted by the audience, for whom this intervention is fascinating. Especially at such moments, the audience sees the actor at work, and they love it. Such moments can inspire a wonderful relationship to bloom between the actor and his audience.

Using his ability to divide his focus of attention, the actor is also able subtly to direct the attention of the audience toward what is happening on the stage—for whatever interests the actor, interests them as well.

The actor's focus is mainly sensory: a matter of using his eyes and ears. But by concentrating he directs his energy from himself toward the objects of his attention. He shares this action with his fellow actors who are also directing their energies toward the objects of their attention. And since they are all "on the same page" in telling the story of the play, the actor also receives energy back from his fellow actors. Of course this doesn't always happen, and it certainly doesn't happen by itself. It is something the actor must work for. Inspiration doesn't fall from the blue sky, or the roof of the theater, it is something that the player must create within himself; he is the one who must blow the wind to belly his own sails.

Through eye contact there is interaction with the audience and through that contact the actor's energy is transferred to the audience, and vice versa the audience's energy is transferred to the actors, just as with pop or jazz musicians. This exchange is a spark that goes through an audience, the ever so mysterious—but not so mysterious—sizzling tension of a performance. It is a tangible communication. This is the real, makeable magic of theater. But even in real-time theater this does not always happen. Audiences do not always respond the way you'd like them to respond. Often they don't know how to respond. That is not their fault. They too must get used to this different approach, to this new convention.

Alertness. Even when the actor is just watching the play rather than playing his role, he is actively attentive. He is *alert,* ready to go and to "intervene." Seeing with his own eyes, and hearing with his own ears, encourages the actor to react *alertly* to what *really* is happening on stage, and not only to what is taking place within the play.

His *alertness* also accentuates the "reality of the acting" itself: his actions and reactions, which are based in that alertness, become "interventions" that are necessary for the progression of the play and the performance. This makes his character's actions more "real": they are things that *have* to happen. At the same time his alertness helps the actor to play his character's actions in a more truthful manner because they are not only based on the reality of the dramatic situation of the play, but also motivated by the reality of the acting itself. He cannot simply act "as if." He can't pretend because the act of the acting has to be true.

Being alert means being sharp, keen, and eager. There is energy to being alert, the actor's energy: he is eager to play his role; he wants to tell the story of the play and his role; he is committed to it. The keenness and energy with which the actor in real-time theater "intervenes" and operates are not necessarily the same as the keenness and the energy of the character he plays. His alertness as actor gives the actions of his character their obviousness and necessity: they are actions that simply *must* happen.

Alertness is not the same thing as *timing,* but it definitely helps the actor find the right timing. The actor's eagerness and keenness not only help to make the actions of the character he's playing clearer and more transparent, they also make these actions easier for the audience to assess and consider, especially when there is eye contact between them and the actor. In this way the actor—not the character—becomes visible to the audience as a *propulsive force* in the dynamic of the dramatic development of the play. This contributes largely to the actor being the narrator of the play. He is not someone who waits passively (in the wings) for things to happen but someone who *makes them happen.* By bringing the play to life with his own energy, he obviates the need for the play to "live a life of its own," propelled by its own mysterious dynamics.

The actor's alertness also imparts alertness to the audience. They start to sit on the edge of their chairs, and they become interested not only in the story of the play and the roles that are played, but also in *how* they are played. Stimulated by the actor's presence as himself and by his alertness, the audience is stimulated to have what Brecht called the capacity of "intervening thinking," which is not unlike what children do when they watch a (puppet) play: they intervene. So the audience has the opportunity to participate intellectually and emotionally in what the characters are doing and saying. They are not just looking at what the people on stage are doing and saying from a distance—taking it in, or being entertained by them, perhaps judging their actions, dismissing the villain and applauding the hero. Instead they are actively experiencing each character's actions as propositions from the actors who invite the audience to form an opinion about it, to take a point of view. In real-time theater, the actor's alertness is conveyed and transferred to the audience by means of the eye contact between them.

In the moment. The real-time actor is *in the moment.* What "lives" on stage is he *and* his role, not he *being* his role. The actor's continuous presence on stage accentuates the real time on the clock, and simultaneously gives the actor himself a sense of continuity within the role he plays, and therefore a sense of continuity of the whole play. *It is the actor who moves the story of the play forward, not the coming and going of the characters.*

Through the choices for the form the actor makes, he shows why it is important for him to perform *this* play, and to tell *this* story in *this* way, to *this* audience. The distance he creates between himself and the character cannot be cold, observing, uncommitted, or impersonal: it is, on the contrary, highly personal.

Finally, being in "real time" helps the actor avoid several troublesome acting problems that plague many actors in performance:

Automatisms and routine in the acting. Every performance is different. The actor must be prepared and allow for new things to happen every night.

Anticipation. Being ahead of oneself, or *anticipating* things that are yet to happen or words that have not yet been spoken, is a sign of the actor's absence—rather than his presence. It is a side effect of his being introverted, or preoccupied with his gestures, blocking, text, or of his waiting for cues, which can easily interfere in the actor's work.

Assimilation in tempo, rhythm, tone of voice, and even mood. If the actor is not really present and in the moment, not really looking and seeing, hearing, and listening, he may rely instead on his routine, and before he knows it, he may find himself speaking in the same rhythm as his partner since actors are naturally drawn toward each other energetically. The slowest tempo almost always defines the tempo of the whole scene. And the lowest energy, including the lowest vocal energy, may define the energy of the whole performance.

If these sorts of problems do occur during a performance, the real-time actor can repair them. In fact, everyone on stage can help with this repair job, because everyone immediately becomes aware of the problem when it occurs, and because, more importantly, everyone feels equally responsible for the progression of the play. It is just a matter of taking that responsibility. Since he is "in the present moment," the real-time actor also has "presence of mind." This presence of mind is more than simply being attentive and vigilant. It is, in fact, the perfect description of the state of being of the real-time actor.

Nothing can go wrong. The worst thing that can happen to an actor is when something goes wrong—and this happens more often than an audience ever notices. If something goes wrong in a real-time performance the actor's situation is similar to what it was in the rehearsal situation:

he doesn't have to deny it. Because he doesn't have to keep up an illusion, he can fix what went wrong. So, in real-time theater there is no "paradox." There's only the actor's heightened consciousness of the theatrical situation.

The actor who is not trained in the technique of real-time acting is used to hiding or denying things that happen outside the "illusion of reality" that he is creating. If something unplanned happens, the illusion is destroyed, and the actor suddenly faces insurmountable problems that can make him lose his credibility as a character, unless he is able to hide and camouflage the repair job he must perform to cover the problem. Diderot, in his *Paradox of the Actor,* describes with hilarity how a skilled actor can pull off this trick. It is a trick, which the actor within the convention of realism must perform frequently.

In real-time theater, however, *nothing can go wrong,* because the actor in this convention is always showing how the illusion is created. He connects his role permanently with the visible reality of the stage situation and his acting itself. So every "mistake" can be repaired, publicly, quietly, and visibly, without embarrassment, just as a child might do it; it is "just" play, after all. The circus artist should be his example: if the equilibrist falls from his rope, he gets up and tries again. Thunderous applause.

The actor who is not used to the quadruple focus he must maintain—focus on the acting itself and the reality of the stage, focus on the actions of the character he is playing, focus on the play and the other roles of the other actors, and focus on the audience—can easily get confused when yet another reality enters his awareness. He may tense up when something out of the ordinary happens. He can feel out of place, observed, embarrassed, or naked. He may lose his confidence, as if the ground under his feet had fallen away. When something that has been carefully blocked is forgotten or handled carelessly, when an actor forgets his text or enters too late, or when a prop isn't in the right place on the stage, or the music starts too late, an actor can feel terrible

But such "mistakes" are inevitable. Usually such mistakes are unexpected. After all, acting is a human activity, and actors are not automatons, and sometimes nothing can be done to prevent a mistake because the disaster hits from outside. For instance, two latecomers once walked into a performance I had directed, entering the theater through the wrong door and crossing the stage to reach their seats. The actors couldn't ignore this, so they simply stopped and informed the new guests of what had happened so far. Another time, during a performance of *Forbidden Reproduction* (based on the novel *Love-Act* by E. M. Austen, Southern Comfort / Frascati, 1987) the actress entirely skipped an important section of the text. Without these lines, everything that followed would have become completely incomprehensible. But the other actor stopped the action and pointed out the omission to her, which showed his alertness and his ability to shift focus. At first the actress who had made the mistake didn't understand, so the other actor got up and went to fetch the script, showed her the text, after which they continued the performance. In *Drums of the Night* (Brecht, Toneel Academie Maastricht, 1988) the only chair we used suddenly broke. The four actresses stopped the play, gathered around the object like nurses over a patient, tried to repair it, to no avail, then put the chair away and continued the action without it. In a performance of *The Tigress* (based on the novel by Walter Serner, Southern Comfort / Frascati, 1989) one actor's shoulder became dislocated. He was so much in pain that he had to stop playing, and ask for a time out. A member of the audience— most of whom were unsure whether this was real or part of the show— put the arm back, and after fifteen minutes, the actor, still very much in pain, resumed the play. He got generous and grateful applause from the audience: nobody had left. In one of the performances of *King Lear* (Toneelschool Amsterdam, 1997) a glass bowl broke, and everybody in the play knew that a few scenes later two actors would have to run barefoot on the same floor. The actress who played Goneril went to find a broom and cleared the stage, while continuing her dialogue with Lear. Another night, the actor playing Lear stopped in the middle of his action because he wasn't happy with what he was doing. He simply told the audience that he would start all over again, and did so. And during one of the *Man Is Man (2)* performances (The Elephant Brigade at HERE, 2007), one of the actresses got sick during the show. We stopped the performance, asked to audience to hang on, and decided that the other actors would alternately play her part, script in hand. It implied a lot of improvisation and "mistakes," but it was still a good performance. Without the focus on the acting itself, and without the actors being present-as-themselves, such choices would never have been possible. Only once (*Brotladen/Breadshop* with Schlicksupp teatertrupp, Frankfurt, 1982), the ensemble of actors couldn't finish the show. This was when children took over the bread battle that was raging (with rolls and baguettes) and chased the actors off the stage.

When they are handled publicly, and with presence of mind, such "accidents" contribute greatly to the real-time quality of the performance. They become wonderful opportunities to demonstrate the presence of the actor. However, it would be a mistake to institutionalize such mishaps and "repeat" them the next evening.

If an actor does not react to such unexpected events, if he ignores the shattered glass, the broken chair, or the text omission, he must try to act *as if* these things were "not happening," or as if they were "normal" and "part of the show," and must attempt to hide the "mistake" with another action that nobody knows about but he himself. But when he does so, the actor can get caught, for he has no tools with which to repair the ruptured dramatic illusion. He may try to keep his focus on the dramatic situation, but meanwhile he can be consumed by a deadly fear about how to save the performance. At its best, he may try to hide the irregularity. But his attempts to do so will usually impact his acting considerably: his attention will wander, he will move strangely, and become insecure. If the audience does notice the accident, he will feel embarrassed at his efforts to hide it. The countless anecdotes about such incidents are a cause of mirth for the insiders, but in the end, they cultivate fear of, and contempt for, the audience and for the acting profession itself. In real-time theater one can eliminate this acting nightmare entirely and bring the acting profession a step closer to being a grown-up art form.

Rehearsal Process and Improvisation

Reading a text. Theater productions of a play usually begin with reading the text. Reading and speaking the text out loud is a way of defining the dramatic actions of the character. Some directors prefer to read a text for a long time before the actors start to move.

I myself prefer to read the text several times in different ways. At the first reading, I have the actors read the whole text, without much interpretation, and not in the roles they are going to play, but simply going around a circle, reading passages one after another (sometimes, especially in educational situations, the roles are not even decided at this point). This avoids the problem of the actor acquiring an immediate fixation on the role he is going to play, and it creates an opportunity to focus, more or less objectively, on the *actions* of the characters, instead of on their *feelings* and *thoughts*. It is an excellent way to just "hear" the play and enables actors to share among each other the meaning, relevance, and importance of a text, without claiming the parts as one's "private property." It also prepares them to play the whole play, and not just their role, as is the practice of real-time theater.

The second step of this reading process is to read the text scene by scene or act by act with each actor reading one role in each scene or act, after which other actors read these roles in the following scene or act. This creates a sense of the continuity of the dramatic action. It helps the actors to understand what's going on in the play, and it puts them in a better position to begin to interpret the dramatic action.

Then, the third time through, I have the actors read the text in the roles they are going to play. Now they can fully focus on the actions of their character and start to define the actions of their characters with a verb. This reading can be repeated as many times as is necessary to find the "dynamics" of the play and the characters, and to create physical and theatrical images.

Different forms of improvisation. Not all productions are based on a play. Sometimes a theater production is based on material out of which a play is constructed. Sometimes a production is entirely nonverbal, or based on physical actions and visual imagery. Whatever the basis for a production, in real-time theater theatrical images are usually discovered through exploration and improvisation.

1. In the rehearsal process for real-time theater, the first focus of attention is on the creation of physical forms, which can embody the actions of the characters. By starting to speak and move, actors gradually get a picture of their characters' psychological makeup and behavior, what they are doing, and who they are. Using their own instruments, they "meet" their characters, and they begin to build their roles. It is very useful at the beginning of the rehearsal period to "walk" through the play or scenes from it.

2. The second focus is on the specific aesthetics of the form and the

theatrical style that are chosen for the play. The criteria for these are subject to the interpretation of the play and are, of course, entirely subjective choices. Together with the physicalization of the character's actions, they result in certain theatrical images, created by the actor through *improvisation.*

3. A third focus of attention is on the particular space in which the play is going to be performed, that is, the kind of stage.

4. Then there are other elements, like the music, the props, furniture, video, and so on, with all of which the actor creates the images for the performance.

It is very useful, not to say essential, for the real-time actor to be trained in improvisation techniques. Such techniques, for example as those developed by Viola Spolin[13] and Keith Johnstone,[14] open to the actor other ways of exploring the givens of a dramatic situation beyond just speaking the text and executing the blocking. These improvisations can be verbal or nonverbal, purely physical or with objects or masks; they can be designed for the individual actor, or for twos and threes, or for whole groups. They can be focused on the actor's ability to relate to the space or they can help the actor to find out what an action is, how to react, and how to follow impulses. Improvisation techniques can also sharpen the actor's *alertness* and *intuition,* enhance his *imagination* and his *sensitivity,* and train him to take risks, to play freely, and to value his creative process.[15]

A thorough command of such techniques will reinforce the real-time actor's ability to actively contribute to the creative process of a rehearsal. A rehearsal process, however, is not the same as a training session in improvisation techniques. The goal of a rehearsal is, after all, the creation of a performance, whereas the goal of improvisation is the process itself. Improvisation in a rehearsal process is a process too, but it must be geared toward a performable, repeatable result.

Improvisations on form: An inexhaustible wealth of images. Generally speaking, there are two approaches to improvisation during the rehearsal process: improvisations based on the content of the play (story, interpretation, character, structure, and the givens of the play), and improvisations based on the chosen theatrical form or style.

Improvisations based on the content of the play are meant to find out more about what Stanislavski (and Viola Spolin) would call the "what" (action), the "who," and the "where." What are the characters doing, who are they, and where does the action take place? There are many exercises designed to find out more about the nature of a character's actions. When such improvisations are verbal and situational, they tend to be "realistic," or imitative of reality, which is natural considering that "realism" is based on our need to get a grip on the world around us, and those who inhabit it. Characters in a play, and the dramatic situations they find themselves in, usually reflect this reality, and the measure of their truthfulness is gauged against the "real world."

To get away from the strict imitation of reality, and closer to the pure essence of a character's actions and to theatrical images, nonverbal, physical improvisations can be very helpful. But in all cases, it is the play and its content that sets the limits of the improvisation. In order to understand the play, its situation and characters, the best thing one can do is to improvise on situations and characters in similar circumstances, that is: by comparison. A director must be very inventive to think up adequately similar situations. (We already mentioned Stanislavski's substitution technique, but that is not an open-ended improvisation, it is part of the actor's preparation.)

Here is one of the exercises I use, inspired by Brecht,[16] to help the actor "meet" his character. As a real-time actor, you can work from your own presence on the stage, using the technique of *telling a story* to find new ways of looking at the character you play, and different ways of playing him (see chapter 5 of this book). For instance, you can do the following:

1. Tell the story of your character through the whole play, or of one act, or of one scene, or even of one particular, seemingly significant moment of the play. Tell the story in the third person. Focus on your character's actions.
2. Tell the same story in the third person and adopt a point of view toward the character. Try to physicalize this point of view. Try to relate to the theatrical space. Always focusing on the character's actions, you can do this exercise several times, from different points of view.
3. Choose one point of view and tell the story in the first person.
4. Physicalize the action and find an image for it.

Through such improvisations you can discover a wealth of options for the interpretation and embodiment of your character. There is no such thing as *the truth;* the truth is many truths. And you, the actor, are free to choose one of them. Now, with this version in mind, you can embody your character, and play the scene.

Improvisations based on the aesthetic form or style in which the play is going to be performed can also lead to discoveries about the content of the play and how to interpret the character's actions and behavior. To be able to do such improvisations, the starting point for the theatrical form must be clearly defined and outlined. (Without this specification of the form the director and actors have nothing against which to gauge the results of the improvisations.) So the director and the actors need to have some knowledge of the chosen form. It may be useful for the actors and director to research the style, to invite experts who can talk about the chosen style, or even better, to do a little workshop on the style—just as they might do if they needed to include a song or a tap dance in the play. Or they might look at picture books, read poems, visit the zoo, watch movies, make an excursion, or visit a museum.

In one of the first shows I directed (*The Comedy on the Servant of Two Masters,* my adaptation of Carlo Goldoni's *Servant of Two Masters,* Nieuwe Komedie, 1974), I asked the actors to improvise within obvious style elements of the commedia dell'arte. At first they came up with late nineteenth-century English drawing room comedy, and it took them a while before they began to act in a cruder, more grotesque, and less civilized manner that was more appropriate for the knockabout style of the commedia. By trial and error, they learned how to do it and found the form.

In the first fifteen years of my career as a director, in which I directed many plays by Brecht, I often started with a clearly formulated theatrical "form/style principle," upon which we would base the whole play, and on the basis of which the actors could improvise. (See the introduction to this book.) *The Exception and the Rule* (Die Einmalige Theatergruppe / The On(c)e and Only Theater Group, Berlin/Frankfurt, 1976) was played as a circus play. All the characters were clowns and the actors improvised every scene as a clown act. To prepare ourselves, we watched Fellini's *Clowns* over and over again. In this way we stripped the play of its social-realist form: the coolie in the play became not only a pathetic victim of the merchant, the merchant was also the victim of the coolie—and that was both hilarious and a real eye-opener. Brecht's *Fear and Misery in the Third Reich* (Toneel Academie Maastricht, 1982) we did in the form of a cheap, basement cabaret. This allowed us to make the scenes of the play into vaudeville sketches, sometimes improvised and paraphrased on the basis of these scenes, alternating with live music and whatever else can happen in a nightclub cabaret, from tap dance to songs and striptease. This form gave the play an acerbity that had an enormous impact. *Ubu Roi* (Het Vervolg, Maastricht, 1987) took place in a restaurant in which four of the last guests—loaded with booze and with enough money in their pockets to amuse themselves at the cost of the helpless waiter—projected their bourgeois fantasies of power on this poor man, who was forced to do whatever they told him, as long as the bill wasn't paid. The actors, who used the design of a nouveau riche restaurant and all the "props" that go with it, improvised the whole play in this grim manner, scene by scene: using food and plates and bottles. For Shakespeare's *Troilus and Cressida* so-called *bouffons* were the starting point: real-life vagabond-clowns, frightening people, hungry and desperate, who, during the dark Middle Ages, mocked the better-off people in the streets of Paris. Just as in *The Exception and the Rule,* we did many nonverbal, physical exercises for this show to build the characters. We used grotesque costumes, loud wigs, and shrill music. For my first stab at Brecht's *Man Is Man (1)* (InDependance, 1988) the Marx Brothers were the source of inspiration for the theatrical form. In each of these productions, the theatrical forms, some of them quite spectacular, added unexpected dimensions to the plays and their content.

Naturally the play itself—the text, and the space between the lines of the text—must provide the key for the use of such theatrical metaphors. Otherwise the chosen style might be merely imposed upon the play, which then has to live up to the demands of the chosen style. I fell into this mistake when I directed Brecht's *Saint Joan of the Stockyards* (TAT, Frankfurt, 1979), for which the dance films of Busby Berkeley inspired me. But the play didn't quite work the way I had envisaged it because not everything in the play fitted within Busby Berkeley's portrayal of a dream world in which his audience could seek refuge from a harsh social reality. In order to make that work, I would have needed another, purely theatrical framework.

In each of these cases, I was looking for what I would call a "second theatrical metaphor," a theatrical vehicle that provides images to tell the story of the play. The desert in *The Exception and the Rule,* and the Salvation Army in *St. Joan of the Stockyards* are the first, "literary," metaphors established in the plays themselves.

Gradually I discovered that I didn't always need a dominant theatrical metaphor for the whole play; instead I could use all sorts of different images for different scenes, depending on the nature of the scenes. Sometimes these images didn't even need to correspond with each other; they could be juxtaposed. They didn't have to be "big" and spectacular, they could be small and rely more on what the stage itself has to offer. With this realization, I discovered the importance of the presence of the actor as himself. From the juxtaposition of scenes and different images for each scene, the actor emerged, almost necessarily and inevitably, as himself. In *Der Brotladen / The Bread Shop* (Frankfurt, 1980), *Fear and Misery in the Third Reich* (Maastricht 1982), and *Mephisto* (1) (Maastricht 1983) I realized that the actor didn't need a justification to be present on the stage, other than the fact that he is performing a play, and that, therefore, he also didn't need an extra form from outside the play to provide his justification, no matter how strong and effective some of these theatrical metaphors might be. The actor could simply take the creation of images into his own hands, set up the images and "stage" himself in them, and he could make a montage of all these image-based scenes into the performance of the whole play.

Improvisations on the form can produce all sorts of different images. Everything is possible, even images from the conventions of realism and the epic theater. The wealth of images is inexhaustible. Different styles and forms can live peacefully next to each other, juxtaposed as they are in the montage form of the performance. The play and the actors create the unity. Every image can have not only its own quality, but also the quality of a "quote"—something between quotation marks. This functions in the same way that modern composers quote themes and styles from the history of music. In my very first experimental production, Brecht's *The Measures Taken* (1971–72), this was already the case: we quoted from the iconography of the social struggle of the late nineteenth and early twentieth centuries and the Russian Revolution. These quotes originated from improvisations on the form. And Louis Andriessen quoted in his new score the original music by Hanns Eisler.

The Illusion of Reality vs. the Reality of the Illusion

Dreams don't fall from the sky. Hardly anything is more beautiful to me than an empty stage: the wooden floor, the brick or concrete walls, the velour curtains or cotton drapes, the grid for the lights above, and the machinery of the tracks at the sidewalls. A special smell lingers in the air, promising that something is going to happen soon. And the memory of past performances and actors inhabits the space. The stage is a romantic space, a space in which worlds are created that don't exist in the outside world, a place in which desires can be fulfilled and dreams can be lived. That's attractive and exciting.

However, as soon as this dream world of passing illusions has to be created, the problems start—not only because these dreams don't simply fall from the sky, and not only because we have to work terribly hard to bring these dreams to life, but because the created illusions are often so clumsy and awkward that we actors and directors ourselves can hardly believe in them.

In the realistic theater, interiors and costumes, either imitated from a bygone era or from contemporary history, can be only as truthful as we want them to be. Each actor knows that the reality he enters on stage is, in fact, only an *illusion of the reality,* a world in which nothing is really real. And the audience knows this too, and knows that they, too, must do their best to believe in the illusion. "Realism," in other words, is something that looks (or attempts to look) like reality, but is not.

In real-time theater the illusionary world of the play gives way to the material reality of the stage itself. The starting point in real-time theater is not the world of the dramatic situation, but the reality of the actor who plays a role in a play. And the world of the actor is the *reality of the illusion* he brings to life.

The stage doesn't represent anything but itself, and therefore it is real and truthful per se. The theater is real, just as the actors are real, the auditorium and the audience are real: they are all really real, all really themselves.

A different use of the same elements. In real-time theater the transformation of the stage itself into an imaginary space is not necessary. The dramatic action doesn't have to be represented or illustrated by a realistic set. The fact that King Lear is in his castle, or on the moors, or on the battlefield, becomes evident in several sources:

- The text itself
- The dramatic action of the characters
- The physical action of the characters
- The imagination of the actors
- The theatrical space of the stage and the things that are on it, like furniture, drapes, props and the way the actors handle them

The same elements are used in the realistic theater, in which "illusions of reality" are created. But behind the so-called proscenium arch, the actor finds himself in an illusory reality, a reality that he can't escape. He adjusts to the iron laws of the "fourth wall." Behind it he is caught in a situation that he is powerless to change, and he must behave according to the rules of this artificial reality. He must do whatever he can to boost the truthfulness of this situation. If, during a performance, at nine o'clock at night, he must have lunch in the house of the Prozorov family in Chekhov's *The Three Sisters,* he must employ acting exercises or some mental preparation. Perhaps he will skip his own supper so that he can play this scene truthfully. And then, during the scene, he may not get to eat at all: the plates are empty, and the wine is apple juice. So many of his actions in this situation are fictitious actions, not real, but fake.

Strangely enough actors and directors often apply these laws of artificially imitated reality even when a production is staged in a more abstract way. The actor is so used to justifying his actions and activities based on the dramatic situation, that he does so in a "realistic" way even when the play itself is not realistic, or not performed in a realistic manner.

In real-time theater, however, the actors, who are on the stage using the elements of text, dramatic and physical action of the characters, their imaginations, and the qualities of the space itself, take these elements in their own hands and make them serve their purpose, which is to tell the story of the play, in direct communication with the audience. Instead of imitating a reality, they create *autonomous theatrical images* of the dramatic action.

In *The Three Sisters* the actors stood for their lunch with the Prozorovs at the end of the first act, more or less in a wide, loosely arranged, line in the center of the stage. Instead of sitting at a table, they chatted about the weather, Moscow, birthday parties, work, and the situation in their provincial garrison town, while standing as one does at a cocktail party. They didn't raise their glasses—there weren't even glasses—but without moving around, or obliging to the rituals of a formal lunch with food and plates and forks and knifes, they played the actions of the characters; listening to each other, and showing on their faces and in their bodies that they were fully aware of what was going on between the characters they were playing, they made eye contact with the audience more than with each other; they created an image of a lively and very alert group of actors on the stage telling the story of the lunch at the Prozorovs. Saying "cheers" to each other without a glass in their hands forced the actors to find the pure physical gesture to inform the audience about what the actors were doing, feeling, and thinking. This way of acting stirs the imagination of the audience.

Real-time acting can be that pure and simple; at least it can look so. In fact, it is sometimes difficult to create such a simple image in which the actors seem to be doing hardly anything, but where a great deal is going on under the surface. Sometimes more elaborate theatrical images, which require more activity of the actors, are easier to achieve.

Conditions of the stage itself. In traditional theaters with a proscenium arch, actors and audience are separated: the actor is in the light, while the audience is in the dark. And while the people in the audience are present as themselves, the actors are there as if they were someone else—and somewhere else. For these reasons alone, in the traditional theater, the actors and audience are unequal.

In real-time theater, this inequality can be eliminated. But in order to allow both the actors and the audience to be present in the theater as equal partners—without interfering with their differing functions—a few things must change in the theater itself, both as an institution and as a building:

1. The proscenium arch has to disappear, so that the actor can no longer withdraw or hide himself behind it. At minimum, a technical means must be found to overcome the way in which the arch tends to separate the actors from the audience.
2. An open space has to be created, in which the actor can be on equal footing with the audience, with whom he can communicate directly: both parties are in one space.

3. The lights must be hung in such a way that they do not blind the actor or keep him from seeing the auditorium and the audience.

In its most simple form, the stage can be a level floor, with the audience rows beginning at that level and then progressing higher on bleachers or on risers, with chairs on them. In this arrangement, the feet of the people in the first row of the audience are on the same floor as the feet of the actors. Even the audience in the higher rows feels the intimacy that this creates, even in larger auditoriums. This simple change creates an immediate rapport between actors and audience:

- There is no deep orchestra abyss between audience and actors.
- There is no curtain or fire screen like those in proscenium theaters.
- Both the actors and the audience can see each other.
- The actors are not pushed away from the audience by bright lights.
- The actors can actually come extremely close to the audience.

This is a true democratic theater, just as the original Greek theater was. In this sort of theater every spectator in every seat can see everything. There are no favorable and unfavorable sightlines, as is the case in the proscenium arch theater.

However simple the arrangement of this so-called *flat-floor* theater may seem, in practice it usually means that such spaces can only be created in existing empty spaces like abandoned factories, or they have to be entirely newly erected. (See also Part III.)

Form and format. The way in which we *interpret* the dramatic action of a character is subjective. It is based, first of all, on the personal ideas of the director and the actors, and, more objectively, on the ever-changing opinions and prejudices of the times in which we live. These cultural predilections have consequences for the *forms* we choose in creating a character. For instance, in Shakespeare's time, Richard III was thought of simply as a murderous court intriguer, but in our time he has been played as a Nazi and as a psychopath.

The choices an actor makes to shape his character and his dramatic action—under the guidance of the director—give the audience signals about how to interpret and understand what it sees. The actor reveals the thoughts and feeling of his character in several ways:

- Physicalizing the actions of the character through movements and gestures
- Speaking the text using intonations and inflections of the voice
- Relating to the other characters and to the space
- Creating theatrical images

In the realistic and the epic theaters, these forms are chosen during rehearsal and are then shown to the audience as *finalized, finished products*. In these theater conventions, the *form* is dictated by a set of "rules" or "laws" that define what is realistic and what is epic. That's why performances in these styles look often similar in many respects. These rules are formalized in the acting techniques being used and in the concrete reality of the proscenium arch theater. Therefore, they are ultimately defined by the conditions of its architecure (see also Part III). The form is at the same time a format.

In real-time theater, the actor's performance is neither *finished nor finalized*. The form may be invented during rehearsal and will be rehearsed, but during the performance the actor takes his character and the dramatic situation of the play by the hand and gives them, in full view of the audience, shape and form—as if he were a sculptor giving form to a figure that he carves out of stone.

If there are "rules" in real-time theater, they are that the form is not fixed, but open and infinitely alterable. In real-time theater anything is possible. It is not a format: realistic scenes can alternate with songs, or a clown's act, or a film fragment, or a highly stylized "Brechtian" scene. Performances in this convention look different from each other.

The architecture of the open space defines the conditions for the infinite possibilities of the theatrical form (see also Part III).

Instruments of the Theater Itself 1: Stage and Stage Design

For the sake of truthfulness and historical reliability, the stage in realistic theater is usually decorated with a set representing the reality. As a result, the theatrical space itself becomes invisible. Instead of the stage, we see living rooms, corridors, kitchens, hotel lobbies, and so on.

In Brecht's epic theater the stage was sparsely decorated and often white. Dramatic situations were stylized and presented in their essence; the stage was turned into different locations by simple means, but the actor still found himself in illusionary spaces: Galileo with his scientific instruments, a desk and a chair, Mother Courage with her cart on a revolving stage, with which she moved from one moment to the next and from one location to another. This filmlike device dealt with time and space in a very effective way. The curtain was replaced by a half curtain and opened and closed between scenes. But the space of the stage itself remained invisible.

Even when sets are an *abstraction of reality,* they can create an illusionary location inside of which the realistic stage situation can be maintained. A *symbolic* set, which provides the actor with an illusionary but concrete location, is a substitute for a realistically designed stage. As long as the theatrical space itself is ignored and not included as part of the design of the set, some sort of illusion of another world is maintained.

When the stage is filled with set pieces that represent Macbeth's castle, or the woods, or the battlefield, the actor still knows that he is actually on the stage—and so does the audience. Therefore, there is no reason we cannot just remove these set pieces and take the stage itself as a starting point. Similarly, more abstract images that symbolize the castle, the woods, or the battlefield, can give way to the stage itself. This doesn't mean that the stage must always be a bare, empty space with very few things on it, as in *Waiting for Godot,* or like the plays Bertolt Brecht directed at the Berliner Ensemble. In fact, the stage can be meticulously and beautifully designed and arranged as a space.

For a production of *Big and Little* by Botho Strauss (Haiyuza Theater, Tokyo, 2000), I collaborated with the Dutch stage designer Peter de Kimpe and the Japanese stage designer Yukio Horio. De Kimpe suggested that we create what he called a "landscape for the play." The two designers created a set that was the stage itself: a unified space, which included the acting space and the auditorium, a single space in which the actors acted and the audience watched. There were no "interiors" or "exteriors" of any kind.

In 2005, De Kimpe further developed this idea of the stage as a landscape for the play. In my production of *Allein das Meer / The Same Sea,* he designed not a set that would represent the dramatic situation, but a theatrical environment. The huge level stage showed its bare walls (which were usually covered with black curtains to hide the storage space they contain); four slabs of stone divided the space roughly in two. The actors moved chairs around to create a new space for every act (the play has four acts). They wheeled a huge table with a collection of tea services from different cultures into different positions. Upstage, in the background, where the actors never appeared, against a cobalt-blue backdrop, stood a copper construction that rotated slowly. Although the play takes place in Israel, this "landscape" didn't represent real interior or exterior situations of an exotic Middle East. Instead, it provided the actors an ever-changing space to create (physical) images for the actions of their characters, and it gave the audience an opportunity to use its own imagination.

Theatrical images in real-time theater use the theatrical space, that is, the stage, and sometimes even the whole theater, to create a space for the play. These images accentuate specific qualities of the space. The idea of such an "empty space" was introduced by Peter Brook in his book *The Empty Space,*[17] and was demonstrated in many of his performances in his Théâtre des Bouffes du Nord in Paris, in which the space itself is always used, disclosed, and taken as real.

The theatrical space itself is disclosed as the location for the performance of the play, where the actor tells his story and displays his theatrical imagination. The stage is designed not to represent, illustrate, or symbolize the material location of the dramatic situation of the play, but to create an overall theatrical image for the dramatic action: the space and the design of that space are a part of the overall theatrical image: *the stage is the set.*

Use of the space. In real-time theater, the physical or material reality of the dramatic situation is less important than the dramatic actions of the characters and the pure theater actions of the actors, which—in combination with the reality of the stage—are the main source of inspiration for what I call "theatrical images": *what* takes place in the boudoir of Madame X is more important than how the boudoir looks in all its realistic details. A theatrical image should express it. The actors, who stage themselves in the empty space of the stage, create these images. In real-time theater we see no "divine magic" (deus ex machina), nor three-dimensional picture-book images, in which changing locations and other illusions are produced, magically controlled by invisible hands in the wings or on the grid.

This starting point for real-time theater demands, first of all, a concrete use of the space: the actors have to be *somewhere*. There must be a place on stage for them to occupy, a place from which they watch the action, and out of which they can move to begin their own actions. Practically speaking, there might be chairs or other places from which they can watch the action, standing or moving around. Current ideas about blocking and mise-en-scène, based on a realistic design of the space, must change to serve this idea: where the actors are on the stage depends on the possibilities of the theatrical space and the theatrical images they create for the actions of their characters. Blocking arises naturally, but it comes last in the rehearsal process. *Blocking* is therefore not a very good word, because it refers to the practice of moving the actors around in their dramatic environment, blocking them from going somewhere else and pinning them down in fixed positions. In real-time theater, their position in the space, discovered during the rehearsal process, results in a *choreography* of the actors in relationship to the space, to each other, and to the characters they play: it is a "dance" between actors and characters.

Use of chairs and other furniture. In my own practice, beginning with Brecht's *The Measures Taken* (Theater School, Amsterdam, Directors Dept., 1971–72), chairs have always been an important element of performances. Their use always has been both practical and aesthetic. But in the Brecht production, it took a long time before we were able to see these chairs purely as chairs, as furniture to sit on, and not to use them as something else, for example a boat to transport rice—an object in the play—or even to simulate a fight with, as we tried to do. The chairs and other furniture or constructions need to have a place on the stage and must be moved by the actors, staging themselves, to serve the purpose of the theatrical images. These are pure theater actions, in which the actors feel the "real time" of the performance they are creating. Furniture is fine on the empty stage, as long as it is not meant to design a living room with.

In *Mephisto* (1) we used simple garden chairs, not to indicate a garden, but to divide the space with in ever-changing compartments, thus contributing to the theatrical images for the different scenes. For instance, in the suicide scene (see the section "Alternating" above), the text and action made it clear that Gottschalk and Miriam were on a railway bridge. Three garden chairs merely defined the space. In *Black Box,* the image of the temple, where negotiations over the estate took place, was created by a row of chairs with their backs to the audience. And at the end of the play, the actors put all the chairs on the wooden stage to create the image of a big but incomplete family since most of the chairs were empty. In *Big and Little* (Haiyuza Theatre, Tokyo, 2000), in the last scene the actors first put chairs on the stage, then one by one sat on them, as if in the waiting room of the doctor, then they left after the doctor had called their names, separating the theatrical action from the dramatic action of the scene, until only Lotte, the main character of the play, was sitting alone, and lonely, amid a field of empty chairs.

I don't mean to imply that chairs are an indispensable element in real-time theater, or that they are the only possible decorative objects. The obvious reason that they seem to be necessary most of the time is very practical: the actors need something to sit on, most of all when they are not acting and just watching. This doesn't mean that actors always have to sit when they watch and don't act. They can also stand. Or sit on the floor. Or lean against the wall. But it is amazing what you can do with chairs, and how beautiful an arrangement of chairs can be. I have also directed plays where there was no furniture at all. Elements of the space itself, simply what is there, can be enough, from the stone rear wall of the theater, the cloths or drapes, ladders, and the lighting grid. When we started working on Brecht's *Der Brotladen / The Breadshop* (Schlicksupp teatertrupp, Frankfurt, 1980), we were offered a newly renovated former slaughterhouse for rehearsal and performance space. We had no money, so when we entered the unusually shaped space I suggested for the very first production of our new group that we use only what we found there: a big table, a ladder, and two black bentwood chairs. And so we did.

As Peter Brook has shown many times, a carpet on the floor can be enough. Drapes, hanging down, or pulled up by actors who are visible to the audience, can be used to create different spaces in which to play, rather than realistic locations. If it is technically possible (and if the theater rules allow), it can be striking if the actors handle these devices themselves, as we did in *Big and Little* (Tokyo, 2000), where at the end of the play, Lotte stood alone in the rain that poured down from a contraption in the grid manipulated by two actors who were visible to the audience. Everything on stage can be used, but nothing *has* to be used:

the space itself is present in the same way as the actors are present. In this sense, the space for real-time theater is very much like the space for modern dance.

Instruments of the Theater Itself 2: Props and Objects

Since in real-time theater everything is present and visible, everything the actors need for their acting is present and visible too. The design of the performance space can include special places for the props you need—on the floor, on a wall, or on a table—instead of having a prop table in the wings or behind the stage. And since the actors themselves handle the props they need, they can be their own prop masters. The design can also include objects that are not used, but are simply there for their own sake, objects that do not represent anything but themselves, but which stir the audience's capacity for free association. In *The Same Sea / Allein das Meer* the slowly revolving copper construction against the cobalt-blue backdrop was such an object. It reminded members of the audience of a house, but also of the Holocaust Memorial in Berlin. People like to give meaning to things, even when there is no specific meaning intended. It is good when the audience can decide for itself what the image might mean. Similarly, the collection of porcelain tea services from different cultures on the big table, had no immediate function in the play, but the actors drank tea from them when they felt like it.

There are many different ways of using props. Sometimes you can use a prop to create a theatrical image. For instance, in *The Three Sisters* there was a small table with a collection of liquor glasses on it. These glasses were only used twice: one time within a scene, when Andrej and Chebutykin mustered their courage with some drinks, and one time as a pure theater-action, when the actor who played Andrej drank a glass of water before he started his long complaint. For the rest of the time, it was just a small table with a collection of liquor glasses on it. Similarly, in *Ivanov (2)* a swinging tabletop hung down from the grid, with glasses on it that Lebedev tried to grab. His lurching for the glasses made him swagger on his feet, without having to play drunk. And in *Man Is Man (1)* (1988) an actress, outside the action but on stage, used a hammer to bang on firecrackers for the fake execution of Galy Gay.

While some props may be present without being used, others may exist to support an action. I have mentioned the sponge with blood that Gloucester used when he is blinded. Similarly, the actress who played Ilana in *Black Box* brought a bunch of flowers onto the stage. She did not give the flowers to her former father-in-law, Gudonski, but instead put them on the floor to be "discovered" by him when he started the play.

In *Man Is Man (2)* (Tisch, NYU, 2007 / The Elephant Brigade, HERE, 2007), a young actress played Galy Gay. In the mock trial in which he is sentenced to death for selling a nonexistent army elephant, he tries to escape his fate by taking his moustache off. But as a woman, the actress didn't have a moustache. She wasn't trying to hide that she was a woman, and therefore *she needed a moustache to be taken off.* Purely for dramatic reasons and the progress of the play, she got a moustache from one of the soldiers who were "trying" her—a piece of black gaffer tape, not a moustache of hair from a makeup artist! This was a very theatrical and dramatic moment: the gesture with which the soldier gave her the moustache was the image of a "kiss of death." Now the moustache could be taken off, but it didn't help poor Galy Gay, because he had cheated and everybody had seen it.

But real-time theater can also refrain from the use of props altogether. When the actor, playing the dramatic action, has found a physical image, he can rely on the text and the image without needing a fully designed location and the props that usually go with it. The lunch with the Prozorov family in *Three Sisters,* as we have seen before, was played without any props—no table, no food, and no glasses for the wine—just the text.

One "rule" for the use of props in real-time theater is that they should not "illustrate" the action. Another is that they can be used to create an image for the action. As a rule of thumb: *if the text mentions props, try to find an image without them; if the text or the space between the lines inspires you to find an image, use props whenever you need them.*

Instruments of the Theater Itself 3: Costumes

Costumes are the clothing the actors need to play their characters. It is important that a costume contribute to the creation of a character and a theatrical image for the character. But in real-time theater, a costume needn't be an imitation of the clothes of a character, or of the clothes we think a character would have worn. Many costumes, especially costumes referring to a historical period, or fantasies referring to a historical period, are often superfluous illustrations of the character. This is one of the most difficult issues in real-time theater, for a costume can entice an actor to imagine himself actually *being* another person. It can help him hide as if behind a mask. In realistic and epic theater this is normal practice, but in real-time theater it can undermine the presence of the actor, which is the basis of the aesthetic.

So in real-time theater, a good starting point is for the costume designer to ask the actors to play in costumes in which they feel comfortable. This need not mean that they must wear their everyday clothes, or that they should not look good. On the contrary, the designer, using his imagination, following his own good taste and having an understanding of real-time theater and acting, can design the right clothes, or find them in stores. The costume the designer creates must help the actor to express the action of his character. Often the behavior of the character and his idiosyncrasies can give a clue to the sort of costume the actor should wear. Another clue is how he relates to other characters in the play and to society. Just as with props and sets, costumes often tend to "illustrate" the function of the character. King Lear is often played in some sort of a nondescript robe simply because he is a king without power, and that seems to be how we think of kings in the dark Middle Ages. Essential is that the designer begins the costume designing process by thinking about the actor who will "take on" the role of King Lear. For, in real-time theater this is exactly what we see: actors who, in the here and now, take on the roles they play. And then the designer needs to look at his actions.

It works best when costumes are invented during the rehearsal process and through association. This allows the actors to participate in the process; it also requires new approaches to design and production. It makes it essential that designers attend rehearsals rather than designing the costumes at their drawing table.

In *Black Box* the actor who played Michel underlined his progress toward an ever-stricter Jewish orthodoxy, by adding more and more black clothes to his initial white shirt and black pants. He changed his clothes on the stage—as the actor—letting the audience see that at each stage Michel needed another piece of costume for the phase he was in.

In real-time theater, actors also often play more than one role. To do so, the actor sometimes must change costumes, but he can do this in the open, where the audience can see him change. This sort of onstage change is always preferable. If the change is very complicated or requires too much undressing, the actor can make an exit—but he must be sure to exit as the actor, not as the character, and then reenter again as the actor, before he starts his next scene.

Those costume changes taking place on the stage often require a costume-changing space, which should be part of the stage design. This provides another place where the actors can be and from which they can follow the action. In *Black Box* this was a brilliantly lit space behind a half high curtain, so that you always saw the actors' legs. Costumes can be on a rack, but they can also be spread around the space wherever the actors need them; they can lie on the floor or on the ramp of the stage, or hang on the back of a chair, or they can be in a chest, like the kind children used to find in their parents' attic (and dressed up from, to play theater . . .). But it is also possible to casually change clothes during the action itself.

Instruments of the Theater Itself 4: Music and Sound

In realistic theater, music often illustrates the dramatic action, underlines certain emotions or the general mood, announces something that is about to happen, or counterpoints the action. This music is usually mechanically reproduced through speakers. On rare occasions, there are musicians on stage or in the orchestra pit. In realism, music is used in the same way it is used in film, and the actors remain subservient to such musical effects. They have no influence on the music, and the music doesn't influence them.

In epic theater, music is one of the most important "alienation effects." Often it interrupts the action. In many plays by Brecht a small ensemble on stage provides music to which the actors sing. Although we have become used to this form, it was an important innovation in the theater of his time. The most famous example is *The Three Penny Opera,* the Kurt Weill songs of which became part of the world repertoire of light entertainment. The live orchestra is one of the most eye-catching features of this play.[18]

The songs in an epic play are not an illustration of the action of a character, but an interruption and a continuation of the action by other means. As soon as the actors step out of their roles to sing a song, they, like the musicians, are supposed to become simply present as themselves rather than as characters. They are part of the music, because they produce it themselves. In most Brecht productions, however, it has become common practice for actors to remain in their roles when they sing.

In many of my real-time theater productions, I have followed the practice of using music as an "alienation effect." I have collaborated with several composers, like Louis Andriessen[19] for *The Measures Taken* (Amsterdam, 1972) and Heiner Goebbels[20] for *The Exception and the Rule* (Berlin/Frankfurt, 1976) and *Saint Joan of the Stockyards* (Frankfurt, 1978).

Just as in the epic theater of Bertolt Brecht, music in real-time theater is an interruption of the action. But in real-time theater, it is not the music that interrupts the actors in their playing, but rather *the actors who interrupt themselves to play some music or sing a song*. In this way—unlike the use of music in the epic theater—the actors contribute actively to the montage of the performance. Whether the music is "live" or mechanically reproduced, all the musical moments in the play together form a *composition* in its own right, telling the story of the play with musical means. This is so even when these moments include completely different genres of music. In *Black Box,* for instance, a Schubert string quartet was juxtaposed to a Shostakovich waltz, punk rock, and klezmer jazz. And in *Mephisto (2)* actors sang Eisler songs alongside other recorded music by Arvo Pärt, Stravinsky, Osvaldo Pugliese, and René Aubry. It is up to the director and the musical director, together with the actors, to create this composition by finding musical moments, not only at the ends of scenes and at breaks between acts, but also in the "spaces between" the action. Even when the actors themselves don't sing or take part in the music making, they are present and listen to the music, just as the audience does.

It goes without saying that live music is preferable to mechanically reproduced music. But an orchestra is expensive, and a good orchestra very expensive. Another possibility is to ask the actors if they play instruments, or if they want to learn to play instruments. Many actors are capable of doing so. The members of the theater group I worked with in Frankfurt, Schlicksupp teatertrupp, all learned to play, though some mastered only a few notes on their instruments. They were not perfect musicians, but their playing was a part of the acting, and their music making became the expression of the dramatic action with musical means, not an illustration of it. During the workshop sessions for *Der Brotladen* (Frankfurt, 1981), and *Flametti* (Rotterdam/Frankfurt, 1983), the actors improvised under the guidance of musicians. In *Der Brotladen / The Bread Shop* the actors often brought their instruments with them onto the stage and into the dramatic situation. During the bread battle at the end of the play, one group of actors "attacked" their opponents with the wild sounds of their brass instruments, which sounded like a battle cry. When the other group responded with shrieking sounds of a violin and a clarinet, the first group moved forward under the cover of their instruments, which they carried over their heads, to protect themselves against the rolls, the baguettes, and the flour with which the others pelted them.

At the end of the show, the actors came together after Washington Meyer's death, and each one repeated one staccato note on his instrument, until a shrill and sad cacophony of notes hung in the air. Then the actor who played Washington Meyer rose up from the dead, took hold of his tuba, and joined the musical ensemble, creating another strong death scene moment. After that, as the actors stopped playing one by one, only one last sad sound remained, the sound of the clarinet. Then this sound faded out too, all the actors put their instruments down and the play was over.

If the music is performed electronically rather than live, I would recommend that the actors themselves operate the sound equipment onstage so that the actors can contribute to the pace and rhythm of the performance as their music making becomes an integral part of the show. This can vary from a simple CD player to a computer-operated sound system. Putting this equipment at the disposal of the actor reinforces his presence as himself, and it adds something extra to the performance. In *King Lear,* for instance, some actors worked on a huge soundboard to create the storm in the act 3. And the battle in act 4, which is only referred to in the text, was played as a musical intermezzo, with the actors wearing thick gloves, as if ready for battle. In *Man Is Man (2),* actors operated the computer in full view of the audience, to create the sounds of slamming doors, creaking floorboards, and gunshots, while other actors, in and out of character, responded to them, as in a radio play. In *Mephisto (2)* the actors sang their Eisler songs to a piano accompaniment, which the actors played through a CD player. In this way, the actors' work with the sound equipment can allow them to interrupt the character actions with pure theater actions while this punctuation contributes to the rhythm and pace of the performance. And ideally, the entire musical composition enhances the whole performance, evoking unconscious levels of meaning, understanding, and emotional rapport for both the actors and the audience.

Instruments of the Theater Itself 5: Light

Then there is light. In realism light functions mostly as the expression of a "mood," as lighting designers and technicians often like to call it. And like "mood music," light-as-mood illustrates the dramatic action and isolates the dramatic situation from the space in which it is performed. This sort of lighting is typical in realism, and color often plays a big role in it; light applied in this way usually underlines the emotional charge of the action. Brecht, on the other hand, demanded bright, white light for his epic theater. He wanted to put the dramatic events of his plays in a clear light that left nothing concealed (except the stage itself). At first this worked as yet another effective alienation effect. But soon the proscenium arch theater adapted this style of lighting, transforming it into a harmless theatrical device.

Large proscenium arches demand strong frontal lighting. Big theaters with large auditoriums, high arches, a curtain, a teaser, and a fire curtain create a great distance between the actors and the lighting instruments, which must, therefore, be very bright. The audience wants to see the actors, and frontal lighting serves the purpose of lighting them, particularly their faces. Much of the light must come from far away in the auditorium to light the actor's faces, even far upstage. Additional light comes from behind the proscenium arch, from the pipes above, and some can be added from the wings. The strong frontal light is mounted on pipes high up in the auditorium, or on balconies and other prominent parts of the auditorium, from where it dives under the proscenium arch and blinds the actors. This isolates them from the audience even more than they already are by the proscenium. Nowadays, even small flat-floor theaters have adopted this sort of lighting, in spite of the fact that, in a small space, it is totally unnecessary.

Brecht, with his Berliner Ensemble, also worked in a proscenium arch theater (Theater am Schiffbauerdamm) where he had to use frontal light. But he purposefully had the lighting grid or pipes lowered so that the spotlights could be hung in such a way that the audience could see the source of the light and observe the lighting changes. This device helped make it clear that the theater reality was an artificial one, and this way of hanging lights is now generally accepted within the practice of the proscenium arch theater.

In real-time theater the most important function of light is to disclose the stage itself and everyone and everything that is on it, not to provide a dramatic situation with a suitable mood, for it is the actor himself who "shines a light" upon the action of the characters. As in Brecht's epic theater, bright light is necessary so that the audience can see the whole space, not just isolated situations. But that is not to say that the lighting must be cold or distancing, as is often presumed. Light, even colored light, can contribute a great deal to the theatrical images that are created for the dramatic actions—as long as the light creates a space for the dramatic actions on the stage, has a function in its own right, and can be seen *as* light.

Light is a seductive instrument, and it is difficult to tell the story of the play with light without being tempted to illustrate the story, and without isolating the dramatic situation from the space in which it is performed. Lighting the space demands technical know-how and insight into the working of the instruments. For directors of real-time theater this knowledge is indispensable.

In real-time theater, a very essential lighting consideration is that the lights not blind the actors. They must be able to see the audience rather than staring into a dark hole where they suspect the audience to be. For this reason, footlights can be deadly for actors, for they make them as blind as moles, forcing them to guess at what lies beyond the light. The audience for its part needs to see that the actors can see them. A flat-floor theater is most supportive of these considerations because its overhead grid allows the light to come from anywhere. A fraction of the normal amount of front light thrown on the actors' faces in these theaters is usually enough to make them visible. Most of the light can come from the sides, from above and from the back, giving the actors more contours, as lights do for dance performances. It is not a problem if some of the action takes place in the semidark or in light shadows.

Lighting in this way and in these kinds of theaters creates one unified space for the actors and the audience. In such a space, the reflected stage light also illuminates the audience as it does in concert halls, so light-reflecting colored surfaces can be very useful in such theaters and as part of a stage design.

If one attempts to perform a real-time production in a proscenium theater, it is almost impossible to create one space for audience and actors. These theaters don't have an overall lighting grid, and if they do, it doesn't help much because lights from the grid cannot be aimed under the proscenium arch, so one must almost always add the auditorium lights to the lighting design. If this is not possible (which is often the case in older theaters) the lighting designer must light the audience itself by illuminating the walls or the ceiling with indirect light, but this must be carefully done so as not to blind the audience.

In terms of its lighting, the so-called black box theater, which is usually a flat-floor space with an overall grid, is still based on the proscenium arch principle: The walls and floor of the black box are black. Because black absorbs light rather than reflecting it, the stage space is not disclosed but hidden on purpose: you are not supposed to see it. This makes it easier to isolate the actors and the dramatic actions they play by putting them in the light. But this choice also isolates the actors from the rest of the theater space and makes it difficult for them to connect with the audience and to create one space, which is so essential for real-time theater.

In a good flat-floor theater, there are many ways to use light to partition the space and create acting areas. Parts of the space can be accentuated so that the space is disclosed in different ways at different times. For some productions, like *The Same Sea / Allein das Meer,* and *Mephisto (2),* stage designer Peter de Kimpe created one general light and smaller accents for each of the four acts, to disclose and accentuate the space from different angles, like photographs of the same space taken through different lenses or with different lighting. For *Black Box* (Amsterdam, 1999) stage and light designer JanJoris Lamers created one space, with ever-changing lighting that had its own rhythm and tempo, independent of the development of the dramatic action of the play. The slowly changing light created the impression of turning around, not lighting scenes, but rather creating light and shadow that glided over the stage and the whole space, thus telling the story of the play in its own subtle way.

It is helpful if the actors themselves can control the lights, just as they can run the music and sound. This intensifies the sense that the actors are staging themselves and that they are present onstage as themselves, for every time they push a button, they are executing a pure theater action. This kind of control can contribute something to the performance, as we have seen in the suicide scene in *Mephisto (1)* with a sound effect, and in *Ivanov (1)* with a lighting effect. But practically and technically, this is often difficult to achieve, because the lighting board must be on the stage. Recently, however, even in proscenium productions, lighting and sound crews and their control boards have left their booths and have been placed in the auditorium, in order to be closer to the stage. In fact, the lighting technicians, using portable boards and computers, can now be very close to the ramp or the edge of the stage, or even on the stage itself. So instead of being anonymous and invisible, they can become part of the performance. Of course this arrangement has consequences for the stage design. If the sound technicians can also be placed on or at the edge of the stage, then they can perform the sound punctuation of the show's action, visible to the audience, as I did in *Der Mann der . . . / The Man Who . . .* Their interventions will be more accurate because of it. Their actions will become part of the dynamic of the performance. And the technicians sitting there, working their boards, become part of the overall theatrical image.

Instruments of the Theater Itself 6: Media—Film and Video

Although theater directors were attracted to the new medium of film from its early days on at the beginning of the twentieth century, its application in a "live" performance stayed marginal for a long time because of the technical requirements for projection. In the 1920s, in Berlin, Erwin Piscator was the first to introduce moving images and still photography projected on screens at the side or the back of the stage. These were black-and-white projections, and silent, and were merely a backdrop to his huge epic spectacles. But when film evolved from a rather primitive medium into a technically highly advanced medium— silent movies became "talkies," and black-and-white pictures were replaced by Technicolor—it also required a highly advanced projection technique, which made its application on stage virtually impossible:

there was no place for a projection screen in the context of a realistic set, and the lights for the stage, mostly coming from the front, or from above, interfered with the projection of film, which also had to come from the front. Other than by switching off the lights altogether and turning the theater into a movie house, it was hardly possible to use film in the theater.

This changed when television was introduced, in the 1940s and 50s, and soon became a medium in its own right, with a projection system of its own: the television set, which very quickly began to dominate every household. When television was followed by video, the medium was ready to claim its place in the theater. At first, television sets became part of the stage, either for immediate projection of "live" television, or for projection of taped material, from a video player through the device of a "beamer," onto the screen. The latest electronic developments of the computer and digital recording and projection completed this technological revolution. At the end of the twentieth and the beginning of the twenty-first centuries television sets on stage made way for big screen projection of video images, "live" or canned, or both, in a "live" performance. The beamer allows for projection from the front and from behind, on a relatively short distance and from all angles, without interfering with the stage lights. Since then projection screens with "moving images" have become regular and increasingly popular features in the theater, and are here to stay.

With its capacity to absorb, or adapt to the newest technology, the convention of realism, often confined within the proscenium arch, applies the devices of film and video mainly as a backdrop, substituting the stage set completely or partially. As an alien, highly artificial, element, it can enhance, if applied subtly and carefully, but it can also disturb the quality of truthful reproduction of reality on the stage. It doesn't matter too much, when, within the convention of realism, stage sets appear to be artificial and ramshackle, as long as the actors are truthful in their performance, and as long as they can maintain the "illusion of reality." But with "moving images" on the stage, one has to think twice before applying this exciting and seductive medium. One doesn't want the actors to compete with the images on the screen, nor does one want them to compete for the audience's attention.

At the same time, film or video projection in a "live" performance creates an opportunity to break away from the strictest realism, even behind the proscenium arch. It is, actually, an ideal tool to create an "alienation effect," as Brecht had envisaged for the epic theater. The realistic dramatic situation on stage can be broken up by images, which belong to a different medium. Directors need to be aware of the overwhelming power of the moving image, *which in a theater performance needs to add to, and be tied in with, the dramatic action.* They need to make sure that film and video images do not become *illustrations* of, or *comments* on, the dramatic situation. Spectators, preconditioned by the familiar presence of television sets in their homes, permanent exposure to computer images, and countless visits to the movies, tend to look at film images first, and will be easier distracted from the dramatic situation on stage, if these images don't *illuminate* the action. Moreover, the bigger and technically more accomplished the projected images become, the more they tend to live a life of their own, close the stage off from the audience, as the "fourth wall" did before, and create a wonder-world of illusions of reality on the stage. The *alienation* loses its *effect* and makes way for a new form of self-contained realism, even when the projected images are more abstract and poetic. Film projection can easily become the deus ex machina of the new age.

In real-time theater this pitfall can be avoided, for instance by having cameras on stage, operated in full view, whose pictures are projected simultaneously as cameramen/-women film them. I explored this for the first time in the performance of Brecht's small play *Die Horatier und die Kuriatier* (Toneelacademie Maastricht, 1979), when cameras were still very big, and the technique didn't allow for more than black-and-white projection. Projection, of course, was immediate and was on television sets, and the camera operator was necessarily present in the performance space. Used in this way, recording and projection become part of the theater action.

Actors can also operate (small, handheld) cameras themselves, and thus have control over the creation and projection of the film images required for the performance. I tried this for the first time in *Man Is Man* (2) (Tisch School of Drama, New York, 2007). After initial hesitation the actors, who usually stay away from everything technical, became enthusiastic filmmakers. The action of creating the video images themselves, projected through a beamer, contributed to the dramatic impact of the story, and the actors were automatically in "real time": when you operate a camera there's not much else you can do. As long as these "pure theater actions" can be integrated with their other tasks, the actors thus participate immediately in the action of the performance, and without creating some sort of "false" magic, they are telling the story of the play with these means, as well as with the other elements they have in their command. Applied in this way, filmed images are being created on the spot, in "real time," close to the actors and the audience, even if their projection is on big screens.

However, the video technique always requires a technician who operates the beamer and the switchboard. It is advisable to have the video technician, just like the light and sound technicians, on the stage or very close to it, so that his actions of producing these film and video images are visible to the audience and can contribute to the rhythm of the performance. This is particularly necessary if existing or prepared film material is projected as well. In *Der Mann der . . . /The Man Who . . .* (Neues Theater, Halle, 2007), the technician operated "live" video images created by the actors, prepared video images created by a video artist, and the sound. His position was downstage, from where he could oversee the stage and the actions of the actors, in the same way as the orchestra for the opera was positioned in pre-Wagner times. The audience observed his actions, just as they observed the actions of the actors: the technician was one of them.

Staging, Blocking, and Choreography

In realism everything has a fixed position in the illusory space. The director usually invents the *blocking* for the actor: the arrangement of the actions on the stage and the positioning of the actors, in relationship to the realistic images. This blocking (mise-en-scène) is often designed on paper, perhaps before rehearsals begin, in the same way as a storyboard is designed for a film. Following this map, the actor can find his way around the stage. Everything depends on the right timing, the proper position, and the progression of the dramatic events of the play. Dependent as he is upon this blocking, an actor who is used to performing within the convention of realism wants to know beforehand where the director wants him on the stage, and where and when he will have to move. "Tell me where you want me to be, and I'll deliver the scene" is something you can hear actors say, who are used to this form. In the epic theater, in its stylized form, the same blocking "rules" are generally applied. Blocking is often what directors in these traditions do more than anything else: rehearsal times are short, and directors often don't have much time for their authors.

In real-time theater, however, nothing on stage has a fixed position before rehearsals begin. Only the space itself is defined. The blocking, or rather the choreography, originates gradually and organically during the rehearsals, in improvisations on the form, according to the ideas for the theatrical form and the imagery. For this process to work, the actors have to develop a sense of space, and of the particular space they are working in. The exercises in "seeing" can help them here. It is particularly important that they become aware of the effect of standing in one line, either "horizontally" or "vertically" in the space. Unless they are purposefully next to each other, without facing each other, horizontal lines (from left to right) are boring; they take the tension out of the interaction between actors and show faces in profile, which might be good for film, but not for theater. Vertical lines (from downstage to upstage) often block the audience's view. So actors have to learn how to create and follow *diagonal lines* in a space, as they position themselves in relation to each other. During performance, especially when the show is performed in different theaters (in Holland, theater shows always travel), the same holds true: the actors must rediscover over and over the arrangements of their actions within the space—both as characters within the dramatic situation and as actors within the stage reality— which includes freedom of movement and improvisation. How they do this is something they must learn during the rehearsal process. *Choreography* as another term for blocking is an appropriate word, for it refers to the movement of the "chorus." In Greek tragedy, twelve to fifteen actors/dancers were the chorus, out of which the actors who spoke or sang individually appeared and manifested themselves. Similarly, in real-time theater, all the actors are on the stage during the performance, as in a chorus, whether they are playing or watching. They move around to position themselves properly. The result is a living, breathing choreography, which has a rhythm and an aesthetic quality of its own.

Because he himself has discovered or largely contributed to the "material" gathered during the rehearsal process, the real-time actor is able to deal freely with this material. He can alter how he uses it to build his character by slightly changing the choreography.

As long a he stays within the limits of the agreements that are made for the actions he plays, the actor is free to improvise with the theatrical forms and the choreography, just as the jazz musician can improvise with the musical material and the score of the melody he plays. If he breaks these agreements, he may surprise his colleagues in an unwanted way. But if the voice of his scene partner suddenly comes from somewhere else than the day before, he shouldn't be surprised: if he listens well, he will be able to locate his partner soon enough.

Rehearsal and Production

The actors in real-time theater create and invoke theatrical images instead of simply being a part of images created and invoked by the director and by the stage, costume, and lighting designers. In traditional theater practice, the images are "givens" chosen by the director and his design team. The actor is cast in a role and is asked to carry out the tasks the director has in mind for him. It is up to the actor, as a professional, to meet the demands of his role and to carry out the wishes of the director. The director guides him to understand his role, to embody his character in a truthful and hopefully passionate manner, and to fulfill the demands of the artistic concept. But usually—and unfortunately—within traditional production methods, there is not much time for exploration, and many choices have been made long before the rehearsal period begins. This kind of tight production schedule caused Peter Brook to reject such a system. He called theater constrained by the pressures of time and money "deadly theater." But such theater still remains common practice; it calls for "genius" directors and "star" performers—artists who accept the system, adapt to it without question, overcome it individually with their talent, and create great art by themselves and without much experimentation or collaboration with others. Many of the others, unfortunately, just "do their work."

Within the proscenium arch theater and traditional theater production, what happens in the play is simply what happens to the characters. Since the set and the costumes are usually designed and built before the rehearsals begin, the actors often find themselves at some point in rehearsal stuck inside theatrical images and costumes that have been imposed upon them. These production practices are related to the dominant convention of realism, but seem to have been established for eternity. At least they are not questioned. The problem really is that these production practices often dictate the artistic process, and even worse: the artistic process is subjugated to the demands of the production system and the budget. Within these production circumstances there is not much room for questioning. One has to break with the system to do so.

For the nonrealistic theater and for real-time theater in particular, other production methods must be applied, especially when the actors participate in the creation of theatrical images with which they tell the story of the play. Brecht, as director of the Berliner Ensemble, developed a rehearsal practice that lasted as long as was necessary to find the right form. This allowed him to have both set and costumes developed along with the rehearsals. Of course, his theater was heavily subsidized.

Real-time theater improvisations-on-the-form need a rehearsal process that is designed to discover the right theatrical images for what the company wants to tell with the play. While working with the Frankfurt-based Schlicksupp teatertrupp between 1979 and 1985, we developed a *collective* rehearsal method in which actors were active participants. This is an experimental process in which the rehearsal space becomes a laboratory. In its first phase—and in its most ideal form—the actors develop their own proposals for scenes of the play, which they show to the group. Although staying away can be hard for the director, it is best if he is not present while the actors are working on their proposals. During the rehearsal period, the actors continuously share their ideas in small showings. Sometimes they may offer several different proposals for the same scene. Everyone in the group can contribute to these improvisations, because everybody "knows" the chosen form. In the beginning, this "knowing" is only approximate, but little by little the actors and the director become experts in the form, so that it becomes easier to make choices. This process makes it possible to refrain from casting roles at the beginning of a rehearsal process, so that every participant gets a chance to contribute to the creation of the roles. Over time, the actors discover which roles they like the best, and eventually they may even be able to choose their own roles. In the end, the actions an actor plays on stage may have been created in part by other actors. During the second phase of the rehearsal process, once the roles have been chosen, each actor can return to the text and further develop his role, adding more depth to the character and making the form his own.

This process requires a completely new way of rehearsing and producing. It can be very time consuming, and perhaps it is possible only when there are no set limits for production: when there is a lot of money—or no money at all. The result of this process is that no actor can think he is the sole and private owner of the role he plays, and the director cannot think himself the sole inventor of the artistic ideas of the production or of the accomplishments of "his" actors, nor can the theater or producer claim the artistic ownership of the production, even if he has put all his money in it.

The fear that this sharing of the creative development of roles will result in an artistic uniformity, or that the quality of the work will be reduced to the lowest common denominator is quite ungrounded. Under these pressure-free circumstances, actors challenge each other creatively, and are pushed to go beyond what they usually do, resulting in a higher level of artistry.

Rehearsal and Performance

This real-time theater rehearsal method leads to a performance technique that makes it natural for the actors to watch each other while they are acting, to be interested in and committed to the work of every actor on stage, and thus to share their work with each other. It is one of the cornerstones for the building of an ensemble.

It is a shame when actors feel—as they commonly do—that everything is different in performance than it was in rehearsal. Often this difference is blamed on the fact that the space has changed—the rehearsal room is replaced by the stage—or on the lights, or on the gaping auditorium they face. But I believe that this difference is actually the result of the way in which rehearsals are conducted and of the performance style employed. In traditional theater productions, the actors and directors share the space in the rehearsal room, but once the actors are on the stage, the actors are isolated and cut off from the audience. Of course, a performance will feel entirely different from a rehearsal if the actors are not actively creating the performance each night—consciously re-creating their roles and concentrating on *how* they are telling the story of the play. If the performance is a thoughtless repetition of what they found in rehearsal—or even of what they found during the previous night's performance—the actors will soon find themselves on the slippery slope of routine and be unable to tell their story well.

In real-time theater the presence of the actor as himself allows him to show to the audience that he is creating the performance here and now, over and over again, as something new. In that sense also the performance is a sort of rehearsal and has an improvisational character, just like a jazz concert.

Ensemble

It is the dream of every theater group and of every director to create an ensemble: a group of actors who really play together, who *are* together when they play, who propel the whole mechanism of a play and keep it moving forward, and who collectively create the musical and rhythmical unity of the performance.

In realism, mostly produced in traditional proscenium arch theaters, ensembles hardly ever occur, even if some companies call themselves "ensembles." Such companies are often big and cumbersome, and almost always they are organized hierarchically. Even when actors have a say in certain artistic choices regarding repertoire and artistic direction, their influence is limited. Sets and costumes have to be designed and built long before the actors set foot in the rehearsal space, so it is rare that what happens in rehearsal can alter the choices that have previously been made. Money dictates the creative process. The creative input of the actors, under these common circumstances, is usually limited to the creation of their own roles. It is very rare that a whole group of actors can actually develop a performance together. Rehearsal schedules are individual, or by scenes. One obstacle to group creation is the availability of the actors. Usually the whole group of actors comes together only toward the end of the rehearsal process, for the technical rehearsals, when all the elements of the performance have to be put together, and the director must bring the separate scenes in harmony with each other. Sometimes it is only during "tech" that all the actors meet each other. The conventions of realism that prioritize the fate of individual characters and that insist on conventional production methods, condemn most actors to an isolated existence within which it can be very difficult to create true ensembles in which everyone, the director *and* the actors, is responsible for the creation and execution of the performance as a whole. If actors do not make themselves aware of the effects of such a production system, and if they do not try to change this situation, the resulting lack of togetherness can undermine the creative work in any form or theater convention.

Creating an ensemble is not something you simply decide to do and then just carry out. Success depends very much on whether the participants in the effort desire more or less the same thing. An ensemble is usually created on the basis of shared visions of the subject matter, or of a specific form, a shared ideal, a similar way of acting, or as the result of a specific rehearsal method.

In real-time theater ensembles come into existence not only through the presence of the actor as himself, but also because of the presence of the whole group of actors on the stage during the duration of the performance, who stage themselves in theatrical images they found themselves. With this important feature, they express their collective responsibility within the form of the play itself, to which they have all contributed during rehearsal. Their collective collaboration in rehearsal expresses itself in the form on stage. By acting and by watching each other while they're acting, the actors tell the story of the play together and as a group. In real-time theater the *ensemble is an organic aesthetic result* of the technique.

Postmodern Theater and the Actor as Author: The Fate of Men Is Man-made

The closed forms of realism and epic theater are dominated by the limitations of the proscenium arch theater and the acting techniques that were developed for them. This has led to a sort of uniformity in styles of staging and acting. We can see this result on Broadway, with its mostly realistic sets and Stanislavski-based acting style, and in German municipal theater, with its mostly stylized sets and Brecht-based stylized, "epic" acting style.

Like the realistic and epic theater forms, real-time theater is a *form* (and a convention) and a *technique* at the same time. The technique, however, is not just the acting technique, but also the technique of making theater and staging oneself. Unlike the "closed" realistic and epic theater forms, real-time theater is a more "open" form.

Real-time theater gives the actor the greatest possible freedom: freedom to move and act, to think and to feel for himself. His presence in the present time enables the real-time actor to play the way he does in an improvisation, without losing the precision that is required to tell the story of the play, and without sacrificing his focus on what he must do to plumb the depths of his character. This freedom does not simply arise: the actor first creates and then "owns" it. He also "owns" the character he plays, the play, and the whole of the performance. This is a different form of ownership than the privatized ownership of the traditional theater.

Actors may encounter serious obstacles in attempting this style, for many theaters adhere to hierarchical conventions even while working on productions that strive for real-time values. If the existing work conditions are taken for granted, the team of actors, directors, and designers may not be sufficiently aware of the significance of the theatrical means they are using and may use techniques, such as the presence of the actors on the stage before the performance, simply as a gimmick. They also inevitably may run into the unquestioned demands of the system.

But if the actor succeeds in liberating himself from these conventions, and if he understands the essential principles of real-time theater, he will be able to re-create the creative experience he knew as a child, when, ignorant of rationalizations and "realism," he still could freely "play" and magically change the world around him into something else. He can recapture that wonderful moment when he realized that he wanted to become an actor. It is a precious experience, full of excitement and joy, that is often lost for actors in the routine of everyday business. The real-time actor knows that on stage he can make everything possible. And this knowledge gives him wings.

In the realistic theater, where everything on the stage seems to be fixed and unalterable and the characters are presented as finalized and finished, their destiny frozen in an illusionary time, the *fate of these characters seems to be finalized and finished* as well, as fixed by the uncontrollable forces of nature.

In the epic theater, where everything on stage seems to be brought back to its essence, and the possible alternatives of people's behavior are presented in a poignant stylized form, their destiny determined by sociopolitical conditions in an artificial time, the *fate of these characters seems to be alterable,* but is in the hands of the demonic forces of society.

In real-time theater, where the actors can separate themselves from the characters they play, they can show that hardly anything in people's lives is inescapable and predetermined destiny, and that most of the *fate of men is man-made.* Real-time theater, as an offshoot of postmodernism, puts the responsibility for the fate of men in their own hands, and thus provides forms for truly modern tragedy and comedy.

His presence makes the actor into a unique person who has a story to tell for which he has found a unique form. He can fully commit to it because he has made the story of the play into his own story. He has assumed the place of the *author,* re-creating with his own means what the writer had in mind. In fact, he himself *is* an author. And so it is inevitable that the audience wants to listen to him, wants to watch him, and wants to participate in such an event. By allowing the audience to witness the *creation* of the images that reflect the reality of the play, the real-time actor restores the communal quality of the ritual that theater once was—in a highly emancipated form, and without its religious connotations.

5 The Workshop

How It Started

The idea for a workshop came to me in 1978 while I was working with drama students at the University of Utrecht on a show called *Figures of Contemporary History,* based on Heinrich Böll's novel *The Lost Honor of Katharina Blum.*[1] Wishing to explore the secrets of epic theater, its methods and techniques, I asked the students to tell a story about one of the characters in Böll's novel. Because I was looking for a theatrical form that would help us transform the novel into a theater piece, this seemed like a good place to start. For me it was also an excellent way to get to know the students (future academics, dramaturges, theater critics, and drama teachers), and for them it was a way to start to acting.

During the following years, at the start of the rehearsal process for other productions, I often began by asking actors to tell a story from their own biography—an incident that had really happened—an event that, for some reason, they remembered. A story like that, taken from one's own life, is stored in one's own memories. It is an event we have actually lived, and something we can easily access. By contrast, the story of a character from a play—fictional or not—is someone else's story, which the actor must then make his own. By beginning with one's own story, one can discover how appropriation works.

The act of telling a story began to transform my own development as a director and acting teacher, and it became part of the technique that I called, at first, *epic,* then *narrative,* and now *real-time acting.*

The Epic Genre in Literature and the Epic Theater

Though *epic* in the narrow sense simply means a *narrative,* a story to be told, the epic genre in literature, as we all learned in school, implies large, compelling stories, stories like the *Iliad* and the *Odyssey* of Homer, or the sagas of King Arthur and Lancelot.

The "epic theater" mixes the "telling of a story" with another genre we know from the classical literary categories: drama (the third category is poetry, which had been incorporated in drama for a long period of time). During the 1920s, Erwin Piscator[2] began to stage large, compelling stories about the struggle of the working class, introducing the idea of the "epic theater" as a new genre. Piscator's plays were built by montage, which was a highly sophisticated and revolutionary way of storytelling at the time. Bertolt Brecht added to this the idea of "epic acting," in which the actor had to act on stage as one does when telling a story. This technique was designed to help the actor create a distance between himself and the role he was playing. This distance is one of the main features of epic acting. Eventually this technique became a style of acting, a theater convention in its own right.

When I introduced my storytelling exercise, I wanted to know whether the act of telling a story—separate from the work of staging the play we were about to rehearse—could help the actor to do "epic acting." The exercise was based on Brecht's suggestion (in *New Technique of Acting,* 1940)[3] that the actors transform the roles of a play into the third person and "tell a story" *about* them. As a rehearsal technique, Brecht's suggestion was designed to prevent the actor from "identifying too quickly" with the role he played, to help him study the character with almost scientific curiosity, and to look at the character from different points of view before taking on the role. With this *alienation technique* Brecht aimed at enabling the actor to play a text "without total transformation" and "not as an improvisation, but as a quote," not *being* the character but instead *showing* him or *demonstrating* him to the audience. Brecht recommended three ways to alienate the words and actions of the character to be portrayed:

- Transposition into the third person
- Transposition into the past tense
- Speaking the stage directions and comments out loud

Alienation used in this sense means "estrangement," making words and actions of characters seem "alien," "strange," "not normal," or "different," looked at with curiosity, wonder, and amazement.

Creating a Distance

When I first encouraged the actors at Utrecht University to follow Brecht's suggestion to tell the stories of the roles they were to play, they simply summed up the facts about the characters. But I wanted them to find a personal connection with the stories. This is why I asked them to tell stories about themselves.

A person usually tells in the past tense the story of an event in his own life: "When I was twelve years old, I went on vacation with my best girlfriend, her parents, and her little brother." Or, "Some ten years ago, I bumped into an old friend whom I hadn't seen for years." Or, "The other day I went to visit my aunt, you know, the one whom I had always loved the most." To give the story more urgency and necessity, one may use the present tense, but the story itself still takes place in the past. Everything that has happened in our lives is lodged somewhere in our memory. Most of it we forget, but some things we remember. By definition, our memory refers to the past, even if the story we are telling happened only yesterday.

At first I limited myself to asking the actors to tell a story from their own biography in the first person, and then to retell the story in the third person, as if they were referring to someone else. Even with this simple change, the difference was enormous. The distance this exercise created gave the actors the opportunity to look at themselves with amazement, the way they might look at a stranger. It also caused confusion: sometimes it made the story feel unimportant to them, although it was something they had experienced in their own life. Sometimes they became almost indifferent to the events, and the distance between themselves and the story grew so large that they ended up merely relating the facts of the story, in the same way they initially told the story of the role. But telling a story is not just a dry summing up of the facts of the event. It also includes the telling of *how* you experienced those events, how you felt about them. That is what you remember—and perhaps that is *why* you remember the story—while the facts themselves may have become blurred or imprecise. Telling the story in the first person, straight from your memory, is an event in itself, and often exciting. If you want to tell your story again in the third person, you have to make this into an exciting event too.

Acting in Real Time: A Technique

In order to connect certain moments in the story with each other, I asked the actors to add *interpretation* and *point of view*. This is how the stories acquired logic and a structure. Then I introduced questions of theatrical form, at first standard ways of telling a story, then freely invented theatrical forms, and eventually leading to solo performances. Finally, I had them tell each other's stories, first in the third, then in the first person—which is almost the same as telling the story of a character in a play, and close to playing a role. More recently I have started to create performance pieces by creating montages of the actors' stories.

Over the years this workshop developed into a training technique for real-time acting, and I sometimes used it as the basis for the performance we made afterward. The stories themselves did not become the subject of these performances, but the acting technique became *the way you tell the story of the play through acting*.

Nowadays when I lead such a workshop, I usually start with exercises that activate the body and mind and train the actor to be *present as himself*: active seeing and hearing, active rest, grounding, relaxation, connection, and trust. (See chapter 6, "The Exercises.")

In this workshop, actors begin to discover a new approach to acting. This approach is not only technical—as the word *technique* suggests— but also mental. The workshop provides the participants with a fresh awareness of how acting works, and a new appreciation of the ways in which actors can participate in the creation of a theater production.

Setup of the Workshop

This workshop is designed for a group of actors, acting students or drama teachers,[4] preferably a group of not more than ten. The workshop itself is divided into several exercises. Depending on the available time and the number of participants, and depending on how fast the work proceeds, one can repeat these exercises several times or do them just once. It is also possible to make different "packages" of these exercises.

An extensive and intensive workshop can take from two to four or even six weeks. Usually this much time is possible only within a theater school or drama department.[5] But it is also possible to conduct an intensive workshop of one week. In that case, one can offer a limited version, according to the needs of the participants, and one must choose which exercises are most important. Unfortunately, it is almost impossible to present such a workshop within the professional theater. I have had the opportunity only on a few rare occasions.[6]

Except for the physical exercises on the floor, the exercises in the workshop are individual and therefore time-consuming. Depending on the number of participants, four to six hours is the longest a workshop day should last. The detailed description of the exercises below is meant to enable readers to lead such a workshop; however, it is highly recommended that one do so only after having first participated in a workshop oneself.

Step 1. The "I" Story

Narrator and audience. The individual participants in the workshop tell their stories to the others, who are their audience. At each stage in the work there are clear changes in how the narrator is telling his story. The more often it is told, the more exciting the story becomes, not only for the narrator, who keeps telling his story in different ways, but also for the audience. They are like the audience of an ancient Greek tragedy who knew the plot very well and were most interested in seeing *how* the story was newly interpreted and how the actors played their roles. They become insiders to the story—"experts" Brecht would call them—and therefore active participants in the process. The narrator and his audience need each other.

Process, not result. It is important for the participants to understand that this workshop is about the process, not about the result. "Right" and "wrong" are terms to be avoided. It is an exploration, like research in a laboratory. The participants "improvise" not by inventing a story, but by groping within their memories, looking for words and images, stumbling through the undergrowth of their subconscious. In this process, they "risk" discovering what is partially unknown. So there are no "mistakes," and every result, including ones that are not immediately useful (for the next step, for interpretation, for application) is an artifact that the participant can learn from and build upon.

Telling a Story in the First Person: The Assignment

Choosing a story. The first thing to do is to choose a story about something that happened in your life, an event you remember for any reason. It doesn't matter how long ago this event happened. It might have happened long in the past, a few years ago, or last summer. The circumstances can be anything: your (early) childhood, or primary school, or a vacation with your parents, or the university where you've been a graduate student, or your wedding day.

It is important that the event be part of your *memory* and have a place in your biography. Perhaps the event made a deep impression on you and changed your life in some way—the loss of a beloved person, the first time you fell in love, or something else that had a lasting impact. But you don't have to know or be able to explain *why* this is so. The story itself, and the way you'll tell it, will make it apparent.

The next thing is to make sure that you play an *active central role* in the story you're going to tell, preferably the main role. Sometimes an actor may choose to tell a story about something that happened to him, an event in which he participated, but only passively, rather than actively. But for this exercise, it is important that the narrator is the "I" character who pushes the events of the story forward. For instance, a story that takes place in a foreign country when a violent conflict breaks out could be an event the storyteller has no control over, unless it is the cause of something he then *made happen*. Such extreme circumstances are likely to strongly affect the story.

The "I" either makes a decision (or decisions) or reacts to a decision by someone else that changes the course of events. This means that other people may play more or less important roles in the event.

Take a few minutes and think of a story you want to tell: choose something that comes to mind, often in a flash ("that time when I kicked my little brother's ball away into the river"). Don't think too long about it. You'll soon discover whether it is the right story or not. If it is not, you can change to another story. There should be time and space for such changes.

When you have chosen your story, don't write it down, but mentally prepare to tell it from memory. Make a few notes in your mind.

There are always people who claim that they can't think of a story or have no stories to tell. By watching the other participants telling their stories, they soon will discover that this is not so: everyone has stories about his past. In fact, our biography is one big storybook.

Preparations: setting up the space and focus. Before you start the first round of stories, look around in the space where you're having the workshop. Make sure the room is not cluttered with "stuff" and personal belongings. Then try to decide, as a group, what would be the best place for the storyteller to be, and for the audience. What the storyteller has behind him—a wall, a curtain, or an open space—is decisive for how comfortable he feels. Very often participants want to begin in a corner, where they feel safe. You may feel vulnerable—after all it is a story from your private biography—and you are about to entrust something precious to your audience. A safe space is therefore important. With the floor exercises during the workshop, the feeling about the room gradually will change.

Where the light comes from is an important factor. Make sure the light doesn't impede eye contact between the storyteller and the audience. Daylight is trickier than artificial light.

When you're ready to begin telling your story, make sure you are grounded. Take a few steps back, away from your audience so that you can easily see them, and make *eye contact* with each member. This helps you to get your nerves under control, and to get your breath in the right place.

When you start telling your story, *focus* on two things:

1. On the "I" in the story. Focus on your self as the active (main) figure of the story. Focus on what you did, on your *action*. As in an

improvisation, you're digging into your memory to find the story. While telling the story, you're piecing the fragments together.

2. On the audience. Having made eye contact at the start, you will find it easier to maintain this contact and to keep in touch with the audience as you continue. The presence of the audience—the other participants in the workshop—compels you to really share the story with them.

Now tell your story . . . and have fun!

Postexercise Observations

1. Past and present. The double focus of attention, on yourself as the main character in your story and on the audience, tells us something about the *nonsimultaneity* of the narrating situation. You refer to something that has happened in the *past,* but you do that *now,* in the *present time.* There is always a discrepancy and a difference between how you experienced the event at the moment when it happened (in the past), and how you tell the story of that event (in the present). *Telling a story, as a form of communication with an audience, automatically creates a natural distance between the action of narrating itself, and the actions and events in the story.*

While you're focusing on your action(s) in the story, you also focus on how you felt in the past and what you thought. Because you want to get your story across, the presence of the audience makes you aware of this double focus.

2. Memory is activated—truthfulness. While you are telling your story, you may be surprised to find that you remember more detail than you initially thought you would. Most of the time we consciously remember only the most important moments of our stories, the decisive moments when something important happened, while the less important moments, the circumstances, and the other people in the story lead a slumbering existence in our memory. By giving words to the events of the story, you activate your memory, and you may find that you are able to retrieve a treasure of fragments of the story, sometimes the smallest details of colors and smells, which were hitherto covered by layers of gray brain cells. This enables you to "connect" with the feelings and thoughts that went along with the action in the story, and bring them back to life.

However, our memory also plays tricks on us. We can never know for sure whether the remembered events, feelings, and thoughts are induced by the present feelings and thoughts we have about the event, or whether they were, in fact, present at the time of the events we are recounting. We can never be sure whether what we remember is a truthful account of what happened. For this exercise, that doesn't matter. *What you think and feel now about what you believe you felt and thought then is just as true as what you actually felt and thought then.* The next time you remember the story, your feelings might have changed. *What makes the story "true" is the way you tell it.*

When Brecht wrote his famous "Street Scene" (see chapter 3), this is exactly what he meant: the account of an accident at a street corner by bystanders who saw it happen is truthful only insofar as the story they tell is told in a truthful and convincing manner.[7] The narrator always wants the version he is telling to be believed.

3. Remembering feelings and thoughts: images, words, and movement. Much of what you tell in your story will come from *visualizing* the events you remember. Focusing on what you "did" in the story (your action), you see *images*. In fact, except for words spoken, like "It was at that point that I said: 'You liar!,'" most of the event is stored in your memory as images, not as text. If you picture the images of your story with your inner eye, you will find words for it. And when you do, the audience will see these images too!

While you tell your story, you *invent the text* for it. Language is the primary tool of the narrator. When you begin, you may not have much control over the words you use, but the more comfortable you become, the more easily you will command language, and the more readily your activated memory will help you find the words you need. At the same time, you will find yourself almost automatically physicalizing the feelings and thoughts that are evoked by the memory of your actions. Your body will quickly become a second essential tool you wield as a narrator. The remembered actions will translate into physical–movements. These movements will be influenced by the *act of telling the story. The narrator is "quoting" the movements of the past, and "telling" them with movements of the present.*

Then there is your "sense memory":[8] while telling the story, the sensorial perceptions that went along with the events of the story may spring back to your mind, sometimes quite strongly. Without realizing it concretely, you connect the images from your memory with the feelings, thoughts, and sensations that went through you at the time of the events you are recounting. *Telling a story is a good exercise in emotional memory.*

Emotional memory, however, is not the purpose of telling the story. It is simply the result of the narrator's focus on the action of the "I" in the story. The narrator serves a double function: he refers to the action of the "I" by telling a story about him, and that action—the action of telling the story—in itself releases feelings and thoughts within him. Discovering this is extremely helpful for the actor of real-time theater, where a similar process takes place. *By focusing on the action in the story, the narrator connects his present feelings and thoughts with his feelings and thoughts from the past.*

4. Chaos and repertoire. At first the situation of telling a story in front of an audience may seem nerve-wracking, but once the narrator settles in, he usually begins to feel comfortable and enjoy it very quickly. Often the story itself will be chaotic. You may jump from one storyline to another without much coherence, or you notice that you "forgot" something important, and that you have proceeded with your story to such a point that you feel you're too late to make up for the omission. Don't worry: you'll get a second chance.

If the narrator chooses to tell a story he has told many times before—a story that is part of his "repertoire"—you can always tell because of its almost perfect form and structure. The words are polished and carefully chosen, the turns and transitions in the story have all been pretested for dramatic effect. I would encourage such a narrator to choose another story.

The first time a story is told is also a special moment for the audience: it is an opportunity to get to know each other a little better. Or, if the participants in the workshop know each other well, they may be surprised at learning an aspect of someone's history they didn't know about before. It is quite rare that a story does not arouse the audience's curiosity: they usually want to know more about reasons why, background details, unclarified matters, and the loose ends of the story.

5. Recognition and assimilation. The stories are told in a group, so there are also group dynamics at work brought about by the situation of telling the stories.

Coming from the memory of the narrators, the stories activate the memories of the audience members. They begin to remember similar events in their own biographies. The livelier is the telling of the story, the more this happens. It is a process of *recognition,* in which one or the other individual member of the audience sees himself reflected in someone else's story, as the story becomes a mirror for something that happened in his own life. This is exactly what happens in theater (and what Aristotle in his *Poetics* called *anagnorisis*).

The more the memory of an audience is activated, the more they will ask themselves, in what way the story could have taken another turn, or ended differently, or how they would have acted under similar circumstances. If the main character in the story, the "I" (who is the narrator), had acted differently, would the event have led to a different outcome? This effect is reinforced by the fact that the audience knows that the event the narrator is relating really happened. This is contrary to what happens in the theater: there the audience knows that the events they are witnessing are invented fictions, or at most, refer to real-life events. They only *seem* to really happen (in the play). And even if they happened in reality, as in documentary theater, they didn't happen to the actor himself.

The second mechanism that occurs is related to the first one, but is much more practical and concrete. It is called *assimilation*. It is something that, in a different way, also occurs in acting. Just as actors tend to assimilate to each other's tempo, rhythm, general dynamics, and even tone of voice, participants listening to stories may get an idea for telling a similar story of their own. For instance, one story about a person's early childhood may release a whole series of early childhood stories. Or a story of playing pranks or of unhappy love, or conflicts with parents, or coming out as gay or lesbian, or accidents with a happy ending, may encourage others to tell similar stories.

Within a group—mysteriously or not so mysteriously—a tone is always set. Sometimes it is very obvious, for example when the whole group looks at one of them, clearly the "leader": what he dares to do, the others dare to do too. If he is ready to take risks, the others are ready too. This form of competition can be helpful, but can also be counterproductive. If no risks are taken, the stories are often innocent, superficial, and stay on the level of anecdotes. But if risks are taken, the stories may acquire an existential quality. It is obvious that this last category of stories is more interesting. For the benefit of the workshop, it is good if the participants work with a wide variety of stories. With a little insistence from the workshop leader, it is always possible for each participant to find a very personal and meaningful "I" story to tell.

6. Commitment. It takes great commitment to connect the feelings, thoughts, and sensations from the past with the feelings, thoughts, and sensations of the present. To do so, the actor must fully physicalize his actions and find the right words for his images, telling his story with real enthusiasm. *A good story is a well-told story.* You must *want* to tell this story, and you must *want* it to be a compelling story, one that keeps your audience members on the edge of their chair.

The first time you tell your story, you will focus primarily on what you remember. You're finding your way through the story, discovering in your memory how you experienced the events back when they happened. The *commitment* with which you tell your story is directed this first time through to *what* happened and the role you played in making it happen: you, yourself want to know. The words you find and the physical expressions of your feelings and thoughts are all spontaneous discoveries, often to your own surprise. They usually don't belong to a standard repertoire.

The commitment the narrator makes to the telling of his story provides the energy he needs to share his story with the audience. It is an essential element of his ability to captivate his audience.

7. Practicalities. Out of nervousness or embarrassment, or simply because he is not used to looking straight at the audience, the narrator often tries to avoid direct eye contact with the audience, by looking over their head into the void, or into the ground. He may look away because he feels uncomfortable with the situation or vulnerable. After all, he is improvising and he is trying to remember.

The activity of telling a story, which is quite normal in everyday life—at home, in a restaurant, or elsewhere—suddenly becomes something special: the storyteller/narrator experiences a heightened consciousness of the situation he is in. This is exactly the same as the situation the actor finds himself in when he's on stage playing a role: he knows he is being observed. Most actors are used to communicating directly with each other, but not with an audience. In order to tell a personal story, immediate eye contact with the audience is essential: after all, you're always telling a story *to* someone. Once you have established this eye contact and you feel comfortable with it, you can always let go of it for a few seconds in order to think about the story you're telling, or to remember something more precisely, and then shift back to the audience. The floor exercises are extremely helpful for this contact with the audience.

Many stories start with "I'm going to tell you a story that happened . . ." or "This is a story about . . ." And while the story is told, the narrator often says: "I remember that . . ." It is clear that he is going to tell a story, and it is clear that he remembers—or is trying to remember—how it happened, so these kinds of phrases are not needed. Try instead to jump into the story by telling something you did or by describing the atmosphere of the story: "It was a dark, cold night, when I . . ."

8. What else is noteworthy? It may take a while before you have your story under control and before you're able to communicate it to the audience. For instance, it may be hard to distinguish between the main issues in a story and matters of minor importance, and you may find that you are paying equal attention to unequal elements. Therefore, after you have told your story for the first time, a brief evaluation of your journey is useful. All previous observations may be reviewed, one way or the other, but make sure that they don't take too much time. One easily gets engrossed in lengthy discussions, which stop the actual work.

The most important thing you want to know is whether the story was indeed an active "I" story. For example, a story may begin: "My brother and I went on vacation without our parents for the first time. When we arrived on the island, we decided to go fishing and were nearly overtaken by a storm." If "I" and "my brother" keep doing everything together, the audience will never see who decided to go back to land before the storm could catch them: the "I" disappears behind "my brother." This happens most often in stories about group or family experiences. It is something to pay attention to the next time you tell the story: the audience wants to see what *you* are doing in the story; they want to know what you are feeling and thinking, and how you negotiate your way through a change or life passage. They want to learn which of the two brothers wanted to go back, who actually decided to do so, what happened beforehand, and so on. An enormous drama might be hidden there.

If the story seems to have a rather passive "I," then it may be better to choose another story. If the story was a "we" story—first-person plural—you may be able to transform the "we" into an "I," but if the "we" seems to be a cover for an "I" who remains invisible, it may be better to select a new story. The most important thing is to determine how "active" the "I" in the story is: What are his actions, what are his decisions, and how does he change?

The brief evaluation, in which all participants take part, also gives you a chance to check your own experience of how the narration went: how you felt, your relationship with the audience, your focus, your digging into your memory, and the unexpected discoveries you made. Very often you remember important parts of the story after you've told it. Keep these discoveries for the second round.

This evaluation can be done at the end of the first round of stories, after all stories have been told. It serves as a sort of inventory of the treasure box. It also gives the audience a chance to express what they experienced and observed.

Before moving on to the next exercise, it may be useful, however, to point out a few other important elements that make up a story, and to note how the process of telling a story works.

9. Themes and historical events. Stories reveal something, and they have a meaning. In most cases, the stories that are told appeal to our collective subconscious. It is very rare that a story is unique and so idiosyncratic that no one recognizes himself in it and nobody's memory is stimulated by its events. The universality of stories allows us to categorize them thematically. For instance, stories may be about such big themes as guilt and punishment, innocent (blameless) guilt, punished recklessness or "hubris," shattered hope, fulfilled (or unfulfilled) expectations, answered (or unanswered) promises, loyalty rewarded, triumph celebrated, pride offended, or love lost. Such themes, occurring in concrete situations, are archetypical and have mythological dimensions; that's why they are recognizable.

It can be helpful to point out such themes and to make comparisons with other well-known stories, myths, plays, novels, and movies. It can even be useful to exaggerate a little, to make the stories seem bigger. The bigger the theme, the bigger the narrator's urge to tell his story, and the greater his ability to transform his story into a unique, "historical" event that has significance not only for him but also for others. But don't forget: *you're not telling a theme, you're telling a story* about (a series of) events in which you play the main part. The story and your actions must be central.

Usually the theme of a story—what the story is really about—will only gradually become apparent during the series of exercises that follow, as the story is further being explored.

10. Given circumstances. There are other important elements that lend the story character and color, that fulfill a dramatic function, and that contribute to the meaning of the story. These are very much like the given circumstances in a play, and they are a part of every story. The better you get at telling your story, the easier it will be to incorporate these elements:

- The time and timeframe in which the story takes place
- The age of the main character ("I") and, if it is important, the ages of the other characters in the story
- Where the story takes place: indoors or outdoors, at school or at home, in your hometown or out of town, in your own country or abroad
- The changes of place in the story: moving from one place to another, from house to school, from a provincial town to the big city, traveling from one country to another, and the dynamics of these movements
- The sensory impressions, the colors, smells, sounds that are unique to the story
- The climate: is it hot or icy cold, does it rain in the story (or does it pour), or is the earth dried out and barren?
- The general atmosphere: the moods and designs of the locations where the story takes place, special occasions (weddings or funerals or spelling bees) or historical moments ("Where were you when Kennedy was shot?")

- Other circumstances that play a role in the story: family circumstances, political, social, economic circumstances, nature, landscapes or anything that gives the story a special dimension or framework

11. Plot and structure. Each story has a structure, a way it is built up, a dramaturgy of how the facts are organized in relationship to each other. The drama, or the dramatic quality, of a story becomes visible if it has a "plot." Many stories have compelling structures of *cause and effect.* But there are also stories in which each of the events stands on its own and together build a story—for instance, one in which a series of accidents happen, independently and without any relationship with each other, but with the same person as their victim, or rather as their "perpetrator." These stories have a looser structure, but they reveal the narrator as the one who creates a story out of them.

Most stories are somewhere between a rigid cause-and-effect structure and a loose structure. This leaves the stories open for discovery, interpretation, and change.

If the premise of a story changes, there is a good chance that the structure will change also.

The first time a story is told, there may be no discernable structure, only fragments, bits and pieces, but by the end of the workshop there will be a structure. There is always a beginning. The narrator begins to tell his story. (The first time through, this beginning point may not be the real beginning of the story. There may be another, better beginning.) And there's always an ending, though this ending too might at first not be the "real ending." Beginning and endings need to be discovered or uncovered. Often there is a "middle": one moment where the story changes and takes a new turn. Sometimes there are more turning points in a story. These are the *transitions* from one phase of the event into the next. Sometimes these transitions are unexpected and abrupt; sometimes you can see them coming. Often such moments coincide with important decisions of the "I," or of other characters in the story. Exactly at these decisive moments the emotions in the story are the most poignant. But sometimes seemingly insignificant decisions (by the "I" or others) can also lead to huge changes. While you find your way through the story, it is a good idea to keep in mind how you want it to end. That gives you a goal to work toward.

The exercises that follow allow the participants to learn, step by step, how to get a grip on the structure of the story. At this point a rough structural analysis of the story should do: where do the turning points occur, and of what importance are they? In that sense the workshop is also an exercise in practical dramaturgy during which you slowly discover the dramatic quality of the story.

Telling the Same Story Again in the First Person: The Assignment

Dramatic conflict. In this second round it often happens that the narrator feels inhibited: he is afraid that his audience will be bored because they have heard the story before. This would probably be so if he were to tell the story in exactly the same manner as before, in exactly the same words, and with exactly the same structure. However, unless the story is "repertoire"—a story the narrator has told over and over—this familiarity is actually very unlikely because the narrator is always discovering something he didn't realize before, and will use different words.

1. As you retell the story, try not to censor or excuse yourself. Trust yourself—and your audience—and try to overcome your inhibitions by deliberately allowing yourself to find new words, or choose a different beginning, something that happened before the moment you had initially thought to be the beginning of your story. The first round of telling the story, your activated memory, and the evaluation will have given you many ideas. Take your time to explore these new ideas. Often totally "new" stories emerge in this exercise on the basis of the same material. During this second round, participants feel often as though they are telling their story for the first time. They had never thought that this story had such significance.

2. Keep focusing on your actions in the story, and on what you felt and thought at the time of the event.

3. Try to avoid commenting on the story, or giving explanations for events or situations: let things happen and let the story unfold.

4. Try to *connect what you are feeling and thinking now with what happened in the past:* actions, feelings, and thoughts. Try to physicalize the feelings and thoughts of the present and the past. Embark on

your journey and allow yourself to float with the stream you're creating yourself. If you allow this to happen, you will discover a lot more of what the story is really about and what it means. You are digging deeper, emotionally and intellectually.

5. As you did the first time, you must also focus on the audience to whom you are telling your story. Keep making eye contact with them. By now they also know the story, and they are looking forward to hearing more details and to finding out how you handle the material this time. This creates a different relationship between you and them. You are partners in the same game: they also have told their stories—they are with you, as you are with them.

6. You may have gained enough confidence now to stop the flow anytime you want: you are calling the shots. If things don't go the way you want them to go, you can take a time out, to think things through, walk around a bit, take a breath, drink a glass of water. You can resume your story at an earlier point and give it another twist. After all, it's just an exercise and an exploration: nothing can go "wrong."

7. Try to pay attention to the *transitions* in the story, to those moments when the situation changes and when you and others make important decisions, or when something that happens has an effect on the actions that follow. Try to get a better grip on it: by creating a structure for the whole story, you are discovering the *dramatic conflicts* within the story.

8. Try to enrich your story with details for which you had previously left no space, details about the place(s) where the story happens, the smells, and all the other elements that give your story its particularity.

Tell your story.

Postexercise Observations

1. Distance and catharsis. You will notice that the distance between you and the story has become a little larger. It's the same situation: you are in the present and the story is in the past, but now you can see this relationship more clearly. You can see yourself in the story more clearly, because you are more in command. You can feel the distinction between now and then; you have created a space in which you can begin to make the connection between the two. In this space you begin to rise above the story.

For the audience, things become much clearer now too, and they recognize more. They realize that they are part of something special: not a secret, but something precious that you want to share with them. This is not therapy, but the situation, which is often loaded with emotion, can definitely have a healing, *cathartic* effect on the narrator as well as on the audience. Another effect of repeating the first-person story is that the audience can pay better attention to *how* you're telling your story. They also sense more space—space, which allows them to connect with both you and the story.

2. Internalizing. The second time around, the narrator begins the process of consciously *internalizing* what before lingered in his memory as scattered images and emotions. Because he is more in command of the telling of the story, and more aware of what he is looking for, the narrator often feels free to dig deeper into his memory. Often he comes up with surprising new takes on the story, new dramatic twists and turns, new insights. Telling the "I" story the second time around often enriches the story with a wealth of images and colorful details. Very often new people begin to inhabit the story, or certain people in the story become more important and visible or disappear. All this is very exciting for the narrator and the audience.

Depending on the number of participants and the available time, you can repeat this first-person story again. Sometimes one or two participants need more time to get a hold on their story. Repetition is good for the story and for you, for you gain a better handle on the story, more oversight and confidence in telling it. The next exercises give you ample opportunity to enlarge the scope of your story and give it the depth you want.

Step 2. The "He/She" Story

Telling the Story in the Third Person: The Assignment

What the first person sees: the omniscient narrator. This time you tell the same story, but now in the third person. The "I" character of the first-person story is now "he" or "she." You, as the narrator, speak in the present about yourself in the past, and *you are looking at your self in the third person.* In the "I" story, the "I" character and the narrator were identical. In the "he"/"she" story they are also identical, but by calling the narrated character, that is, the original "I," "he" or she," or by his or her (own) name, you create an artificial distance between yourself and the story.

Nothing changes in the narrating situation: the narrator tells his story to his audience. But in this setup you see the events of the story before your inner eye and you tell *about* them. You see yourself *move* through the story and observe your actions as if from a helicopter overhead. Having told the "I" story once or twice, you are pretty well aware of the events of the story, so it shouldn't be too hard to do this.

You may think that you as the narrator are a completely new "I," but you don't become someone else; *the narrator is not a role you are playing: you are still you.* You know all about the story, not only because it is your story, but also because as narrator you are like an *omniscient writer,* hovering *above* the story. This means that you don't have to explain or justify why you know what you know: you just know it; it's your privilege. You don't have to say: "I happen to know this young man, whose fiancée is called Julia;" you can just say: "Robert has a fiancée called Julia."

The narrator doesn't play a role in the story, except that he is always present as the narrator. That is the only sense in which he is a part of the story.

Now tell your story.

Postexercise Observations

1. Neutrality doesn't exist. At first this depersonalization is a strange experience. Often the artificially created distance can make the narrator feel lost, as if by creating this distance between himself and his story he has lost something that was unmistakably and uniquely his. But this is not so. You as narrator must realize that your story is and always will be your story, just as plays, which are performed over and over again in new forms, perhaps for centuries, remain the same play: the text is the same text, the story is the same story. Only the interpretation will be different.

However, the third-person character (who was the original "I") must still experience what happened in the story from the inside, as he did during the "I" story. So you must make sure that "he"/"she" stays connected to his or her action. And you, as the narrator, must stay connected with the "I" character of the story, his action, thoughts, and feelings.

The distance you create between yourself and the story allows you to be in charge of the story and of everything that happens in it. You can be more at ease and bring in details that you felt you didn't have time and space for when you told the story in the first person: details concerning the main "action" of the story, or details concerning the actions of other people in the story, atmosphere, and circumstances.

Looking at it from a distance, you can see the changes and transitions in the story more clearly. Some things become more important, others less so. Again, don't be afraid of boring your audience by telling them a story they already know: they are insiders and by now just as committed to your story as you. So you have to keep being committed to telling it.

For understandable reasons, it may not be easy to distance yourself from something that is so much your own, and it can be particularly difficult to let yourself have an unfavorable view of what "he" or "she" did in this story. We tend to be kind to ourselves, so many narrators fall into telling their stories in a neutral manner, just summing up the facts. That, indeed, can be boring. In fact, you can't really tell a story in a neutral manner. Neutrality as such doesn't exist.

Moreover—and this is very important—*the narrator always has his own feelings and thoughts about the story.* After all, you are observing your own actions from a distance, and it would be strange if you did not have any feelings or thoughts about them. The events are the same, but you can feel and think differently about them than you did before, when you told the story in the first person.

2. Point of view. With everything we do or say, we feel things and think things—even when we think we are not thinking. In fact there is nothing in our life to which we don't relate in one way or the other, emotionally or intellectually. Even if we are indifferent about people or things that happen in the world, and even if we are dismissive toward people or things that happen to us, our indifference and our dismissal are the ways we relate.

Brecht used the word *haltung* to describe the actor's point of view toward the character and his action. Literally translated, *haltung* means "attitude" (see also chapter 3). With a *haltung* or an attitude we express what we feel and think about another person, or about ourselves, about his actions, about his behavior under certain circumstances, about his relationships, or his position in society.

When you first told the story, in the first person, the way you related to it arose spontaneously. Now, telling it in the third person, you discover that you have to make up your mind about it. You must consciously choose the way you, as the narrator, want to relate to the events in the story and the actions of the original "I." This *point of view* is the *perspective* from which you choose to tell the story. It is a step toward making a different *assessment* of the event(s), a step toward finding a different way of telling the story, a step toward a new interpretation of the facts, and eventually toward a new arrangements of those facts, a new structure for the story.

Telling the Original "I" Story in the Third Person, from Someone Else's Perspective: The Assignment

Insiders and outsiders. In this exercise we'll try to tell the story from someone else's perspective. This person could be someone who plays a role in the story or someone outside the story. But this other person can't be neutral. Each person always relates to the story, in one way or another. This "new" narrator has a point of view, an opinion about the actions of the original "I"; he has thoughts and he feels something about those actions. This exercise is meant to help you in choosing a point of view other than your own, and to practically experience what it means.

If you choose a person from within the story, then this "insider" has a relationship with the original "I": he is involved in his actions. Take, for instance, the story of a twelve-year-old girl who goes camping for the first time and is put to the test by her camp peers. In this case you could choose to tell this initiation story from the point of view of one of the camp leaders, who might be terribly *proud* of the girl when she passes the test successfully.

If, on the other hand, you choose a person from outside the story, then this "outsider" is not directly involved in the actions of the original "I" and has not actively participated in the events of the story. Take, for instance, the story of a young woman who breaks off a long-term relationship and now has to tell her parents. In this case you could choose to tell the story from the point of view of her mother, who might be very *disappointed.*

It is also possible that the "outsider" might be someone who was on the mind of the original "I" when the events of his story unfolded. Take, for instance, the story of a boy who goes joyriding in his father's car. You might choose to tell this story from the point of view of the father, someone who is "in" the story only because he is "in" the mind of the original "I." And this father might be very *angry* after he finds out about the joyride.

When you choose someone else from whose perspective to tell your story, you always are choosing a point of view. Whether this point of view is factual or not is irrelevant. It can be entirely made up or imagined. It is simply a possibility, an option. The "camp leader" might just as well be *concerned* and *worried,* instead of proud. The "mother" might be *relieved* instead of disappointed. And the "father" might be *forgiving* or *indifferent* instead of angry. It is important that you assume what this other person, insider or outsider, might feel and think about the actions of the original "I."

By looking at yourself from another point of view, you acquire another view of your role in the story. Often this knowledge is very revealing.

Form, content, and the narrator's instruments. When we express ourselves, we hope that there are no misunderstandings about what we think and feel. Misunderstandings about how to "read" a person's real feelings, thoughts, motives, and intentions often lead to a breakdown in the communication between people, and sometimes grow into insolvable conflicts. So we want the signals we give to the outside world to be clear and unambiguous.

Under normal circumstances, if we have nothing to hide, we usually succeed at this clarity: we are pretty transparent and easy to read. But circumstances are often not "normal" at all. Then we may hide on the "inside" what we really feel and think. The chosen point of view may help you to get to that "inner truth." The narrator has to know about the differences between the outside and the inside.[9] And if he doesn't, here is a chance to explore them.

Therefore, as you tell your story, it is important that you keep physicalizing: your gestures, facial expressions, language, intonations, and volume of your voice need to make clear what you are thinking and feeling. It doesn't suffice to say to yourself: this one I'm doing *concerned,* without searching for the place in your body where "concern" lives, how it feels, what sort of vocabulary you need for this particular point of view, and how you speak. The *form* in which you express yourself says everything about what you think and feel, about the *content.* Or to put it even more strongly: this form *is* the content. In telling a story, in playing a role, and in daily life: *How* you tell your story (the form) says everything about *what* you want to communicate to your audience (the content).

You must "translate" or "transform" the point of view you have chosen into physical and visual expressions. As the narrator, you must not only use your body and your voice, but your whole emotional instrument, your brain, your senses, and your imagination. You also use your memory and your life experience. And in all this, it is your task to be as precise as you can.

Before you begin with your improvisation, take a little more time to think about all this, and make some mental notes.

Choose a person from inside or outside the story, from whose point of view you are now going to tell the story.

Postexercise Observations

1. Justification and "character." The narrator who is trying this exercise almost always wants to explain how he knows what he knows. When working with an inside narrator, this storyteller might say: "I happened to be there, when Gary . . ." When working with someone outside, he might begin: "I have a friend, and she told me this crazy story about how she . . ." But you do not need this kind of justification, any more than a character in a play needs to justify his presence on stage. You are the omniscient narrator, like a writer who can know everything about his characters. How and why you know all these things, is not important. The best way to avoid this trap is to focus on the actions, feelings, and thoughts of the original "I." And just as you did before, try as the new narrator to connect your point of view to those feelings.

Another danger is that you may start creating a character for the new storyteller: you may end up creating a new "I" story in which you might focus more on "your" own actions than on those of the original "I." To prevent this, keep focusing on the actions of the original "I." Be careful to limit yourself to the point of view of the camp leader, the mother, or the father. And look from there to the actions of the original "I." Don't try to impersonate these characters, but find a way of *expressing their point of view, physically and emotionally.* The audience will then say, "Oh, clearly, that was the father," for your point of view is related to and derived from the function he has in the story.

While you retell your story, you will find new physical and emotional expressions for the point of view you have chosen. The audience may recognize this viewpoint, identify with it, sympathize with it, or hate it, and so on.

As nothing is written down, you are once more on a journey of discovery. Your body and voice will most likely express new feelings and thoughts, and you will discover new words and images as you go along.

2. Five exercises in one. Telling the story in the third person serves multiple purposes:

It is an exercise in *interpretation:* every story can be told from different points of view. Every time you change the point of view or your perspective, the story changes, which often leads to surprising insights and discoveries about the meaning of the events and the role the original "I" plays in them. The story itself supplies the key to whatever point of view the narrator chooses. Not every point of view will work or make a good story. Sometimes a radically contrary point of view can throw a new and unexpected light on the original story. You (the original "I"!) need to have the courage to choose such a radical point of view.

Often a story contains a strong change, a striking transition from one situation into another, for instance when a tense situation transitions into relief. It is possible, but not necessary, that at such moments the point of view of the narrator changes as well. But it is also possible, at such moments, to stick with your original point of view. In later exercises, you may add more nuances, so that the chosen point of view becomes merely a guideline.

Telling the story in the third person is also an exercise in finding precise *physical expressions* to give form to a point of view. In this exercise *externalization* begins. For instance "confused" is not the same as "worried," and "worried" is different from "afraid," and "afraid" is something other than "terrified." All these emotional states have different physical expressions: they feel different and they look different. You have to find these different emotions in your body and your voice so that you can embody them. Just like the actor, you as the narrator have to be able to make them visible by the way you tell the story. In this way, telling the story is also an acting exercise. I like to compare this process of expressing one's thoughts and feelings in an adequate and precise manner to what the sculptor does, or the painter: discovering shapes and choosing colors.

It is also an exercise in finding possible *motives and intentions* for the actions of the original "I." When you tell the story from the point of view of a third person, you may gain an insight into the possible background of the story. It is a practical study in behavioral psychology, and if you are able to stay connected with the actions, feelings, and thoughts of the original "I," you will be able to embody those newly discovered feelings, thoughts, and actions.

It is an exercise in creating a *distance,* which makes it possible to observe and assess the events in the story. At the same time, it forces you to commit fully to the story itself in order to make it as compelling as it was in the first person. Moreover, you must find the way to do this without changing the actual facts of the story.

Finally, for the classroom audience it is an exercise in *observation.* They learn to see how you are expressing a chosen point of view, and whether this new interpretation changes the story. If you succeed in embodying the chosen point of view, this can be an exciting experience for the audience, for now they are paying attention not only to the content, the facts of the story (and, by the way, they will quickly notice if you leave out something important), but also to the form, the way you are telling the story.

3. Deeper meaning. With this exercise you are able to analyze the material of the story, to unravel its mysteries and secrets, and get closer to its core, its complexities and deeper meanings. A new understanding of the story may disclose what lies behind the superficial facts. This third-person exercise makes it clear that a story can be interpreted in many different ways, at least as many as there are participants in the story. If we include all the other people outside the story, then an almost endless range of possible interpretations appears.

In postmodern times, it is recognized (and allowed) that every participant in an event has his own version of it. Any interpretation of the events of a story has become relative. If you put all the interpretations of the same events together, you have the basic stuff that modern drama is made of: a source for both tragedy and comedy. We can make the story tragic, comical, absurd, or grotesque, or even all at the same time, without changing the facts.

It doesn't matter whether what the narrator tells from his point of view is true. *The truth* doesn't exist anyway; there are only truths. The only truly important thing is whether you are truthful in the way you're telling your story, and whether, therefore, the audience believes your new version of the story.

Telling the Original "I" Story in the Third Person, from Different Points of View: The Assignment

The pure narrator: deconstructing the story. This exercise is the same as the previous one, except that now the narrator doesn't derive his point of view from a person inside or outside the story, but comes up with a point of view himself. You should undertake this exercise when you have grown accustomed to viewing your own story from a distance, and when you no longer need to justify your knowledge of the story or the point of view you are taking. You can choose any point of view you want. It doesn't have to be your own personal point of view. It's a suggestion for an interpretation.

Working purely from a point of view, the emphasis now rests more upon your ability to find an expression for this point of view, a *form*. This is where the pure narrator begins to emerge, and where the externalization takes shape. Now it's just you—the narrator. Even if it isn't your own *personal* point of view, you have to *own* the point of view you choose. It has to be convincing. The way you express and give form to your point of view is the way you embody the actions, feelings, and thoughts of the original "I" of the story (who is still you).

Giving up the protection from another person, inside or outside the story, is hard. Therefore, try to begin with this: from the narrator's point of view, look at your own story with *wonder and amazement:* "Isn't it strange that he did this or that, and not something else." *Question your own actions:* "Why did he do that?" This will change the tone of your story, and you will find new words for it. If you just sum up the facts, you will end up telling your story in a linear, chronological order. But when you start questioning your actions, wondering about them, being amazed about how these things were possible, the story can open up to different approaches and interpretations.

Being in command of the facts of the story, and of the important moments of change and transition, this is the best moment to begin to "organize" them in a new order. You should be able to *deconstruct* the story: taking it apart and putting it together in a different way, leaving linear dramaturgy behind. Depending on the point of view, you might start at the end of the story, or somewhere in the middle, perhaps at a significant turning point, and then go to the beginning, or to another significant fragment of the story. You also can return to a specific significant fragment of the story over and over again, so that meaning is derived from its repetition. The moments of transition in the story will change because of this; they won't disappear, but they may gain a new meaning. However, keep in mind that it is not your intention to manipulate the facts, but to use the facts to make your point.

Giving up linear dramaturgy and the chronology of the story is very hard. The previous exercises have been preparing you for this moment.

Many points of view. There are innumerable points of view from which to tell a story, although not every point of view will work for every story. A point of view might derive from what the other characters in the story do, how they behave and think. For instance, you might feel proud of your son, or you could be disgusted by the outrageous behavior of an eccentric aunt. Or a point of view may grow as a reaction to events, things that happen and in which people are involved: people might have an opinion on the war or politics or Halloween parties. A point of view might even spring from a reaction to inanimate objects: some people hate garbage cans; other people love roses. Just as there are verbs for actions, there are words for points of view, usually adjectives and nouns or combinations of them. Usually they go together with a preposition: outraged *by*, indifferent *to*, ashamed *of*.

Here are a handful of points of view, from which one might tell a story: *with wonder/amazement, enthusiasm, or admiration, in awe, proud, impressed, intimidated, relieved, satisfied, grateful, hurt, offended, indifferent, disgusted, indignant, angry, worried/concerned, condescending, arrogant, reproachful, gleeful, pitiful, hateful, bitter/cynical, regretful, sad, contemptuous, afraid/frightened/scared/terrified, frustrated, depressed, despondent, indulgent, disappointed, confused, wronged, passionate, strict, happy, ironic, surprised, understandingly, bewildered, resentful/rancorous, determined, forgiving, hypocritical, suspicious, paranoid, ashamed, irritated, disparaging, amused, mocking, impatient, ecstatic, jealous, resigned, dedicated, discouraged, doubtful.*

With these points of view you, as the narrator, can relate in one way or the other to the actions in the story of the original "I." All these points of view reflect emotional and intellectual states of mind. They live in your body: they are "attitudes" ("haltungen"). You know them, you're familiar with them: you use them every day in your life. Try to find them and to express them physically. The key for your choice of point of view is to be found in the story itself and in the actions of the original "I." You must ask yourself, how one can look at your story?

- Make a choice from this list, or come up with a point of view yourself. It can be helpful to announce the chosen point of view to your audience as you begin, so that they can focus on how you're accomplishing what you have set out to do.
- In the first exercises you might have been scurrying around in the space, not very aware of the possibilities of the space you're working in. Try to acknowledge the space and expand your territory by using it for the physicalization of your story.
- By now you are sufficiently the master of the material to condense your story to a maximum of ten minutes.

Now tell your story.

Postexercise Observations

1. Hidden points of view. It is often not easy to take on one of these points of view, express and sustain it throughout the story. In reality it can be a fine line, for different emotions often blend with each other, or change within one story, especially at moments of transition. For the sake of the exercise, however, try to stick to one point of view, at least as a guideline and for the sake of clarity.

Very often the point of view is taken from the outcome of the story. In such cases it is easier to maintain the chosen point of view. But it is also possible that with every segment of the story there is another point of view, and with the transitions a new one appears. Or the story has a big turning point, where everything changes by surprise.

Sometimes you may discover that a new point of view acts as a hidden motive, behind the chosen point of view: for instance, when you want to show shame but you actually exhibit sadness, or when you want to show suspicion but you exhibit contempt. Doing so, you discover that your sadness arises *out of* shame, or your contempt *out of* suspicion. These are contradictions and inner conflicts within the narrator. They help you discover the contradictions in the actions of the original "I," the difference between motives for these actions and intentions: the betrayed lover shows anger but feels justified; the mother, "relieved" that her little daughter is not hit by a car when she ran across the street, doesn't hug her, but slaps her in the face.

2. The narrator's own feelings and thoughts. In the he/she story, the narrator expresses what he thinks and feels about his own actions and behavior by *connecting* these feelings and thoughts with those of himself as the main character of the story. But in your role as narrator, you will also discover that there are feelings and thoughts that are purely yours, and not immediately or necessarily expressive of your point of view on the actions of the "I" in his story. The greater the distance between yourself-as-narrator and yourself-as-the-"I," the more you will become aware of this and the more space you will have within yourself to express these feelings and thoughts. You must then also find physical forms for the expression of these emotions of the narrator-as-himself. Through the way you use your body and your voice, the audience will know how and what you feel and think while telling the story. In this free space you are *present as yourself.* At such moments you can enter "active rest" and take your time to switch from yourself-as-the-narrator to yourself-as-the-"I"—or you can simply pause and drink a sip of water, walk around, collect your thoughts. I have often seen how effective it can be when a narrator throws in a gesture of irritation (about something outside the story) or impatience (with himself, when he couldn't find the right word, or image) or despair or joy: a shrug of the shoulder, a fluttering of the hand, a sigh, a sudden jump and a cry, or a smile. If you stay in eye contact with your audience, you share these moments with them. They will love you for it.

Step 3. Theatrical Forms of a Story

Before history there are stories. Telling a story is an archetypical form of theater (see also Part III of this book). In folklore, the story has always played a central role. In what is called the *oral tradition,* famous stories from historical and mythological times and from a long ago past have been passed on from one generation to the next. In some parts of the world—on the Italian island of Sardinia, for instance—this tradition still exists. There, groups of three singers travel the island, visiting villages and small towns and telling their stories in community centers or under the shady trees of the central square. Nowadays, no one understands the words of these stories, which are often sung in a monotone and have a special accelerating rhythm (with stops in between), and yet everyone knows them.

Before they become history, there are stories. When—embellished with metaphor, poetry, and imagery—they acquire a distinctive form and become repeatable in this form, they become theater. In this workshop we are dealing with stories from our lives, which can potentially become history and then theater.

Stories in daily life. There are many forms of communication in which the story plays a role, and which have a theatrical quality. Every sermon from the pulpit and every public speech, though it is not "theater," is in fact a theatrical form, and sermons and speeches often use story as an important element. The legend of the birth of Christ is an example of a story that, when it is told in the living room around the Christmas tree, acquires an almost casual form without losing its religious and mythological dimensions, as if it happened yesterday in a not so faraway country.

And in daily communication, story also plays a big role. When children come home from school, something may have happened that bears telling in the form of a story; friends tell each other tall stories in the pub; neighbors tell stories about other neighbors—we call such stories gossip. A joke that circulates in clubhouses and offices is a story in a very strict and stylized form, a story with a punch line, which demands a certain craftsmanship to be able to get it right. Rumors are stories, too.

Theatrical forms of stories of today. Dario Fo, the Italian playwright and theater director,[10] is an actor who tells stories. While telling a story, he creates a multitude of characters all by himself. Cabaret artists have emancipated from stand-up comedians to storytelling actors. These performers create a multitude of characters often in multilayered story-forms. They give their stories a theatrical form of their own. These stories demand artistry and craftsmanship to perform.

These modern storytellers have something else in common: on the stage they are present as themselves, in the here and now: Dario Fo is Dario Fo. They recount the stories of their characters and the events they are involved in by playing them, without ever trying to hide their own identity and personality.

Different story forms. To give the story a distinct theatrical form, you can choose from existing—more or less current—and more or less theatrical story-forms. Here are a few examples of story forms we are surrounded with in our daily lives:

- Eyewitness report (for example, of an accident or a natural disaster)
- Radio/television report/commentary (for example, of a royal wedding, a football game, or a memorial)
- News report
- Public speech (at a political or union rally, wedding, funeral, jubilee, the opening of the Olympic Games)

- Sermon
- Lecture
- Lesson/instruction (in school, university, swimming pool)
- Demonstration (for example, of the workings and wonders of a lawnmower)
- Sales pitch (by a street vendor, or a screenwriter who wants to sell his film to a studio boss)
- Press conference (for example, the police spokesman speaking about a crime, or the U.S. president speaking on the growth of the economy, or the president of the Motion Picture Academy announcing the candidates for the Oscars)
- Guided tour in a museum, with real or imagined pictures
- Pleading (for example by a defense or prosecution lawyer for the judgment of a jury)
- Tall story (in the pub, or the locker room)
- Gossip (going around among neighbors, in families, circles of friends and colleagues)
- Confession (at the family dinner table, or in a Catholic church, in the presence of a priest)
- Joke (with a punch line)

Most of these story forms have a basic *format* but are of an improvised nature, like the eyewitness report and the television commentary. In terms of content they depend on what happens on the spot and in the moment. A lesson, a sales pitch, and a press conference have a more or less fixed content, dependent on the subject matter, but the words are often improvised. Gossip is mostly improvised and can be inspired by the accidental meeting with your neighbors on the stairs, but uses certain key words that return over and over again. The words of a confession in the Catholic Church are improvised, except for certain formulas and prayers, used by confessor and priest, but the situation is ritualistic and almost scripted, with the "actors" playing the roles of sinner and priest, and the confessional as fixed location.

Other story forms, like the speech at different occasions, the lecture, the sermon, or the pleading in court, are usually prepared, but often the speakers depart from the scripted text with an improvisation, an ad-lib. Often, as part of the lecture, the lecturer may recount an anecdote: a story within a story. In a joke, the course of events is fixed, and so are the construction (dramaturgy) and the punch line, but, except for the punch line, the storyteller usually tells the joke in his own words.

Less commonplace, but still stories that can play a role in our daily lives are the following:

- Horror story (with a high fear factor, for example, the appearance of ghosts at a certain time on a certain spot in the woods, or of the Loch Ness Monster, or of UFOs in the night sky)
- Fairy tale (existing fairy tales or stories that take the form of a fairy tale)
- Heroic story (about superhuman achievements or achievements that get superhuman proportions, like the climbing of Mount Everest, or the biggest fish ever caught in a lake)
- Poem
- Song
- Lullaby

The heroic story, the fairy tale, the song, or the horror story may be used in particular daily-life situations, but they have a more literary character. For example, the horror story around the campfire, or the story told by a tour guide during a visit to a medieval castle in Romania, has literary ancestors like *The Odyssey*, or *Dracula*. Therefore these forms have to meet certain literary demands of style, as high-flown language for a heroic story, or rhyme for a song, or certain formulas, like "Once upon a time . . ." for a fairy tale. The fairy tale also has a moralistic ending.

Other story forms: from puppet play to performance piece. All these story forms can be used as a vehicle to tell your story or can be adapted for use. But there are also purely theatrical forms that you can use, for example a *puppet play,* or *clowning,* or *stand-up comedy.* The *song* is a purely theatrical form too. Usually it needs a stage, but songs can also be sung outside the theater, and songs can be made up, words and music and all. And there are many forms of song, from ballad to rap.

There are also "free," newly invented forms. You as the narrator/performer can invent a theatrical form especially for your story. Such a form might be purely theatrical and therefore more abstract than existing theatrical forms and formats, but no less concrete in its execution. Attending a funeral, or having a meal with guests or a tour through a museum, is concrete enough, but a story can also be danced or put into cartoon form or presented as a journey through the mind or as an ever expanding complex mathematical equation or a chemical formula worked out on the blackboard.

Many of these invented story-forms are inspired by reality or the imitated reality of film and television, like quiz and talk shows, police interrogations as in *Law and Order*, or therapy sessions. But I have also seen pure poetry and pure dance, and heroic and cathartic journeys through big cities (as in James Joyce's *Ulysses*), or through barren and overwhelming landscapes, messages from uninhabited islands or letters, or audiotaped confessions, or forms that combine several such existent forms: they are theatrical images for the story.

Solo Performance. Telling Your Story in a Theatrical Form: The Assignment

From subjective to objective, from descriptive to active, from past to present. While keeping the most important elements of the previous exercises, such as the *focus on the action* of the original "I," and the *connection* with his thoughts and feelings, you create a *solo performance* of your story, by applying any of these different story-forms and formats.

Your story, which has been *subjective,* even when you told it in the third person and from different points of view, will be *objectified* through the theatrical form you choose. The theatrical form forces you to look at your whole story from yet another *distance.* What in your story was *descriptive* becomes *active* in and of itself: *you perform the actions and tell them at the same time.* This requires finding new words, and other images; or cutting down on words and replacing them by images. Words, images, and movement now become the vehicle for the action, and nothing has to be explained. What has been in the *past* becomes *present* in the performance.

What you have internalized in the previous exercises you now will externalize through the theatrical form.

You can tell your story in the first person or in the third person. This depends very much on which form you choose. But you can also switch during your story from first to third person, from "I" to "he," allowing yourself, alternately, to "live" your story and to "quote" yourself, giving your own actions a theatrical frame. You might also use the second person—*you*—like this: "Just imagine, you wake up one morning, the sun shines, it is later than you thought, but you have time at your hands, so who cares? You leave your house, and the next thing you know, you are lying in a bed, surrounded by doctors and nurses." Now first person: "Where am I? What's going on? What happened? Did something happen to me?" Now third person: "He had left his house, later than usual, and he had the impression that things were slightly different but he couldn't exactly say what it was . . . Now bear in mind, that he . . ."

The space between the "I" and the "he" and perhaps the "you" creates a space for theatrical imagination. Switching between them gives you the freedom to make jumps in time, to change the chronology or the cause and effect of the story, and to create theatrical images. You become an author-performer. Many theatrical forms depend less on words, and more on images. They have the quality of a *performance piece,* where the performing of the piece becomes the story: the form *is* its content.

To choose a story form, use actions and images from your story as an inspiration for the theatrical form of your performance.

Performance in real time. If you choose to tell your story in court, as a lawyer for the defense in a litigation case, the story will take a different form than if you tell it as a fairy tale or a horror story. The chosen form and the point of view of the first or the third person has an influence upon the performer, just as it has on the main character of the story. If you choose the point of view of a lawyer, then your story is in the third person, and the main character, the original "I" of your story, is the defendant. The point of view of the lawyer will be very different from the feelings and thoughts of his client.

The performer can assume the role of the lawyer, referring to his client in the third person, in which case he creates a *dramatic situation* and a *theatrical framework.* But when he steps out of this role, he can transform into the defendant in the first person. In between, he is just himself, the pure narrator who can step into the shoes of the defendant to listen to the verdict of the judge who then addresses him in the second person as "you." I once saw an actor perform such a story, switching effortlessly from himself to role and back, and arranging the stage for the different transitions in his story.

Many combinations are possible, switching from one perspective to another; in between you always can go back to yourself. You can take a break for a glass of water. While you tell your story and while you play a role, and even when you are not playing at all, you stay in *eye contact* with the audience. You are always present; and your performance is always in *real time*. Show the audience what you're doing, how you're creating your piece.

If you stick to playing the pure narrator, you create the possibility of "demonstrating" both the defendant's and the lawyer's behavior. In such a form, you simply "quote" the court situation, showing different characters and players, rather than creating a dramatic situation and taking it for real. If you do this, don't forget to take a point of view and to commit yourself fully to the story.

Preparations: concept, scenario, theatrical tools, space, and duration. After choosing a *specific form* for your performance, you develop a *concept* and a *scenario*. It is advisable not to write a full script. It could undermine the spontaneity of your narration and performance. It is sufficient to have a scenario, which leaves room for improvisation.

As the performer, you are free to use the material of the story and the different points of view that you have tried out. The form will inspire you to new ones. Additionally you can use everything you need for your performance: *costume, props,* and *music, recorded text* and *video.* But keep it simple. Use mainly the available light.

Next you choose a *space* for the performance. If the workshop is held in one room and there are no other rooms available, you have to decide where in the room you want to be, and where you want your audience to be. If you are working in a big building, you might be able to find a place that is particularly appropriate for your piece: the hallway or the stairs, the little-used storeroom or even the bathroom, as long as your audience can see your performance. Do not make your space into an illusionary space. It is not the location of your story, not the living room, or the boathouse. Think of your space rather as a theatrical space that you design according to your wishes and your imagination. Let yourself be inspired by the space, by the way the light falls through the windows, or how the paint has flaked off the wall. Sometimes the space is the inspiration for the form. A well-used space always adds to your story.

When you choose your space, you also choose the particular place for your performance, and for your audience: where do you want to be, where do you want the audience to be? Do not create too elaborate performance spaces, which need a lot of time to arrange.

The performance shouldn't be longer than seven to ten minutes. All the previous exercises should enable you to condense your story into a short time. Images replace words and express the essence of the story.

Staging yourself in public. You, as the narrator, must do everything yourself. You are in charge of everything from ushering the audience in to turning of the air conditioning. Everything you do you do in public, visible to the audience: arranging the space, changing your clothes, putting on the music. You also do your performance preparations in public, just like percussionists who get their sticks ready and violinists who tune their instruments. This helps you to establish *eye contact* with the audience right from the start.

Like a real-time actor, you-as-performer are staging yourself. In your performance, there are no other actors/narrators or imaginary characters you have to mime. If there are other characters, you can "quote" or play them, and let them talk and act directly and actively. You have no helpers whom you can ask to perform certain tasks for you. *Creating your piece is part of your performance.*

The actor as an author-performer is someone who not only does what the director asks him to do, but someone who creates his role, contributes to the performance as a whole and is responsible for it.

An audience, even in these kinds of solo performances, remains an audience, so be careful not to make your audience into a character in your story. Their "role" is to watch you. But as part of your performance, you can make special arrangements for them. You might seat them in a jury box or a classroom, but don't make them act as jurors or students, for their focus is different from yours: they know less than you do. You address them as audience, and it is your task to engage them, to give them the opportunity to assess your interpretation of the story . . . and to make them sit on the edge of their chairs.

Rehearse your story several times, by going through your scenario from transition to transition (cue to cue).

When everything is ready, when you are ready, you can begin. Have a good time.

Postexercise Observations

1. Evaluation of the performance. In the performance you have the opportunity to test the theatrical form you have chosen for your story. You can find out about its effectiveness by the reactions of the audience. The audience members know the story, so they are the experts: their reactions are from "inside" and genuine. Performing your story in a particular form gives you a different energy. You realize it has to come across. This awareness adds to the story and the form you have chosen. You want to make it work: a good story is a well-told story.

By arranging yourself into the story, by inviting the audience in and seating them, by putting on the music or lighting a candle, you are *present as yourself* from the start. Did this help you throughout the performance to make and keep eye contact with the audience, and to stay with yourself, especially on moments when you have to make a new arrangement, turn off the music, blow out the candle, or just take a small break to go from one place to another? Did the use of the third or the second person in parts of your story made this possible for you, too? Did you lose yourself in the form at any point?

What were the specific form elements you have used? Try to be as specific as you can to describe them. Try to find out from your audience if they have seen what you have tried to accomplish.

Try to find out, with your audience, how far the form you have chosen adequately expresses the story as they know it. It is most interesting to find out if and how the chosen theatrical form has added to the story, not only for yourself, but also for the audience. Did the arrangement in the chosen space work for you? And for the audience? Did the music work? Did dancing help you or get in the way? Was the costume change necessary? Did you notice moments, during the performance, where the staging or the dramaturgy could have been simpler?

Step 4. Someone Else's Story

Natural distance and critical examination. With telling someone else's story, we go back to the former storytelling situation. But now the narrator tells someone else's story rather than his own. This marks a big change: you're still telling a story, but no longer the same person as the original "I" of the story. He is another participant of the workshop. The distance between you as the narrator and the original main character of the story is obvious. Therefore it is quite natural to tell the chosen story in the third person. It also gives you an enormous freedom to try new points of view, without changing the objective facts of the story.

But as you enter this new point of view, be aware that this is a critical investigation, not a critique of the original narrator. It is not your job to offend or hurt him, but to find meaning.

Often the original narrator will be surprised—or even shocked—by the new light that is cast on events of the story and his actions: "I never looked at it that way," he might say. More often than not, the original narrator will suddenly see the humor of the situation he has been recounting, and laugh at his own story, or he may be moved to tears to hear his story told by someone else. In any case, he will almost always acquire new insights into the events of his story, into his behavior and his hidden motivations.

Telling someone else's story comes very close to playing a role. For what else are we doing when we act than telling the story of someone else: a character? This exercise suddenly makes it very clear that an actor *always* tells someone else's story when he acts. By personally connecting to it, he tells it in his own way, with his very own and idiosyncratic ways of expression.

Telling Someone Else's Story in the Third Person as a "He/She" Story and Choosing a Point of View: The Assignment

Point of view and connection. Everyone in the group may choose another member's story to tell, but make sure that no story is left out. Although certain stories might be more attractive than others, for the sake of the exercise it is important that all stories get a chance. The best way of doing this is for each person to simply take his neighbor's story. As a result, there is a likelihood that some of the men's stories will be told by women, and vice versa, but this is good: the story is *material* for the narrator. Just as an actor can play any role, regardless of gender, age, race, or ethnicity, so a narrator can tell anybody's story.

The setup for this exercise stays the same as in previous exercises: you ground yourself and make sure that you make eye contact with your audience. Direct the focus of your attention onto the action of the main character of the story (the original "I"), just as you did with the first "he/she" stories: on his thoughts and feelings, which, by now, you know very well. To find a point of view to use, you can choose from the same list you used for the first "he/she" story. But now you *must discover a personal connection* with the story—even if the point of view you are presenting does not represent your own opinion. You find it in the way you're telling the story. To make this perspective visible, you must find a physical form for the point of view. In this way you "appropriate" the story of the other person and make it into your own. Usually the natural distance gives you the freedom to do so.

Now tell the story.

Postexercise Observations

1. Different dramaturgical structure. An unexpected interpretation, coming from a chosen point of view, can lead to a different dramaturgical structure of the story, as we have seen before. The difficulty the original narrator might have had in altering the story, or in making jumps in time, can now be overcome more easily, because you are not locked into the original narrator's idea of cause and effect. You are free to detect other causes and effects, other motivations for actions, other intentions, in short other interpretations of the facts. The loyalty of the original narrator to his story does not impede you—in a way you are in a better position to deconstruct the original story than him or her.

2. Language and imagery. In addition, the language will change. You tell the story in your own words, and because you're another person, you will automatically use different words and create other images. The freedom you have will stimulate your imagination. You will be more physical and livelier in movement and gesture, and freer in the use of the space.

If you use the same words as the original narrator, they will literally be quotations. "Play" the quotation marks. By referring to them in your version of the story, you also quote the actions of the original narrator, doing what the eyewitness in Brecht's "Street Scene" does: describing vividly the events that happened in the story. The audience sees you, the narrator, and the original narrator of the story. By fully *committing* yourself to the point of view you choose, you "show" or *demonstrate* the actions of the original narrator. Doing so gives you a chance to signal that there is also something at stake for you. And because you must make that personal connection, your story will be just as truthful and convincing as when the original "I" told his story.

3. The story of a role. This last exercise can be applied by an actor to his preparation for a role in a scripted play. It allows him to acquire a thorough understanding of the behavior and the actions of a character, and to find ideas about *how* to play his role. The more radical he is in this process, the better. Brecht suggested that an actor try speaking his text in the third person in order to create a distance between himself and his role. I would add: if you tell the story of the character in the third person, choose a point of view in order to find out exactly what the dramatic action of the character is or can be: how he acts and how his actions can be interpreted. If you don't do this, the exercise can become nothing but a summing up of the facts, a summary of the things that happen in the scene or the play. For example, the actor who plays King Lear might tell the story of the events in the first few scenes of act 1 of the play, explaining what he, the actor, thinks and feels about Lear when the king divides his realm between his daughters—not just the facts: first this happened, and then that happened, and then . . . It is advisable in this preparatory exercise to use strong counterpoints of view, for example, not pity or compassion, but contempt. You can do this for each scene, for a whole act, and for the whole play.

Telling Someone Else's Story in the First Person as if It Were an "I" Story, from a Point of View: The Assignment

Unlike the previous exercise, in which the narrator connects to the behavior and the actions of the original "I" through his point of view, the narrator now tells the story of the original "I" in the first person, just as if it were his own "I" story, *but without identifying with the "I."* The narrator shows or demonstrates the behavior and the actions of the main character of the story, in the same way as he did when he told his own story in the first person. With the help of a point of view, or perhaps of all the points of view that have been explored so far, the actor creates a physical form in which he expresses what he believes the original "I" feels and thinks.

Tell the story.

Postexercise Observations

1. Self-created safety net. Telling someone else's story in the first person, you-as-the-narrator, can show your own feelings and thoughts more freely and more strongly than when you tell your own story in the first person. While you use your own instrument to express the feelings and thoughts of the original "I," you also explore the free space between yourself and the original "I" and use it to switch from one sequence of the story to the other, to make transitions, to take time to think, to make connections between different parts of the story, to repeat certain parts, or to take a small break. In this free space, you feel that you have nothing to lose, and that nothing can go wrong: it is a self-made safety net.

2. Audience as witness. The audience of participants in the workshop knows that the story you tell is not your story, but someone else's. The audience becomes a witness to *how* you create your version of the story. They have a better opportunity to assess the behavior of the original "I":

they have become 'experts,' just as fans at a baseball game are experts.[11]

This puts the audience in the same position as when they see an actor playing a role, for in the theater the audience always knows that the actor is not telling his own story, but someone else's. The eye contact ensures direct communication between them *about* the character's behavior and actions, and a silent understanding between storyteller and audience.

Step 5. Montage of the Stories

Different formats of the workshop. Ever since I first developed this workshop, I have thought of creating a performance piece out of the stories that were being told, and many students and actors have asked me to do so. In 2004 at Princeton University I had enough time and the right number of students to try it out. It gave me the opportunity to shape the workshop in its complete form: the "I" story, the he/she story from different points of view, the solo performance, followed by the story of someone else, and finally a montage of all the stories as a performance piece.

This ideal situation does not exist everywhere. Therefore there are different formats for doing this workshop and still getting the most out of it.

Format 1. The "I" story (minimum two times) and the he/she story, followed by someone else's story. In this reduced version, there is no performance at the end. With twelve participants you can complete this program thoroughly in twenty-five hours.

Format 2. The "I" story (minimum two times) and the he/she story, followed by a solo performance piece. Depending on the available time and the number of participants, the workshop teacher can decide how many times he wants to do the exercises before the participants create their solo performances. With twelve participants it is possible to complete this program thoroughly in twenty-five hours.

Format 3. The "I" story (minimum two times) and the he/she story, followed by someone else's story, and a montage of all the stories in one performance piece. With twelve participants it is possible to do this in thirty-five to forty hours.

Format 4. The "full monty": the "I" story, the he/she story, a solo performance piece, someone else's story, followed by a montage of all the stories in one performance piece. With twelve participants it is possible to complete this program in forty to fifty hours.

Making a Montage Piece of All the Stories as a
Performance Piece: The Assignment

The group as a whole defines the theme or themes that connect the different stories to each other. This gives you an indication of a possible order for the montage. There are also other parameters, which you can use for the composition of the piece, for example, the different locations of the stories or the different theatrical forms that were used for the solo performances.

If you have been working in format 3, you choose individually a story you want to do in the montage. This might be someone else's story, but it could also be your own story. If it is someone else's, it doesn't necessarily have to be the story you have been working on in the previous exercise(s).

If you have been working in format 4, you do the same, but then you can also choose certain theatrical forms of the previous solo performances that were especially appealing to you, either to be performed by yourself, or by the original performer, or by all participants.

Then you decide which parts of the stories should be told, and in which form: as "I" story or as "he/she" story, or as a "you" story. You also decide which stories become monologues, which parts of the stories will be acted out in small scenes, or dialogues, and which will appear as "quotes" of a situation within the theatrical framework of the piece. One of the characters in these small scenes will most likely be the original "I" of the story; other characters are to be played by other participants in the workshop. But someone else can also play the "I," at least for a part of the story. There are endless possibilities for combinations, depending on the theme and what you want to say with the montage.

Then together you make a scenario, and you decide upon an order for the stories. You can break the stories up into several parts, combining them with material from other stories. Most stories can be divided up in three or four sections. Deconstructing the stories becomes a logical thing to do. Connect the different parts with each other by association of content, theme, or shared features of the different stories, such as constellations of characters, locations, the weather, or quality of events. The resulting collage or montage might not be linear and may be devoid of rational logic, but together a new logic will surface, a new theme of all the stories together.

At this point, for the first time in the workshop, you can write down a text. Stories or parts of stories become monologues, or a song, or a poem, and scenes demand dialogue.

You must also decide how you want to arrange the space in which you mount your montage, and where you want your audience to be, where you want to be when you are performing, and, when you are not playing or telling your story, how to circulate in the space, how you can improvise a *choreography*. And you must make sure that the participants can do all the staging for themselves. Keep it simple!

Then, if you're working in format 4, you turn to the theatrical forms that were applied in the solo performances. Together you decide which of these forms you want to keep and use again. And you add new ones. For instance, you might decide to transform a solo dance from one of the stories into a choreography for all the participants, or you might all sing a song. You choose music for the piece and decide when you want to play it. You might use live or recorded music, and you decide which props and costumes you want to use. All these elements together provide you with theatrical images with which you create your piece.

Write the scenario down on a big piece of paper, with indications of the different parts and specifics as to "who is doing what," and what sort of theatrical elements you are using (music, dance). Design this written scenario in such a way that you can read it. Hang it on the wall or put it on the floor together with all other pieces you're using, so the participants can look at it for support. It's also a way of showing to the audience that you're staging yourself in public.

Then you are ready to rehearse the piece once or twice, to find the choreography of the piece, and to make any necessary changes. Finally, you invite an audience from outside and perform your piece, almost in an improvised manner—not forgetting to make eye contact with your new audience.

With this montage piece you can present the results of your work. It makes a beautiful, rewarding conclusion for the workshop.

6   The Exercises

Active Seeing and Looking

Being present requires of the actor a raised awareness. This begins with really *seeing* and *looking*. The actor enters; he looks around and sees the stage, along with everything that is on it, including the other actors. He need not fool himself, nor the audience: he sees the stage for what it is. He doesn't have to act "as if" he were seeing something else or hallucinating something that is not there. What he sees is real and concrete, here and now. And the act of *seeing* is itself real and concrete. It is an active kind of seeing.

Here are seven simple but effective exercises to help actors develop such active seeing.

1. Stand still, feet firmly planted on the ground anywhere in the space, and see what is in front of you (see also the later section on grounding). See what is nearby and what is in the distance. Try not to stare. Then move your eyes up and down, left and right, and see what you see out of the corners of your eye. Now move your head, left and right, up and down, keeping your shoulders in place, and see what you can see: the space to the left and right of you, the ceiling, the floor. Now move your upper body left and right, and see what you see now: an even bigger portion of the space. Turn yourself around on the spot by moving your feet and making your

upper body follow this movement—making sure your body isn't twisting into a corkscrew; observe the whole space and everything that is in it. Take your time for this exploration of the ever-enlarging horizon, and make yourself aware of what you see by silently naming it: ceiling, wooden floor, windowsill, crack in the wall, green exit light, and so on.

2. Include the other actors and make eye contact with them; then choose the person who is nearest to you and make eye contact. Don't talk. It may take a while before you can really let the other in. Making eye contact is one of the most important things actors can do to be present: *you see that I see that you see me.* Real eye contact causes a mutual reaction of recognition, and it is a silent greeting. You may also feel how unprotected you are, how vulnerable. Focusing on another person with your eyes immediately calls up emotions that show themselves on your face. Allow what comes up to express itself: smile when you feel like smiling, cry when you feel like crying, laugh when you feel like laughing. Allow yourself to become present without consciously trying. Allow yourself to *connect* with yourself, to relax within yourself, to let all tension go, and to feel *free* in your body (see also the section on connection). Stay in eye contact with one person for a little while. Then choose someone else.

3. Form a large, standing circle, ground yourself, and look around. Make eye contact, one by one, with the others in the circle. Now the previous partner exercise becomes a group exercise: everyone sees everyone else, without talking. This demands a higher level of concentration. Take time for everyone, but not too long (you want to make eye contact with all the others, also) and not too short (you want to make *real* eye contact). Don't rush; try to find a balance between the two. After one round, ground yourself, and take two or three steps forward, so that the circle becomes smaller. Now do the same thing again. Getting closer to each other makes the task easier and safer, but take your time to give everyone the attention he deserves. Take a few more steps, until you form the smallest possible circle, standing freely next to each other, shoulders and arms almost touching, but not squeezed together. Again, make eye contact, going around the circle with your eyes, and allowing any thoughts or feelings that arise to be mirrored on your

face and shared with the others without talking. Now, walk backward, step by step, continuing to make eye contact. Don't look
down at the floor. Try to maintain the contact until you have
made the widest possible circle. Then dissolve the circle.

4. Start walking around the room, crisscrossing through the space.
Walk at a leisurely pace, remaining at ease, and look around. See
what you see on your journey. Don't rush; take your time. Stop
whenever something you see attracts your attention, identify it
and, silently, name it: chair, table, hole in a curtain, missing rung
of a ladder, spot on the wall. Allow your eye to notice details of the
space; stop, and start walking again. Now, as you move through
the space, keep walking without stopping as you identify the space
and the objects in it, including the other actors in the space, who
are doing the same thing. Make eye contact with them, saying
"hello" with your eyes, and allow your feelings to show on your
face. Don't talk, don't touch each other; just keep walking without
stopping, maintaining your leisurely pace. Stop. Now pick up the
pace, start walking with more energy than before, and keep doing
what you have been doing, but now use your voice, give the objects their names out loud, and say "hello" with your voice to anyone you encounter on your journey. Note that the energy with
which you walk corresponds with the way you talk. Your *walking
body follows your eyes*. It may take a while before you are able to
walk normally and lose the self-conscious feeling that you are
playing at walking. And it may be a while before you really see
what you see and really notice who else is there in the space—the
way you would *really* pay attention if you were surprised by a la-
dybug that landed on your hand—rather than acting *as if* you
were paying attention. Take care that you don't stare at things,
with your eyes gazing blankly into space. When that happens, you
are actually looking inside yourself, and as a result, you're not really present in the space.

5. Choose a position in the space. From there, look at another point
in the space, or at an object. The choice is a conscious decision, a
selection you make without hurry. Now point your eyes at the
chosen spot and then walk deliberately toward it until you have
arrived next to it. Then identify it by calling it by its name, using
your voice. Now turn around and choose another spot and direc-

tion. Repeat this several times. The energy with which you walk toward the chosen spot can be different each time. You can saunter, or you can rush or move with deliberate steps, making sure that the volume of your voice when you arrive corresponds with the way you walked toward that place. In this way you also explore the space vocally. Don't forget that there are others in the space as well, who are doing the same thing. Try not to bump into each other; make eye contact with them when you meet someone, without losing the focus on the spot you're walking toward, only allowing yourself to be interrupted for a moment. Take your time for everything, and be aware of the whole space, of everybody and of everything that's in the space. If you lose your focus, start over from the same starting position.

6. Form a group in one corner of the space, making sure that everyone in the group can see the whole space. Now one person leaves the group and runs diagonally through the space to the opposite corner. He comes to a standstill, turns around, sees the group on the far end of the room, and then loudly and clearly says, "Hello" (or something like that). The group answers him, and he walks back toward the group at a normal tempo, making eye contact with them, narrowing his focus as he approaches from the whole group to the individual members of the group. When he is as close as he can get without losing sight of the whole group, he comes to a standstill and says "hello" again, making eye contact with everyone. At the end of the exercise, the person who crossed the room enters *active rest* (see exercise 3 under "Active Rest"). Then the next person makes his run. By keeping focused on the group across the room, the runner will soon stop feeling self-conscious about his walking body.

7. Walk through the space at an energetic tempo. See what you see, making eye contact with everyone you meet. The side coach calls out the name of one person; the group comes to a standstill, while the person whose name was called walks on, crisscrossing through the others who are spread out over the whole space. The walking person must find his way through the group while making eye contact with everyone. At first this act may feel a bit nerve-wracking, and you may want to hurry, but if you keep focused on the task of making eye contact, you will calm down. Don't stop walk-

ing, but take the time you need for the moment of eye contact. The others do not move but follow the mover with their eyes, turning around when necessary, using their whole body—without forcing themselves into a corkscrew. The walker knows that all eyes are fixed on him, but after a while he may discover the supportive nature of being watched like this.

In addition to increasing his own sense of presence, the actor will find that these exercises also help him develop a physical awareness of his relation to the space—an awareness he needs in order to move freely.

This awareness of the space is something to practice every day before going on stage, especially on tour, when every stage is new and different. In real-time theater, without elaborate sets, each new stage becomes part of the performance, so it is important to explore the stage before the performance starts. Take the time to look around and to picture yourself in different positions in the space.

Active Hearing and Listening

1. Stand still in the space; keep your eyes open and listen to the sounds that come from the stage, from the theater building, and from the world outside (there is no theater in the world so well insulated that police sirens are never heard).
2. Turn your eyes toward each sound you hear, thus coordinating seeing/looking and hearing/listening: Look toward the sharp ticking of a spotlight cooling down, toward the cracking of a floorboard, toward the breathing of your fellow actors, or toward the sound of someone entering the space. Identify the sounds for yourself.
3. Walk through the space, looking around while you walk. Make eye contact with the other actors and mumble something (words, some text, a story . . . anything you like). Then speak louder. And louder. And louder. Now decrease the volume of your voice gradually, but keep walking at the same tempo and keep making eye contact. Come to a standstill. Ground yourself. Listen to the sounds you hear in the room, outside the room . . . your own

pounding heart. Keep your eyes open. Identify the sounds to your-self.

4. Resume walking and start telling a story (out loud, but to yourself) while making eye contact with the others and taking in the room. When the side coach calls a name, the whole group comes to a standstill and stops telling stories, except for the one whose name has been called. He continues walking through the group, making eye contact with each individual member and telling his story to that person. They listen and follow the speaking actor with their eyes (see also the previous exercise, with walking through a group and making eye contact). Note that it becomes easier to follow an actor with your eyes when you really listen to him.

5. Two actors stand in the middle of the room back-to-back. Allow yourselves to feel each other's back, but don't lean on each other; stand on your own feet. After finding your balance and tuning into your breathing, start a conversation—about anything at all. Don't look over your shoulders: the communication depends upon just really listening to each other. As soon as the conversation is established, start walking away from each other on a diagonal, continuing until each of you reaches the farthest corner of the space. Keep listening to each other, without looking back. It may take some time to suppress the temptation to look, but not looking heightens the focus on hearing and listening. The greater the distance between the two of you becomes, the louder you get (in this way, this exercise is also good practice in coordinating your hearing/listening with your vocal volume and your movement). Once you reach the farthest corner of the space, come to a standstill, ground yourself, wait a moment, and then turn around, all without interrupting the conversation. Make eye contact with the opposite actor, and start walking toward each other. The volume of your voice decreases. Through your eyes you can let your partner—and the onlookers—see that you are listening to each other. Whatever happens between the two actors during this conversation is happening for real. This is exactly how actors need to listen to each other.

6. All the actors stand in two rows opposite each other and close enough to make eye contact, and to start a normal conversation at a normal volume. As soon as the conversations are established,

start moving away from each other by walking backward. Gradually allow your voice to rise in volume. As you move back, be careful not to lose eye contact. If you do, your conversation will get lost within the cacophony of sounds from the other conversations. How far you can move away from each other depends upon the size of the space and the volume of your voices. You will be surprised how far you can get without losing the conversation. At the farthest possible point, stop. Keep your conversation going and walk back toward each other, not in a hurry but at the same tempo you took when you walked backward. Gradually the volume of your voice will decrease. When you are very close again and everyone has returned to his position in two rows, end your conversation. Usually at that point you will find yourself completely relaxed, and you will have no difficulty maintaining your focus on each other. Moreover, what might have started as an artificial or superficial talk has become a real conversation in which both of you are completely engaged.

7. Half the group stands in the space, each person separated from the others. Make sure you can see the other half of the group from where you are; they are your audience. Everyone at once, start telling a story to the audience. The side coach calls a name, and this actor continues with his story, while the others become silent and listen. The speaking actor makes sure that he tells his story to the audience as well as to the others in his group. The others in the group make sure that they see him while he is doing this, allowing their eyes to lead their body so that they can see the speaker. After a minute or so, everyone resumes telling his own story until another name is called.

Active Rest

Active rest is not a contradiction in terms: it is a state in which the actor can *connect* with himself without losing energy and focus. It is, in fact, the opposite of being introspective and introverted. The actor can attain a state of active rest through active listening and seeing. The activity of really looking at and listening to what happens around him brings the actor both *inner rest and alertness at the same time*. It can help him overcome the self-consciousness he may feel about his physical presence—his body, how he looks, and what he's going to say or do— and any self-consciousness he may have about the activity of listening and seeing itself. Active listening in the present moment can enable the actor to react to everything he sees and hears without *anticipating*. It keeps him from becoming "virtually absent" and leaves him always *ready to go*. Active rest enables him to see the audience, to accept it and to appreciate it as a natural and essential part of the performance. Moreover, the active rest of the actor can help the audience feel at ease with the situation, too, for they perceive that, like themselves, the actor is present and curious about what he is seeing and hearing.

Here are a few exercises to help you achieve the state of active rest, and to prevent overconcentration. Take your time with these exercises; do them quietly and in silence.

1. Stand still, grounding yourself with both feet on the floor; then, leaning slightly backward, shift the weight of your body from one leg to the other. Doing just this much, moving your focus from yourself to the outside world, you have already achieved "active rest." Notice what you hear and see and make eye contact with other people in the space. This is active rest. Now shift to your other leg and turn around on your spot, moving your feet when you need to avoid twisting into a corkscrew; let your body follow your eyes. Every time you come to a standstill, you enter active rest.

2. Try this same exercise in other standing positions—assuming any stance in which you feel completely at ease with yourself and your body: leaning against a wall, or with your hands on your back, with your arms across your chest, with chin in your hand, or with both hands on the back of a chair . . . but avoid positions with spread legs or both hands on your waist: these positions lead to rigidity. A so-called freeze is unnatural. From this position, suddenly propel yourself forward, returning to active rest in another standing position somewhere else in the space.

3. Now try the same exercise while sitting: sit down in different seated positions, positions in which you can easily observe the space and the other people. Stay active and don't let your body collapse; avoid losing your energy—laziness is deadly on the stage.

Free your body from any tensions you may feel, and be ready to move at any moment. Get up with a sudden movement, and then find active rest in another sitting position somewhere else in the space.

4. Start walking through the space at a normal walking tempo. Look around, registering consciously what you hear and see, making eye contact with the others when you meet them. Take your time for everything you do. Now come to a standstill and repeat the first active rest exercise (grounding, shifting your weight to one leg, etc.).

5. Walk along one wall of the space and choose a part of the wall or an object (big or small) to look at. Come to a standstill and look at the object in the way you look at a painting in a museum (*really looking, not just acting as if you were looking!*). Make sure you really see what you're looking at. Repeat this several times, taking the time you need to make your choices in the space: make a decision about where you're going, and then keep giving your full attention to the chosen object or part of the space. Come to a standstill, turn around, and see the whole space and everybody and everything in it. Enter active rest without shifting the weight of your body from one leg to the other. Note the inner space you have created within yourself.

Grounding, Centering, and Relaxing

In order to be present, the real-time actor must be relaxed. In a relaxed state you can feel your body. Your breathing drops into your center, not too high in the chest or the throat, but somewhere below between your pelvis and your solar plexus. This is your *center*. It is very important you are able to breathe calmly and steadily, because your breathing supplies the fuel for your energy.

Being *relaxed* is not the same as being laid back, lazy, indifferent, or resigned. It brings you *inner rest and confidence*. To find real relaxation, you must be *grounded*.

Here are three consecutive exercises to help you to go from being "grounded" to "relaxed."

Exercise A: Grounding

1. Come into a circle as a group. Stand still, legs slightly apart, feet directly below your hips.
2. Keep your eyes open, your head straight on your shoulders, and try not to stare. Let your arms hang down along your body, drop your shoulders, and drop your jaw (lips slightly apart). Bring your attention to how you are standing on the floor, and feel the ground under your feet. Feel the warmth of the soles of your feet standing on the ground. If you pay attention, you can feel the blood rushing through your veins; if the room is very quiet, you may hear a buzz in your ears. Let yourself become aware of your body and of the space you're in.
3. Unlock your knees, allowing your rear end to drop down. Let your shoulders drop a little more, permitting your breathing to become calm and regular. Allow your diaphragm to descend so that your breath falls deep down into your belly. Don't force anything, but allow it to happen. Do this exercise slowly. Always keep looking out with your eyes: it keeps you active. If, when your attention moves downward, you find yourself turning inward, it can happen that the blood withdraws from the head and you get dizzy. In that case, sit down for a while, head between your knees, and recover. Then try again. Remember: if you keep your eyes open and don't stare, you stay active and you won't get dizzy.

Exercise B: Centering

1. In the standing circle, bring your attention to your waist, the area just above your pelvis: this is your *center*. This is where your breath begins, and it is from this center that all of your energy flows. Now allow your attention to move from your waist down to your toes: beginning with the thighs, then the calves, ankles, and finally to the feet and toes. Feel the weight and the warmth of your lower body.
2. Now bring your attention back to your waist and think yourself tall, moving your attention up your spine, continuing all the way up to the ceiling. Bring your attention to the top of your head, feel

your hair, make very little movements with your head, as if you were painting the ceiling with a fine brush—but keep looking out. Without effort you have stretched your body.

3. Now return to your center. Keep your shoulders, jaw, and rear end relaxed and your knees unlocked.

Exercise C: Relaxing

1. Close your eyes and, with your inner eye, try to see the path you took before you entered the studio: from the moment you got up and had your breakfast, or left your house, or any other moment of the day, until you entered the room for this workshop or class. Recall particular events, someone you spoke to, a telephone conversation, something you saw happening on the street or in the subway, or what the weather was like.

2. With your inner eye, picture your position in the room: who or what is in front of you; who or what is next of you; who or what is behind you. Take your time; don't rush.

3. Now picture yourself standing in the room as if from above, hovering, as it were, in a helicopter over yourself.

4. Think of something pleasant that happened to you in the last twenty-four hours. Your face will automatically reflect what you feel at this moment.

5. Open your eyes. Make eye contact with each other, looking around the circle. Share what you feel with your partners. You have arrived in this room, at this moment, and you *are* with your classmates or workshop partners. You are grounded.

The following exercise helps you to go from relaxation to being grounded. Exercise D: From Relaxing to Grounding

1. Lie down on the floor, anywhere in the room, with your arms next to your upper body, palms up, your eyes closed, and with enough space around you. Bring your attention to each part of your body, part by part, beginning with your toes, then moving slowly upward, through your feet, your ankles and lower legs (calves and shins), your knees and thighs, your pelvis, your lower back and

your belly, your spine and your torso, your chest and your back, your rib cage, your shoulder blades, your shoulders, your neck and the nape of your neck, your upper arms, your elbows, hands, and fingers, your head and the crown of the head where it touches the floor.

2. Feel the warmth of the floor under the particular body parts you are focusing on. Your body is giving in to the floor, but at the same time you can feel the floor's resistance. Where parts of your body are not in direct contact with the floor, for instance at your ankles, your knees, your lower back, neck, and wrists—in short where most of your joints are located—try to think these body parts toward the floor, without moving them: let them relax by themselves.

3. Put one hand on your stomach and breathe deeply into your belly. Check the rising and falling of your belly with your hand. Breathe in with your mouth closed, and out with your mouth open, without any resistance. Let yourself feel your breath moving through all the parts of your body as they open by themselves. Do this with ease, without forcing anything. You will notice that once your breath has filled your belly, your chest and rib cage open up. There is a lot of space in your body for all this breath.

4. Once you can fill yourself completely with a deep, quiet breath, breathe out, making a sharp "s" sound. On the next breath, breathe out making a sharp "f" sound. Don't push: If you don't push too hard, it can take a long time before you are out of breath and have to breathe in again. Then breathe out with a full "sshh" sound. This sound will require a much shorter time before you have to breathe in again.

5. Now, breathe out with a full "a" sound, then "o," then "u," and finally an "e" sound. Open your mouth as much as the sound requires, lips and jaw apart. Use an aspiration (an "h" sound), as in "haaa," "hey," "hoe," "huuu," "heee" to lead into the vowel. Use your mouth as a sounding board, so that the "a" and "o" sounds become round and full, and the "u" and "e" sounds sharp and shrill.

6. Let your breath encounter obstacles in your body, things like the pain of a scar, or stomach cramps, or emotional pains, and breathe

out with a sound—any sound—that accords with how you feel at that moment. Don't force anything; just let the sound happen. Your diaphragm has become so relaxed by this time that it may move quietly and automatically on its own. If you find yourself laughing or crying, let it happen. It is simply a physical reaction: your diaphragm flutters. It means your body is completely relaxed.

7. Now stretch out on the floor, with or without a sound. Yawn if you feel like it and start to move around while lying on the floor. At this point, have the side coach turn on some music. Roll over on your side, pull your legs up into a fetal position and, placing your hands next to you on the floor, slowly unfold yourself until you are standing. Feel the weight of your full body. Open your eyes, look around, make eye contact with others, and check how you are standing on the floor.

8. Staying in one place, begin to move separate body parts, starting from your center, at first in small circular countermovements and then in bigger movements. Slowly begin to move through the space, always from your center, until you dance . . . and fly. Use the music and use your imagination.

9. Slowly make your movements smaller and smaller as the volume of the music diminishes, so that as the music becomes inaudible, your movements become invisible. When the music fades out, come to a standstill. Listen to the silence in the space and to your breathing.

10. Try shifting to a moment of active rest, or try looking around in the space and making eye contact, or walking around. Notice how free you have become, how much space you have inside of you and around you.

These exercises all lead to the same result: that you become aware, that it is *you* who is there, not someone else standing in someone else's shoes, or wearing someone else's clothes, or doing someone else's actions, or speaking someone else's text. You can feel comfortable with and within yourself. When you walk, you can really feel the floor under your feet. The steps you take are conscious steps; you're not floating as if in a dream; you're going somewhere: from here to there. You know what you're doing, and why you're doing it. You choose your goals and you arrive there.

Connection and Trust

Active rest and being grounded and relaxed contribute to the *self-confidence,* the *self-awareness,* and the *courage* the real-time actor needs for his presence on the stage as himself. They open him up, help him to have access to himself and be *connected.* Being connected means, first of all, being in touch with your center and with your instrument, not by being introverted, looking inside yourself, but by looking outside yourself, by actively seeing and listening, by grounding and by employing active rest as a moment of active relaxation. But to feel connected you also need to *trust* yourself and trust is a mental condition, which can be brought about by trusting your body.

These exercises help you to create a safe space. A safe space ensures that the real-time actor always safely returns to being himself and connects to himself. Thus he learns that he can keep this connection with himself always alive. And conversely, because of the distance between the actor and his role, and because of his condition of "active rest," the actor never loses this connection when he is acting. There is always enough time and space for him to be himself. Within this self-created safety net, he always has access to his own instrument, to his intuition and his senses, and to the "material" that he has collected and stored in himself, that is, all the "information" he needs to embody the character: the text of the play, the ingredients for the theatrical form, and all the practical agreements that were made during the rehearsal process for the "blocking" or the choreography, the handling of props and costumes.

Here are a few exercises that can help you find physical connection and trust. Some of these are very common exercises, but they deserve a place in this context.

Exercise A: Isolations

These are well-known *isolations,* actively isolating the body parts from each other. Do each movement twice, keeping your eyes open. Ground your self as described in the exercises on grounding. As you work, bring your attention to each body part, which can move independently, starting from the head down.

1. Lift your head up a little—out of its socket, as it were. Then slowly lower your chin onto your chest. Feel the stretch in your neck. Reverse this movement, your hair grazing the air, until your head has returned to its original position.

2. Lift your head up and bend it backward toward the back of your neck. Feel the stretch in your throat. Now move the head back into place in the same manner, your hair grazing the air.

3. Tilt your head sideways toward your left and right shoulder. (Do not lift your shoulders up toward your head. The shoulders stay in place, your arms hanging down.) Feel the stretch at the sides of your neck.

4. Bring your attention to your shoulders one by one, first the left, then the right. Lift them up—out of their hinges as it were—toward your ears (not moving your ears toward your shoulders); move the shoulders gently back down again, and pull your arms gently down by your fingertips (feel the stretch on the inside of your arm), and return the shoulders back to their neutral position. It may feel as though you have moved a great distance, while in fact your shoulders have moved only a few inches.

5. Lift your shoulders up and bring them forward, as if you were lifting them over a threshold, and return them the same way. Repeat in the reverse direction.

6. Move your shoulders in a circle around the joint, both at the same time. It can feel like quite a circle.

7. Bring your attention to your torso, your whole upper body. Place your hands on your hips. Lift your upper body up, out of your middle, and slide it forward—moving from your center (not from your breastbone), sticking the chest out between your shoulders while leaving your shoulders in place. When you return the chest to center, you can feel the difference. Then slide your upper body backward between your shoulders, as if ducking slightly, but keeping your shoulders in place.

8. Lift your upper body up again and move it sideways, left and right, as if it were moving on rails, leaving your shoulders in place. Move your chest in a circle.

9. Place your hands on your hipbones and tilt your pelvis forward, backward, and sideways. Make a circle, as if your hips were touching the inside of a barrel.

10. Lift up your legs, one by one, and circle your lower leg around your knee, to the left and to the right.

11. Circle your feet around your ankles, both clockwise and counter-clockwise.

12. Stretch out your arms and circle your hands around your wrists, clockwise and counterclockwise.

13. Finally, stretch your fingers, forward and backward.

14. To finish off, you can do a nice stretch by rolling down along your spine, counting your vertebrae, until your hands touch—or almost touch—the floor. Then roll up again, the same way, lifting your head last, putting the spine back in place.

15. Now put on some energizing and rhythmical music. Bring your attention to your center and, starting from there, move as many body parts as you can at the same time, independent of each other. Begin with small movements, but then let your movements grow bigger and bigger, until you can no longer stay in one place, so you start to move around the room. (This movement is like the end of exercise 4 in the previous section, only more energetic.) Let the music inspire you. Use your imagination. Soon you may find yourself dancing. Make eye contact. Then make the movements smaller again and more refined. As the music slowly fades out, stay in one place as your movements become smaller, and smaller, until finally, the music and your movements stop and you are no longer moving. Listen to the silence.

Exercise B: Walking

1. Look around the space. As the music begins, bring your attention to your center.

2. Start walking, as if you are being pulled forward by a string attached to your center. Listen to the rhythm of the music. Walking like this is light and easy. You could walk for miles without getting tired.

3. Allow the rhythms to converge until everyone is walking in the same rhythm. Walk as one person, crisscrossing through the room.

4. Walk through the whole space, to the outer reaches of the room and in toward the other walkers, but without touching each other; step sideways, or backward, but never stop; move in and out, like

waves breaking on the beach. Listen to each other's footfalls, hearing all the different rhythms.

5. Walk as a group from one end of the room to the other. Do this several times, turning on your heels as you get to the other end.

6. Some members of the group stay behind, and after the others have reached the other end of the room and have turned around, they move toward each other. Try to move fearlessly through each other. Repeat this several times.

7. Now spread out again. When the music fades out, come to a standstill. Listen to the silence again.

Exercise C: Floating:

1. Form a line of six or eight people at one end of the room. (The other participants remain at the other end of the room.) Stand close to each other, but not touching. Feel the presence of the others next to you, but make sure you're not squeezed in too tightly. Let your arms hang down and let yourself feel free and relaxed.

2. Agree as a group which foot will step first when you move. Look out toward the group at the other end, not at the floor. Try to be aware of each other's breathing and to breathe as one person.

3. Without looking at the others, allow an impulse to start all of you walking at the same time. Trust yourself and trust the impulse that runs through the group. The impulse might come from the breath. It will happen, perhaps not right away, but definitely within a few minutes.

4. Once you are walking, you are floating. Make eye contact with the onlookers. The longer the distance you have to walk, the better.

5. Come to a standstill when you have reached the other group. Enter active rest. Make eye contact from where you are with everyone in the other group.

6. Dissolve the line. Repeat the procedure with the other group.

Exercise D: Falling:

Form a circle of about eight participants standing very close to each other, but as in the previous exercise, not so close that you feel squeezed in. Lift your hands in front of you to nearly shoulder height, palms facing forward.

Let one member of the group stand in the middle, eyes closed, grounded and relaxed, arms hanging down, knees not locked. The person in the middle allows himself to fall into the arms of the group, forward, backward, and sideways. With attentive hands, the group catches the person who falls and gently lifts that person back onto his feet in the center of the circle. Then the person in the middle lets himself fall in another direction. Repeat this several times, until the central person feels completely limp and relaxed and feels that he is truly in safe hands. Let the feeling of trust arise by practicing it in this physical form.

All exercises should be done with side coaching.

Mephisto (2), by Paul Binnerts / Klaus Mann, Hummelinck Stuurman
Producties, Amsterdam, 2006. (Photo Ben van Duin.)

Mephisto (1), by Ariane
Mnouchkine/Klaus Mann,
Toneelacademie Maastricht,
1983. (Photo Rob van Berlo.)

Black Box, by Paul Binnerts / Amos Oz, Southern Comfort / Hummelinck Stuurman Producties, Amsterdam, 1999–2000. (Photo Sanne Peper.)

King Lear, by William Shakespeare, Toneelschool Amsterdam, 1997. (Photo Jean van Lingen.)

The Exception and the Rule, by Bertolt Brecht (The On(c)e and Only Theater Group, Berlin / Frankfurt am Main, 1976). (Photo Susanne Esche.)

Forbidden Reproduction, by Paul Binnerts / E. M. Austen, Southern Comfort / Frascati, Amsterdam, 1987. (Photo Hans Verhoeven.)

Fear and Misery in the Third Reich, by Bertolt Brecht, Toneelacademie Maastricht, 1982. (NOS Photo.)

Der Mann der . . . / The Man who . . . , by Peter Brook / Oliver Sachs / Marie-Hélène Estienne, Neues Theater, Halle, 2007. (Photo Falk Wenzel.)

Flametti, Schlicksupp teatertrupp, Frankfurt am Main, 1983. (Photo Leo van Velzen.)

Allein das Meer / The Same Sea, by Paul Binnerts / Amos Oz, Neues Theater Halle a.d. Saale, 2005–6. (Photo Falk Wenzel.)

Man Is Man, by Bertolt Brecht, Tisch, New York University, 2007 / The Elephant Brigade, HERE, 2007. (Photo Bob Moyers.)

Big and Little, by Botho Strauss, Haiyuza Theater, Tokyo, 2000. (Photo Peter de Kimpe.)

Der Brotladen / The Breadshop, by Bertolt Brecht, Schlicksupp teatertrupp, Frankfurt am Main, 1982. (Photo Bob van Dantzig.)

Part III

Real-Time Acting and Theater in Historical Perspective

7   Origins and Conventions

A Different Look at Theater History

Since realism became a style and a convention in the theater, playwrights, directors, and actors have resisted its overwhelming consequences. This began in Stanislavski's time and lasts until today. Many concepts counter to his psychological realism have been developed since then. Real-time theater—a new convention in its own right—is one of these counterconcepts.

As we have seen in Part II of this book, in real-time theater a distinction is made between *acting* and *play*. To fully understand this distinction, it is good, if not necessary, not only to get a grasp on the technique of real-time acting, but also to know and understand where *play begins*, how it over time *evolved* into *acting* and eventually mostly *disappeared* from the prevailing theater culture. In the course of history, playing and acting became almost entirely one and the same thing. The truth is that in regular theater there is not much room for *play* in its original form and meaning. Real-time theater creates a place for it again.

An actor may be able to apply the technique of real-time acting, but it is even better if he knows *why* he is restoring the element of *play* into his acting. This requires an insight in the historical developments that led to its disappearance. It will help him to see his work in a broader perspective; it will help him, practically, to overcome the many pitfalls of realism, and it will help the theater in general to accept this new form, which is, perhaps, not so new at all.

That is why this part of the book is dedicated to the historical perspective of real-time acting and theater. However, it doesn't offer a comprehensive history of the theater, which can be found elsewhere,[1] but it highlights aspects of the history of acting in relationship to the *origin of acting,* to the broad issues of *realism,* and to the development of *theater architecture.*

Our Need for Realism

Aesthetic conventions in the theater have always been connected to the prevailing techniques of acting. In ancient Greece, Aristotle gave a brief description of the theater practice of his time, and he drew up rules for the written drama in his *Poetics.*[2] More than 1,500 years later, during the Renaissance, Aristotle's rules were rediscovered, and during the Classicist revival of the seventeenth century they were applied to the prevailing acting style and technique, which was declamatory, and called rhetoric. These conventions were not deeply challenged until the middle of the eighteenth century. And it was only at the end of the nineteenth century that the first acting conservatories were founded, based on new pedagogical methods and systems of acting.

Theater of all styles and forms tells stories and presents us with an artificial reflection of reality. More than literature and the visual arts, the performing arts are by their nature and origin close to the original magical rituals, which aimed at *getting a grip on nature.* Acting and dancing still have the features of a magic ritual, even when we are not aware of it.

Since its beginnings, theater has offered its audiences images of human reality and society. These images are based on the interpretation of that reality. What theater often gives us is not a representation of reality itself, but a *representation* of what we make of reality: an interpretation (in artistic terms) of an interpretation. A theatrical interpretation may be metaphorical, symbolical, allegorical, or naturalistic, but it will always be a reflection on the realities of the world, life in general, human existence, or what some philosophers call the "human condition": a reflection of reality in the widest sense. Theater even aims to disclose what lies behind visible reality or what we take to be reality. For all these reasons, theater is never really *realistic,* in the sense of a perfectly detailed photographic imitation of reality, however hard it tries to be. Theater, by its nature, is *artificial,* an art form.

However, as theater has developed over many centuries, it has tended more and more toward a depiction of life and the world that *looks like* life and the world. This may, in part, simply be the result of the fact that, from a certain moment on in its development, actors represented characters. And these actors were human beings, just like the people who watched them. Aristotle, in his *Poetics,* called for anagnorisis, by which he meant that the actions of the characters on stage should be recognizable: their actions should be sufficiently real, concrete, and truthful. Hamlet, almost 2,000 years later, claims that the theater "holds a mirror up to nature," meaning that the theater reflects life in a recognizable manner: in other words, when watching a play, the audience looks in the mirror. Then, at the end of the nineteenth century, naturalists demanded that the reality of life, good or bad, beautiful or ugly, be a subject of investigation and depiction in the arts, if necessary in all its gory details.

Along with the development of the architecture of the theater as a building, the stage as the performing space, and the forms and styles of acting, this view has led to a theater convention, commonly known as *realism,* that has dominated the last 150 years of the history of the theater. In spite of its inherent artificiality, the theater has to a large extent successfully represented life and the world in a realistic manner, by imitating and copying them. This, I believe, is not only due to technical innovations, or psychologically based ways of acting, but also to our *existential need to get a grip on life and the world around us.* This existential drive has led to what I call our *need for realism.*[3]

Child's Play

Of the three performing art forms, theater, dance, and music, theater is closest to what the child does when he plays. Yet there are differences. The child doesn't create a work of art; what he creates is an entirely fantasized world, but one created in imitation of reality. This world is just as true and real for him as the "real" world is for the adults. The child also takes part in the adults' "real" world at his own level of under-standing and perception. The only difference is that in the real world he can't stop the action, and in his play he can.

The child learns by imitation. He copies the grown-ups he sees. By imitating their sounds he learns to speak; by imitating their vocal inflections he learns how to express himself emotionally; by imitating their gestures he learns to express himself physically. Slowly a child takes possession of these instruments of expression, which allow him to maintain himself in the world. Talk becomes language. Physical expres-sion becomes behavior. Later, adding his developing mind and senses, his developing emotional instrument, and his growing power of judg-ment, he learns to make conscious choices and decisions, and he un-derstands how to engage in conflict.

When a child plays, he imitates the reality around him as he ob-serves it, adding his unlimited imagination, not bound by the rules of the "real reality," and fired up by the bedtime stories and fairy tales he had been read or has seen on television. He enacts situations and at the same time narrates the story he is enacting, adding "stage directions," which include the "rules of the game" determining how to play or what somebody has to say. And every so often, he even steps out of the play into the real world to ask for cookies or go to the bathroom. Often his play can move from one location to another, from the street to the bed-room, from the office to the train, from the train to the farm. He breaks the barriers of time and place known to grown-ups but unknown to him. He is a master of improvisation. And he is serious about it, because for him his play is *real*. His "imagined reality" is just as real as the real-ity of the world around him: it is part of that world and merges with it. Even more so: through his play he is shaping that world, which gradu-ally becomes his world.

All this happens in the undivided time of the *present,* in the "here and now." The child, whether or not he is "playing," is always 100 percent present in the here and now, even if he uses the past tense for the stories (and the stage directions) he invents. This is why, completely uninhib-ited, he can fully dedicate himself to this invented, self-created reality.

All this happens completely unconsciously, one could say instinc-tively. Still, without knowing it or being aware of it, there is a reason for this behavior. By imitating reality through play, the child gets a grip on the unknown world around him. It's a way of getting to know the world and modes and patterns of behavior. To me it seems that in his play-making the child assuages his hidden fears of the unknown dangers the real world holds in store for him. There is something magical in this kind of child play. It's a tool for survival that prepares the child for what is to come. Because of play, the world doesn't look so overwhelming and threatening anymore, and life is fun . . .

Primitive Ritual: Awe, Fear . . . and Hope

In a similar way, it seems, our primitive ancestors staged magic *incantation rituals* to get a grip on the reality of the unknown powers of the surrounding world. Hunningher says, in his book: "That the function of play was originally protective is more especially seen in the play of primitive people, who as adults, of course, reflect in their games the problems of their mature life, the struggle for food and the preservation of life."[4]

The world had many life-threatening dangers in store for primitive people: droughts, floods and locust plagues, hurricanes and torrential rains, heat and cold, earthquakes and volcanic eruptions, ebb and flood, night and day, the moon and the sun, the winter and the summer; and the earth was inhabited by all sorts of species and wild animals, which could bring about sickness, death, and destruction.

Nature also bestowed our ancestors with their benevolent powers: it nurtured and was beneficial, contained an endless variety of animals and plants and trees that brought relief and provided food, shelter, and protection.

Our primitive ancestors created ritual dances and songs that *imitated nature* in all its incomprehensible forms. In these rituals, men explicitly acknowledged higher powers, which seemed to reign over mankind and the harsh *reality* of their day-to-day existence. Because these higher powers of nature induced awe, fear, and hope, they had to be appeased, pleased, implored, called upon for help and intervention, and, in case of positive results, thanked.

In order to imagine these overbearing natural powers and to make those powers more approachable, people in primitive tribes gave them a *physical* appearance. Through *imitation* and *representation* of attributed actions and characteristics, they were *played* in *communal rites,* in which all members of the tribe took part. In what Hunningher calls "games" they often appeared behind masks, which bear a human resemblance: behind the mask were human beings, who moved—*danced*—and made noises—*sang*—to resemble the natural powers they were representing.

Whatever the unknown power brought about, good or bad, the rain, for example, was thought of as possessing a soul and the powers of will and decision making. It could therefore be personified or played. It was as if, far above us, there was "someone" who made the rain by deciding to throw huge buckets of water over the earth, as if Nature thinks just as people think. Our primitive ancestors created song and dance rituals that contained images of what they were afraid of and hoped for; for instance, they threw buckets of water over the earth in times of drought in hopes that the rain would come. The cold and icy winter might take the form of a polar bear who causes hardship for human beings, and who is engaged in a fierce battle with the approaching summer. But the polar bear was played by a human being behind a mask and clad in a bearskin. Similarly, the jungle itself was animated and shown as a spirit who makes people go astray or gives them protection, a spirit, Ariel-like, which can be represented/imitated/ played with the help of masks and (animal) sounds. In the *personification* of these higher powers lies the origin of all *play*.

We have to bear in mind that none of the existing theories are conclusive as to the origin of the theater as a cultural medium, simply by lack of evidence, and they are therefore highly speculative, just as nobody knows exactly how these rituals were "invented," and theories about that are speculative too. But it is not implausible that they originated in the same way as child's play comes about: "then you were cold, and I was the winter," "then you were the tiger, and I was the hunter." Child's play, after all, is nothing other than a representation and imitation of an attributed/imagined/imaginary action. And, like the primitive ritual, his play also serves the purpose of helping the child understand and get a grip on the world around him.

Unlike the often chaotic and unrepeatable child's play, these magic incantations or rituals became repeatable because seasons seemed to appear in cycles, rain came and stopped, days became longer and shorter, the sun came up and went down, and so did the moon. These ritual dances took on a *repeatable form* and were performed according to certain rules and a defined form.

Thus, by performing these rites, men hoped to gain *control* over the otherwise uncontrollable reality. Rituals gave them protection and helped them shape their world. As Hunningher says: Play "creates order to bring a certain part of the chaotic world under control."[5] While at first these ritual dances were a tool to get a grip on the threatening reality of the surrounding world, they were also, unknowingly, the origin of all theater: the more control man gained, the more *play* gave way to *performance,* in which the performers confirmed their control over nature.

Gods and Worship Ritual

I believe that religion is, like ritual, a practical phenomenon, something that grows from the practice of life. However irrational it might seem, there is logic behind it. I also believe that religion began when ritual incantations of primitive societies were *successful,* or were believed to be successful—when the rain came or stopped, when people didn't get lost in the jungle anymore, when, most importantly, the winter was followed by spring. When this happened, people could *believe* in a rainmaker who brought the so much needed rain, a jungle spirit who showed the way and kept the wild animals at bay, in a cold-maker who chased the sun away (winter), and a warmth-maker who chased the cold away (summer). People could pray to them, implore them, and beseech them. Sometimes it "worked": their incantations bore results. Sometimes it didn't. Then you tried again. You repeated the ritualistic dance until you were successful. This is, I believe, how our ancestors discovered the seasonal cycle. At a certain point they must have known or understood that the summer always comes back. As long as they kept performing their rituals accompanying the seasonal cycle, the seasons would return. It made sense to perform them. However disconnected from their origin, this is still what Christmas (the return of light) and Easter (the return of life) represent for Christians, just as Hanukkah and Pesach do for Jews. Although we know now that the lighting of a Christmas tree doesn't lengthen the days, we keep celebrating solstice, the return of the sun, saying thank-you to the natural powers, just as we say thank-you for a good harvest on Thanksgiving Day by eating a turkey. Our festive holidays merely confirm what we have known for a long time.

Once people felt they could exercise control over certain natural phenomena, those phenomena began to assume the human shapes, which people had given them in their ritual dances. By personifying the natural powers, they represented them, and by representing them, they created the gods. The natural powers acquired names. The sea *became* Poseidon, who ruled the waves and the high winds. The sun *became* Apollo. Thunder and lightning *became* "Chairman" Zeus, the most awesome of all, who capriciously presided over all the gods and all people, and had a say in everything in heaven and on earth. People could worship the gods, pray to them. This happened in what is called the cradle of our Western civilization, Greece, as it happened in other cultures and civilizations as well: The *ritual incantation* made way for the *worship ritual,* which is equally motivated by awe and fear, and consisted of the imitation of actions that were now attributed to the gods. By urging them to listen to their supplications, men hoped to exercise some influence on them and to lessen the distance between gods and humans.[6]

From Ritual to Performance

Acting originated as a form of *physical representation* of something— some spirit or being or action—that people imagined and attributed power to. It was the representation of an attributed, imagined, and imaginary action of an unknown power by the *concrete, visible, physical action of a human being:* the unknown natural power became a *character,* performed or embodied by a *priest.* When our primitive ancestors saw that their incantations were successful, they needed to be able to *repeat* them. This is how their rituals became performances: the representation of the gods became more than pure play. Human empowerment made ritualistic *play* into *performance.* At first the whole community was involved in these song and dance performances, but some of them must have been better at it than others, so I imagine that those who were particularly good in the act of personification and representation singled themselves out, and took another position in the community. Some of them then became priests, who later became the first actors. The priests who represented the gods were *playing roles* in a ritual that could be *repeated.* This inversion was a monumental developmental step forward.

Although the community stayed intact, now there was a hierarchy between executing members and non-participating members: the priest, who not only had knowledge and access to the gods, also had power over his fellow men, and was often the king. When acting begins, there is also an audience and, however primitive it may be, a theater, a place where people watch the performance. But theater was at its inception more a step toward a social and psychological emancipation than an artistic act. The qualification "artistic" is of a later date.

The human need to control the world is central in the development of religion from primitive ritual. But men had other means to exercise control: their intelligence and their capability to create something out of raw material, to invent tools, to make weapons, to build houses, to till the land. They also had language, which developed slowly, but became a powerful tool. The threats of Nature remained, and people still lived in awe and fear of the gods, but with these tools men gradually gained more and more control over the immediate reality of the world around them. They learned that they also had the power of will, judgment, decision making, and reflection. Sometimes along the way they came into conflict with the forces of nature, the gods. Sometimes they made the wrong judgment and the wrong decision, and then the gods punished them. Priests and religious institutions made people fear such punishment.

Stories and Mythology

It took thousands of years before primitive rituals made way for religion, where believers worshipped the gods who ruled the world from one central command post: in Greek mythology from the nearby Olympus. Likewise it took thousands of years before ritual song and dance developed into theater and drama.

Once the rituals developed into religion, the representation and imitation of higher powers that theater presented developed into *mythological stories,* a series of events that recounted how men negotiated and rubbed shoulders with the gods in order to gain control over the reality of the world. Orpheus and Hercules became mythological demigods because of their heroic feats: Hercules won, Orpheus lost. Agamemnon,

Odysseus, and Oedipus were kings, generals, and mortals of such mythological dimensions that they became the subjects of stories or myths: they won *and* lost in their conflicts with the gods, who also set the rules for the conflicts of men among each other.

In these stories, humans lived, fought, and suffered side by side with, and often against, the gods. They were always subjugated to them, they always had to obey them, but they also challenged their power and their moral authority. By naming these mythological figures and gods, and by placing them in stories alongside normal human beings, humans brought these fearful powers closer to the human realm and placed them under greater control. In this way, concrete relationships between the fear-inspiring higher powers and mortal human beings were built. The stories of how men dealt with the gods, and the gods with them, became ever more powerful. Their lives and feats became examples for men. They reminded people of the order of the world, of how reality is shaped.

These narratives were performed in danced and sung ritual, but they also could be told, over and over again, and were passed on from generation to generation, sometimes over centuries, in what is called the oral tradition. As it happens in the development of mankind and society, practically all phenomena begin somewhere and, over time, begin to live a life of their own, away from their origin. This is true for customs and languages, as well as for the way societies organize themselves, and, I assume, similarly for dance and song. Thus, over centuries, presumably, the tales gradually drifted away from the original stories and the original rituals. As a natural cause of events, they evolved, like song and dance, into independent cultural phenomena, further and further away from their point of origin. In the course of centuries, they were embellished with hyperbole and filled with metaphor, and they lost their literalness. Homer's *Iliad* and *Odyssey* are beautiful examples of time-embellished stories, and when they were written down, they transformed into poetry and literature.

From Story to Action

It is from these epic stories and from the earlier dance rituals that drama originated. In drama, as in the original ritual incantations, the acts and actions attributed to gods and mythological figures were enacted. But drama *shifted* the focus *from story to action.* Stories were organized in a "plot." In a story one thing happens, and then the next thing happens—one thing after another. A story organized in a plot gives reasons for what happens.[7] The awe-inspiring protagonists of these stories now undertook actions and spoke in the first person. This is how theater as we know it came into being, and at this moment *actors who were not necessarily priests came to exist.* And while these performances originally took place in sacred places where religious worship was celebrated, soon they were banned from there. After that it didn't take long—time is relative here: it took a few centuries instead of a few millennia—before theater and play separated themselves entirely from their ritualistic and religious origins. This began when the representational parts of the ritual became too elaborate, too worldly to be allowed on sacred ground. Then these representations began to live a life on their own, becoming more and more a performance or a "show." One can easily imagine how this happened.

The same progression can be seen in the growth of the Halloween parade in Greenwich Village in New York—which began as late as the 1960s, but evoked primitive rituals expressing the fear of the approaching darkness of winter—the event very rapidly turned into a commercial street carnival. One can also imagine the "scandals" such ritual-based performances provoked. Once outside the sacred place of the temple, and using the same performance techniques and expanding them, theater began to tell other than religious stories. And it needed a place of its own: a theater. This is what happened in ancient Greece, which is considered to be the birthplace of the theater.

Some thousand years after the collapse of the Roman Empire, when Christianity had conquered the Western world, and one God replaced the multitude of gods, a similar development took place. Growing out of the Jewish religion, Christianity skipped over the primitive stage of ritual incantation and started right away with the worship ritual. Believers worshipped God's envoy on earth, Jesus Christ, and they believed that Jesus' father, God, high above in Heaven—much further off than the Olympus—looked down and watched over us. The fact that God had become more and more an abstract figure is a sign for how far men in the Western Hemisphere had come in gaining control over the visible and tangible reality of the world around them. God was still a manlike figure to whom people could pray for their well-being. But he was no longer the kind of god who controlled the seasons: the sun and the moon took care of those themselves.

But the monotheistic concept developed play, acting, drama, and theater just as the polytheistic concept once had. And just as mankind made giant steps forward in controlling the overwhelming powers of nature in ever-shorter periods of time, so did play, acting, drama, and theater develop in ever-shorter periods of time. Within a few centuries their subject matter changed, their ways of expression changed, their mode of performance changed, their spaces for performance changed.

One characteristic remained, however—and was even reinforced by secular theater, whose subject matter was now the life of ordinary men. This was the *underlying need to understand and get control over life.* For all theater deals with a fundamental life force: *fear, expressed in tragedy, and release of fear, expressed in comedy.* The stories this secular theater tells are about how men and women are deep down driven by fear, and how they overcome it. Whatever form they take, the stories that theater tells enable humans to get a grip on the reality. Even a farce like *Noises Off* by Michael Frayn, the Irish playwright—an ingenious and hilarious contemporary play showing the mechanisms of a theater production backstage—is based basically on the fear that these mechanisms *won't work.*

The Birth of Written Drama and the Secular Actor

In Athens around 450 BC, for the first time in human history—some four centuries after Homer—written plays were performed: what had at first been attributed to the gods in magic rituals and then embodied in human form as in song and dance now acquired a literary-dramatic form and was physically performed. First there was a "dithyrambe" based on Dionysian ritual with dance and song; now there was a script and a performance. This couldn't have happened without the existence of the other forms of story-telling, song and dance that had been developed over the centuries. And it certainly didn't happen overnight. That was a huge step: fear and awe had, apparently, diminished so much, and the measure of human control over life and nature had so greatly increased, that men could now apply *literary and dramatic metaphors* to contain and express these powerful emotions, and thus to suppress them and keep them under control. It was not that the emotions were gone, or that the fear had gone, but rather that men now had the confidence and maturity to deal with them in a different way, and reflect on them.

Athens at the time was what we would call a modern civilization, a thriving city-state, with huge power, both within Greece and outside its borders. It had a functioning political system, the first democracy, of which many less-developed countries in our own age might be jealous. It was a well-organized society and had a flourishing culture. With so much power delegated to common men, perhaps it is not surprising that it was in Athens that drama came to supplant magic ritual, religious worship, and storytelling. Drama was an essential element and an expression of the Athenian emancipation. It was a cultural expression from a primitive society into a city-state that ruled over others and strove for the hegemony over the complete Greek peninsula and beyond.

After this historical moment, when written drama became the basis for performed drama, we can observe a complicated, twofold process. The higher powers (the forces of Nature: gods and mythological figures) were impersonated, first in a literary and then in a physical form on stage. Meanwhile, the religious component vanished into the background. The people became participant-observers: an audience who had to make the connections themselves by empathizing with the characters portrayed. The audience consisted of the whole city of Athens: theater, at that time, was still a communal experience, in which all members of society participated. The chorus in the earliest dramas was a representation of the community itself. In its dancing and singing, we see the remnants of its origins in ritual. But then this chorus grew smaller, until it was reduced to a body of fifteen to sixteen singer-dancers, out of which the protagonists and antagonists emerged. With this step true drama was born.

The *priest,* who had been an *intermediary* between the people and the higher powers that ruled over them, was now an *actor* who had no religious function, but was the secular intermediary between the performed drama and the people. His sole task was to personify, to represent, and to imitate and perform the world of gods and mythological figures. His performance was no longer done in the temple, but outside.

To demonstrate the ancient connection (and perhaps to keep an eye on it), the high priest of Athens made the back wall of the temple available for this first theater (Dionysus Eleuthereus), and he had a seat of honor reserved for himself in the front row. The spectators—the people of Athens—participated in the Dionysian festivals (rituals!) celebrating spring, where plays were performed enacting stories and myths they all knew.

One and a half millennia later, and more than a thousand years after a new beginning of Western culture, a similar thing happened for Western drama all over again, now based on the Christian religion. Again a primitive form of performance developed from worship ritual to drama, and again literary and pictorial representation made way for physical representation. Stories about the life of Christ, written down in the New Testament, existed next to the sung ritual performance during Mass. The Good Friday liturgy, which had been sung since the early beginnings of Christian religion, was finally written down and performed as drama in the eleventh century in St. Gallen Abbey, Switzerland.

Within the boundaries of the Church, the priest became an actor. And then the priest stepped back in favor of the actor. Theater and drama as a form of art was born once more.

As long as this primitive form of theater was a religious exercise, based on Christian rituals, it could stay within the confines of the Church. But alongside this late development, residues of Greek and Roman performing arts and popular culture—clowns, jesters, jugglers, magicians, buffoons, puppet players, mimes, singers (troubadours), and story tellers—had roamed the country and entertained the people in marketplaces and city squares for almost a thousand years. In late medieval Europe, the jongleurs and troubadours of popular culture inspired theater just as the Thespis players (primarily dancers and singers) had inspired the actors of the first Greek theater. So, as soon as these highly appreciated worldly elements began creeping into the serious religious performance, the Church could no longer tolerate this expanding theater, and banned it from its premises. What was left were religion-based performances in pageants on the street. And soon a new secular drama and theater began, one of worldly powers, of knights and kings, and of the people. And over the following centuries the theater—first in comedy, and then in tragedy—gradually lost its royal glamour, until by the early eighteenth century it had come down to simply telling the stories of human relationships.

XXX-Large: Bigger Than Life

From its origins in ritual dance, through Greek tragedy and comedy, to the religious and secular drama of the Middle Ages, the reinvention of classical drama during the Renaissance, the Elizabethan drama, the classicist drama of the Baroque period, the commedia dell'arte and the more advanced forms of comedy, indeed until the nineteenth century, the theater never attempted to be a precise and realistic representation or imitation of real, concrete, and perceptible reality.

Apart from the technical difficulties that theater would have had to overcome to represent "reality" on stage—the problems of pictorial and architectural *perspective,* which played such a big role in the development of theater architecture—for all this time theatrical representation dealt with imaginary or imagined realities. Until deep into the nineteenth century, theater was artificial in its form and not "realistic."

In Greek tragedy, it was clear that the characters on stage were "higher powers" or larger-than-life figures, and the audience could observe their status in the huge, oversized human figures that the actors, who also wore masks, assumed. This magnified form was an expression of the fear men had for these higher powers, and at the same time it was a way to intimidate the audience in order to inspire fear and awe.

This was a residue from the time when these higher powers of nature had to be appeased. This is why, in his *Poetics,* Aristotle maintains that "catharsis is a cleansing *of* and *by* fear and pity." This catharsis is an echo of the primitive magic ritual, which was a collective, communal affair in which every single person of the community participated. In Athens, we must remember, the whole community of citizens attended the theater, participating in this annual ritual. The audience and the actors alike experienced the Aristotelian catharsis, as they all took part in the communal experience of a theater performance. In this performance the masks and the costumes reminded everyone of the original ritual dance. And the *cothurni,* the high-soled shoes helped to create the XXX-large, magnified human figures representing the gods and heroes in these first plays.

In Sicily, which in those days was a colony of Greece, there still exists a puppet play tradition, which uses oversized figures and masks, towering high above the people who carry them and the audience. This tradition, kept alive over the centuries, was an inspiration for Peter Schumann's Bread and Puppet Theater, whose performances always have the character of magical rituals.[8]

Distance from Reality

The written drama of the late Middle Ages became more and more secular at the time the Reformation began in northern Europe, and shortly after the flourishing of the Renaissance in southern Europe. Religiously inspired mystery plays and pageants, and didactic-moralistic allegories made way for the representation of worldly powers, who commanded the people. Magnified reality was established through historical distance, as in the tragedies of Shakespeare and Marlowe: King Lear, Macbeth, and Tamburlaine were all primeval, larger-than-life kings. A little later, in France, the classicist tragedies of Corneille and Racine presented plays about the kings and princes of ancient Greek and Roman times, and mythologies unfamiliar to their audiences.

This sense of distance and grandeur also existed in the language that was used in serious drama. At first, performances used church Latin rather than colloquial idioms, and later, in humanistic imitation of elevated speech, performances assumed the artificial language of rhetoric, which in the Renaissance was considered to be the highest of all the seven art forms, the art of recitation and eloquence. For centuries serious drama was written and performed in rhyme and verse. The language of the theater was, moreover, of an *allegorical* nature, and the way actors stood on stage and moved had an *emblematic* nature. In the performed form of this drama, tableaux vivants made way for "Grand Recitation," supported by meaningful, emblematic gestures, physical attitudes, and certain ways of standing and moving, all of which were described in a codex that in the Low Countries was called *Welstand:* the right way of standing. This way of acting was not at all "realistic." These actions did not sound or look like the everyday reality the audience saw around it; instead they presented stage characters with the sort of stately grandeur with which kings and other authorities presented themselves to the world and their citizens in parades and other displays of their power, with which they incited respect and awe and probably also fear. These spectacles also provided entertainment for the people.

What was true for tragedy was even truer for comedy, the theater genre that started as a *satyr play*, a parody of tragedy. Once it became an autonomous form, beginning with the comedies of Aristophanes, comedy distanced itself from reality by making a joke of it, magnifying and satirically exaggerating reality, as modern comedy still does. While far from "realistic" in its theatrical form, early comedy was down-to-earth, farcical, loud, and often gross, and it brought reality closer to the people. Its characters spoke a colloquial language. In commedia dell'arte the performance was distanced from reality by masks and grotesque costumes, while in the more advanced "bourgeois" comedies of Molière and later Goldoni distance was achieved through magnified absurd situations and satire, types and caricatures, and through the use of refined language including rhyme and verse, reflecting the culture of the upper middle class. But within this more refined style, the audience could easily recognize the Pantalone and Dottore characters of the old commedia.

New Drama in a New Theater

Although inspired and legitimized by the rediscovered classical dramas of ancient Rome, the language and the acting style of the new serious drama of the Renaissance came directly from the stately and static tableaux vivants of the Middle Ages. That is surprising, because this new drama was much richer in plot and character than the tradition of "rhetoric" had, thus far, allowed. Compared to the two-dimensional allegorical characters of mediaeval drama, the characters of the new serious drama were three-dimensional, flesh-and-blood beings of a kind that had previously existed only in the cruder form of comedy. Hamlet's reflections on acting indicate that Shakespeare—and one might assume, others as well—apparently recognized the friction between the content of the plays he wrote and the means actors used on stage. But the way the actors made gestures with their hands, especially in tragedy, or serious drama, was full of emblematic meaning, only understandable for the educated cultural elite in the galleries of the Globe

Theatre in London. And these "handstands" had to be precisely executed; otherwise their meaning could be misunderstood.[9] But as Shakespeare inserted comic elements in his serious plays, he possibly demonstrated the friction between the demands of the overriding theater convention of the cultural elite, and what he and his colleagues (as actors, directors, writers) might have felt as a constraint: *the ruling convention kept the element of play at bay, and didn't allow a more realistic depiction of life*. It was not until two centuries later, in the eighteenth century, that this issue became the subject of a serious practical and scholarly debate.

Perhaps another reason for this delay lies in the development of theater architecture, which at about the same time took a radical turn. This new theater building, which was a combination of Renaissance and Classical principles, was designed for the existing acting style, or to put it another way, the existing acting style adapted itself to the new theater architecture. In the course of history, developments in drama and acting soon began to diverge from the new trends in theater architecture, but this divergence was not noticed until the end of the eighteenth century, when it was too late to do anything about it.

In the "three-dimensional," dynamic, and complex dramas that were written and performed in many different traditions all over Europe after Shakespeare's time, character and situation came closer and closer to reality and were more and more recognizable and true to life. Theatrical architecture developed in the opposite direction.

Teatro Olimpico: An Architectonic Miracle

With the construction of the Teatro Olimpico[10] by the innovative Italian architects Andrea Palladio and Vicenzo Scamozzi in Vicenza in 1584, twenty centuries of theater history came to an end: the theater, changed from an open-air outdoor art form into an indoor art form. In earlier days, churches, temples, and palaces had given a modest place to forms of theatrical expression, but as soon as serious theater became a secular art, it had taken to the streets as a place to perform: actors, copying their comic counterparts, erected platforms in marketplaces and courtyards, against the back of the church or the wall of a palace; or they mounted their performances on moving carts, drawn by costumed horses, which they took over from religious pageants.

With the Teatro Olimpico, commissioned by the Olympic Academy of the northern Italian city of Vicenza, theater developed from a "low" art to a "high" art, from an art for the mostly illiterate populace to an art for the elite who could read and write. The board of the Academy wanted a theater for themselves in order to study, revive, and promote the "classics," which had been recently rediscovered. At the same time, they wanted a theater that could integrate classical architectural principles with modern perceptions of perspective in the visual arts. The Teatro Olimpico was a wonder of late Renaissance architecture.

The auditorium of this theater resembled the auditorium of classical Greek and Roman theaters: steep ascending rows around the orchestra. The "orchestra" of the theater was not fully round, as in the ancient examples, but half-round and deeper than the lowest row of the auditorium, a sort of pit. The audience in the theater's first row looked down upon the musicians in this pit. The actors stood on the "proscenium," which, as in the Greek and Roman theaters, protruded from the back wall, which was the actual rear wall of the theater house, the *frons-scenae*, three stories high. The proscenium was a slightly raised platform; in reality it was the ground floor on which the *frons-scenae* stood, and like the orchestra below the first row of the auditorium.

Everything in this Olympic theater was made of wood, which was painted to look like marble. The biggest wonders of this theater were the *portas* in the *frons-scenae*, one big main gate and two smaller side gates. Unlike the Greek and Roman theaters, whose monumental back walls were closed and sometimes decorated, these gates were open. Through them the audience could see a painted cityscape: the streets of Vicenza, of course.

Although these three gates opened to a space behind them, this space was very narrow, and useless. Hewing to the newly discovered rules of perspective painting, the ground in this narrow space ascended steeply, and the roofs of the painted houses that lined the painted street descended proportionally toward a final painted backdrop that completed this city panorama. From seven yards away, the optical illusion of a very long street was very convincing. Palladio and Scamozzi had introduced the almost perfect *illusion of reality,* which was then, and still is, the main principle of "realism" in the theater: what is shown on the stage *looks like reality.* This illusion is so strong that even when you stand on the proscenium in front of it, you think you can walk through the gate and onto the street behind it. But if you try, you almost fall head over heels backward, because the floor beneath your feet rises so steeply.[11]

The "realism" of the Vicenza backdrop is somewhat ambiguous, because no actor could walk the picturesque streets behind the gates: after walking one or two yards, his head would rise higher than the painted rooftops, and would undermine the illusion. Although they were not used to move much in the rethorical tradition, the actors must have been a little disappointed. So in the Teatro Olimpico, plays were performed "against the wall," on the proscenium. The illusion of reality was purely pictorial. Moreover, this illusion was only perfect for those in the audience who sat directly in front of the main gate, right in the middle of the theater seats. Unlike the Greek and Roman theaters, and unlike the open-air theaters of the Middle Ages, where everyone in the audience could see everything, now there were good seats and bad seats. The theater lost its democratic character: The high-ranking members of the Academy could witness the plays from the center, while the low-ranked members, the aspiring members, the students, had to view it from the seats from which the perspective was faulty.

The Deceived Eye

This architecturally advanced theater quickly gained new technological devices and became enormously popular at the expense of the boisterous open-air theaters. This was true not only in Italy but also in Spain, where the plays of Calderón, Lope de Vega, and Tirso de Molina had previously been performed in courtyards, with a black curtain for "night" and a white curtain for "day." And it was true in England, where, until then, Shakespeare's, Marlowe's, and Johnson's plays were performed in specially built, but relatively simple and primitive theaters like the Globe and the Swan where the audience was divided between the "groundlings" who stood in the open air (and in the rain), and the higher classes who found cover beneath roofed galleries.

The design of these round theaters had been copied from "bear pits," primitive stadiums for bear fights, while the raised acting platform against a half-closed back wall of what apparently was a house or a palace was taken from the marketplace and courtyard theaters that were known all over Europe. Just as in Spain, Italy, and in the Low Countries, the actors in these Elizabethan and Jacobean theaters played on practically bare stages, which had few decorations and which were not at all "realistic" in their design. And everybody in the audience, groundlings and upper classes alike, could see everything.

After the Teatro Olimpico in Vicenza, this changed rapidly. Royal courts and other houses of the nobility, which thought of themselves as patrons of the arts, enabled the transition to elitist indoor theaters. They took over the patronage of the arts from the Church, underscoring the new, secular nature of the theater. Theater became fashionable in the higher circles of society and an integral part of the culture of the nobility. Some of these seventeenth-century court theaters still exist, like the Royal Theater of Drottningholm in Stockholm. These theaters are characterized by the seventeenth-century Baroque: the trompe l'oeil—deceived eye—effect, the advanced pictorial and architectonic illusion, which offered dazzling perspectives and suggested a reality that wasn't there.

Acting in the Wrong Setting

The open gates of the Teatro Olimpico were just a first step. Soon, the whole *frons-scenae,* the gated wall, disappeared. Only the frame itself remained: a huge portal, an arch, or a *manteau* as the French called it, with two decorated side columns and a ridge on top, a "proscenium" in front of it, and an open stage behind it. The stage was *raised,* and sloped gradually upward so that the audience, now *seated below,* could see. The perspective was created by "wings": painted cloths, parallel to the sides of the portal, which were hung horizontally behind each other, each protruding a little further onto the stage, until, at the back of the stage house, a painted backdrop prolonged the illusion to infinity.

Although the actors found themselves in what seemed to be a vast space, they couldn't go to the deepest parts of it, because standing there, they would look ridiculous and disturb the illusion. The only way to give actors a little more space was by extending the stage area upstage, so that the steep slope could flatten, with the result that over time stages became in some cases three times bigger than the auditorium.

The deeper (and less steep) the stage became, the more problematic it became for the actor: the space was there but could hardly be used. The more the technical innovations were perfected, and the more the pictorial and architectonical illusions were refined, the less the actor fit into the setting. In order not to disturb the illusion, he had to stay downstage, close to the audience. But in order to maintain the illusion behind the arch, the proscenium area in front of the arch had become narrower and narrower. So now the actor could move neither forward nor backward, but was confined to a small area on the proscenium, between the side columns of the arch, the portal, and what was called the "first plane," between portal and first wing. On the "second plane" actors hardly could move: they had to come forward or were part of the set, as a chorus. In this setting there was not much space left for the element of play. Actors were put in their place: *mis en scène,* as the French expression goes. Acting was pretty static.

The frontal declamatory acting style of the two-dimensional Greek-Roman proscenium theater, of the theater of the Middle Ages, and of the open-air theater of the early Renaissance was never compatible with the three-dimensionality of the illusionist Baroque theater, which dominated theater architecture from 1584 till the end of the nineteenth century. So for a long time drama was performed in the wrong setting, and in many respects it still is today. And for an equally long time it seemed that the "rhetorical" style of acting was the best style of acting for this theater. It was an accepted and respected art form, but, as we will see, it was a compromise. As drama itself developed, many actors must have felt a growing frustration with the kind of acting they were to perform.

Oohs and Aahs and Opera

The "Italian theater," as it became known, soon took hold in England. Architect Inigo Jones,[12] inspired by Andrea Palladio, built sets and stages for court masques. Later, after Cromwell's Puritan ban on theater of 1642 was lifted in 1661,[13] the Italian theater with its proscenium arch became the standard for English theater architecture. The half-round open-air theaters of Elizabethan and early Jacobean times became obsolete. Sooner or later the same thing happened in other European countries, in each country in its own way, at its own tempo, and according to its own cultural development.

In the beginning, the painted wings were pivoting panels, based on the classical *periaktoi,* which had been revived during the Middle Ages. Soon these triangular constructions became painted flat screens, or wings. Intricate machinery with pulleys, wheels, and shafts, all made of wood and hand-operated, was used to pull the panels back and forth or quickly reverse a wing to show another scene. If four panels on either side of the stage were simultaneously reversed by a team of operators with good timing, a palace interior could, in a trice, be transformed into a square or a harbor or a garden—to the delighted oohs and aahs of the audience, for these increasingly spectacular changes took place without a curtain, so that everyone could see. This spectacle was what it was all about, and the more spectacular, the better: sea battles engulfed the stage, and chariots of the gods rode through the clouds. The actor must have looked small in the midst of these dazzling spectacles, especially when the stage had grown to be larger than the auditorium.

But all these open-curtain scene changes were also very noisy and sometimes took a long time. So music and dance were introduced as interludes to muffle the noise of the changes and to kill time. Soon music and dance gained an independent status in the masques at the British court and the ballets at the French court.

When singing was added to the masque music, opera was born, and it developed very quickly. Early in seventeenth-century Italy Claudio Monteverdi had composed the first opera.[14] He was the godfather of this new genre, combining theater with music and singing. And it was perfect! Perfect for the new theater and the declamatory acting style: Opera was spectacular, it was loud, its music quelled outside noise, the singing was static, and it required big gestures.

Soon these operas of spectacle-with-music won the upper hand over pure drama, the spoken word, and acting. But there was only one venue for both genres: the Italian theater—the ground plan of which, in principle, remains to this day the basis for many, even new, theaters, in spite of the fact that it is actually a theater for opera, not for spoken drama.

It is a miracle that both art forms—still rivals for the throne of "high art"—have survived beside each other on almost identical stages for so many centuries. For within these Italian-style theaters, the spoken drama did not disappear: the "word" stood its ground against the "music." The actor may sometimes have been thought of as an illusion-disturbing element, but respect for the author, the poet, remained. Even Monteverdi himself acknowledged the author, saying, "The word comes before the music." And if playwrights didn't always write great poetry, still, they wrote for the stage, where their verses publicly could be recited. I don't think, however, that it is accidental that Italy, the birthplace of the opera and the baroque theater building, became primarily a country devoted to opera, while the northern European countries, where the Italian theater structure arrived more slowly, were able to continue their literary tradition.

Toward a Truthful Representation of Reality

Before the theater moved from the marketplace to the indoor theater, performances were noisy affairs. The rough and tumble of jesters and comic actors, the actors of mystery plays, pageants, allegorical morality plays, and (classicist) tragedy all had to deal with an audience that didn't keep its mouth shut during performances. And this didn't change much when the theater became an indoor event. The theater was a social gathering place. The audience talked during a performance and commented on the acting or the play, or on the outfits of other members of the audience, so actors had to make themselves understandable, with thundering voices and mighty gestures. The rhetorical style of acting in serious drama and the bold gestures of masked comedy were the right combatants to survive in this situation.

But the emancipation of society, as seen in the plays that started to be written and performed once the theater moved indoors, demanded a more realistic way of acting, one that more nearly reflected reality itself, one that seemed more "truthful." Hamlet, in the scene with the actors, urges truthfulness and makes fun of big meaningless gestures.

The growing need for truthfulness came from two sides. An actor could hope that he achieved truthfulness in his character, but it was the audience that judged his success. In the classic movie *The Children of*

Paradise by the French filmmaker Marcel Carné,[15] which doubtless gives a romanticized image of the period, we see a scene in which the audience ridicules affected and untruthful actors. And in 1747 Rémond de St. Albine had already argued, in his influential book *Le Comédien,* in favor of a form of identification of the actor with the character he played, saying that the actor must have the same feelings as the character he embodies.

Indeed, actors became more and more like other human beings. The language they spoke became more and more like the language that normal people spoke, and as more and more emphasis was placed on feelings and emotions as the driving forces in human actions, actors could rely less and less on artificial means of expression. More and more they had to rely on internal motivations and the psychological truthfulness of a character. But this development also caused confusion: who was the actor when he played a role: was he himself, or was he the character he played?

The Paradox of the Actor

Denis Diderot, one of the leading men of the Enlightenment,[16] pointed out the problem in this issue of identification in his essay *The Paradox of the Actor.*[17] Must the actor display emotions that he had evoked within himself, as Saint Albine had argued, or should he pretend? In other words, did he present the "truth" or an artificial but truthful *form* for the emotions of his character—and for the reality of the world of the play? Diderot, as a true rationalist and encyclopedist, chose the second option: the mind has to rein in the emotions.

The actor, Diderot maintained, must find a means of expression for the feelings of the character he plays, thus creating a controllable and repeatable form . . . leaving his own, personal emotions out of it. In this opinion Diderot was in agreement with existing tradition.

In his *Paradox* Diderot engaged in a Socratic dialogue in which he acknowledged the emotions of the actor as an element in the process of creating a role. But he foresaw one big problem if the actor were to allow his own feelings to gain the upper hand over those of the character he played: mediocre acting. That, Diderot maintained, would harm the truthfulness of the performance.

The truthfulness of the actor is what the audience *believes* to be true. If the actor has to *pretend* in order to create this belief, that, said Diderot, is his art. In other words: if this "deception" is unavoidable, then the actor must employ pretended emotions, but ones that cannot be distinguished from real feelings.

But how can the actor do this except by using his own emotional instrument? This is the true paradox *of* the actor that Diderot pointed out in his discourse without mentioning it: while he acts, the actor must *hide* the fact that the emotions he portrays are *not* his own feelings, but those of his character, and he may experience enormous confusion about how to do so. The actor has to *pretend truthfulness!* He must use his art to falsely show truly believable emotions!

Of course, it is impossible for the actor to eliminate his own feelings, so in order to portray the "truthful" emotions of his character, he must bring himself very close to the character. For the first time in theater history, the actor was forced to approach the inner life of a character, not just demonstrate exterior and artificial forms of expression. Doing this did not leave the actor as cold and untouched as Diderot wanted us to believe. And yet Diderot was right: the actor doesn't have to be sad when his character is sad. Instead, he has to be able to "play" his own physical and emotional instrument, to give his character's sadness a truthful form.

Confusion and Controversy

Not only the actors, but also the audience, became confused by this paradox; they began to identify the actor with the character he played. The silent agreement that the actor is not the same as the character he plays began to unravel. Of course this didn't happen in one day; there were several decades of transition. Diderot wrote his *Paradox* at the end of the eighteenth century, but it was not actually published until 1830. Apparently by then, the problem had become urgent.

Around the same time as the publication of Diderot's booklet, the French writer Victor Hugo[18] argued in the preface to his drama *Cromwell* (1827) for an "acceptable reality" on the stage. But this plea for truth at first led only to greater historical authenticity in the designs for the huge stage and in the actors' costumes.

By the middle of the nineteenth century, theater practitioners were divided between those who insisted on the realistic, believable, and truthful representation of reality on stage and those who held that theater should present a nonrealistic, artificial, and imaginary reality. In this controversy, the problem of emotion and emotional expression played a crucial role. But the paradox of the actor was not the only obstacle to "realism" on stage. A greater problem was the theater itself, the "Italian" theater with its giant "proscenium arch."

The Meiningers

Around 1860, Duke Georg II of Saxe-Meiningen (in the eastern part of Germany, not far from Weimar) initiated a breakthrough of this impasse by staging realistic reconstructions of historical designs for his productions of plays like *Julius Caesar* and *Macbeth*. Shakespeare, of course, had staged his plays on a bare stage and in Elizabethan costume. But the Duke of Saxe-Meiningen, a passionate man of the theater, not only created an authentic-looking Roman set for *Julius Caesar,* dressing his actors in historically accurate Roman costumes, but also opened up the stage and replaced the painted wings and backdrops with three-dimensional constructions.

For the first time since the theater had moved indoors, actors could now roam the whole stage, which the duke also made more level than before. Because they had more freedom of movement, the duke's actors could act more truthfully. They started to move around and to use their body to express themselves, not just the text. With this innovation, staging, blocking, and mise-en-scène suddenly opened up.

The Meiningers, as the duke's ensemble was called, stunned international audiences with the truthfulness of their acting. The duke paid special attention to the mass scenes, which were wonders of choreography. Their influence upon the ideas of "realism in the theater" was enormous.

8 New Conventions and Innovations

Positivism and Naturalism

Driven by enormous technological and scientific innovations, the secularization of society accelerated, and the persistent needs of humankind to overcome the threats of nature led men and women to take upon themselves the responsibility for their lives. The idea of presenting a truthful, believable representation of reality on the stage and in the other arts received an enormous boost by the middle of the nineteenth century when the philosophy of positivism proclaimed that all natural phenomena could be explained scientifically, and when Darwin proved that all life-forms had a natural origin.[1] The world became even more controllable, and God was pushed a few steps further out into the cosmos.

For the arts, the door to reality was opened for good. The school of naturalism demanded that the reality of life, good or bad, beautiful or ugly, be a subject of investigation and depiction in the arts. In the visual arts this trend was strongly enhanced by the advent of yet another invention of the "scientific age": photography. This new form of accurate documentary representation made it possible to "register" the reality of the world-as-it-is. It must be said that it took a long time before photography became acknowledged as an art form, but nevertheless this new medium had an enormous impact on people's perception of the world around them.

The (short-lived) dogma of naturalism spread from the visual arts and literature to the theater when, in 1881, Emile Zola published his pamphlet *Naturalism in the Theatre*,[2] in which he pleaded for the truthful depiction in the theater of everyday life in all its details, however bad or ugly, in the same way as he and others did that in their novels. Meanwhile, however, the theater itself—the building in which performances took place—had developed in the opposite direction.

Edison, Wagner, and the Fire Department

When the theater-makers tried to follow the novelists into the brave new world of naturalism, they found that it was much more difficult to be "truthful" on the stage than on paper. Then a few amazing developments came to their rescue. The first was the invention of electrical light. Light on the stage had developed from candlelight, to light from oil lamps, to gaslight, all of which only dimly lit the stage. But with Edison's new invention, the stage could be lit completely and in a manner that mimicked reality.

Now the ideas of the Duke of Saxe-Meiningen could be achieved as never before. Sets, with interiors and exteriors, completely designed down to the smallest details, were placed on stage, creating the perfect *illusion of reality*, instead of painted wings and back drops that had offered only a fantastic optical illusion. As these realistic sets provided a convincing image for the naturalistic depiction of reality, the actors not only shifted their activities from the proscenium to the stage behind the arch, *but they also could be seen*. They now had the freedom to move, which they must have missed ever since the theater had moved indoors. And they began to feel at home in these on-stage interiors, even though at first these sets were only partly painted and made of cardboard and wood. These realistic sets permitted a fundamental change in the way the theatrical space was used.

At the same time—and at the other extreme—Richard Wagner was demanding what he called "total" theater, in which the auditorium and the stage were completely separated from each other so that his operas could become "mystical happenings." Between stage and auditorium he created a pit for the orchestra. Now the music was only heard, and the singers lived behind the "proscenium arch," in their own mystical world. The audience sat in the dark, while the opera heroes were in the light—electrical light, that is. The spoken drama and the opera still shared the same theater building, and this building had to accommodate both genres. The proscenium, the small strip of stage before the arch, didn't quite disappear, but it became obsolete.

The municipal fire departments gave an extra hand in this stunning process, giving these developments a definite and final push. Because of the many theater fires that had happened in the course of history, fire departments ordained a metal fire curtain between the side columns of the arch, which could completely close off the stage from the auditorium. If a fire occurred on stage or in the auditorium, the iron curtain would rattle down. Behind this curtain was the stage; on the stage was the set, which wasn't even allowed to be built onto the proscenium; and the lighting positions were adapted to this new architecture. The "iron curtain" and the frontal lights pushed the actors and singers back behind the proscenium arch.

In most proscenium houses the iron curtain still exists. And the fire department is still present in the person of a fireman who stands backstage at every performance. This fireman in the wings is perhaps the only person—apart from the stage technicians—who can observe that what the actors do on the stage behind the proscenium arch is actually make-believe.

Fourth Wall and Peephole

At the end of the nineteenth century, theater director André Antoine[3] in Paris emphasized the separation between auditorium and stage by asking his actors to turn their backs to the audience. He wanted to bring true-to-life reality on stage. If, Antoine reasoned, actors were to really feel at home inside their realistic interiors, why should they keep facing out at the audience as in the old declamatory style? The audience, however, was furious. With this move, the *fourth wall* was born, and the separation between an auditorium filled with an audience of real people, and stage filled with actors who *played* real people, was complete. Now there was an invisible, virtual wall between audience and actors. The audience could see the actors, but the actors could ignore the audience, which became a vague, amorphous crowd whom the actors could no longer see anyway because of the blinding, frontal light.

Now the audience watched the performance like people peeping through a keyhole into a world that exists on its own. They, who had once been spectators in a public place they shared with the actors, became instead voyeurs of apparently private events. Voluntarily or involuntarily, the theater became introverted. The people who moved within this clandestine space were no longer actors who portrayed characters, but characters played by actors. And the theater acquired a new untouchable and absolutist nature. The audience, which had hitherto been present with every performance—sometimes loudly so—was suddenly intimidated. From now on they could only cough or whisper softly.[4] Every other sound or action was seen as a disturbance, not only by the actors, but also by the other members of the audience.

Stanislavski's Psychotechnique

Of course it was not only technical devices, like lighting, and the demands for architectural verisimilitude, that led to "truthfulness" on stage. There were more factors at play. To make a seemingly real performance, the actor also had to act truthfully. Oversized gestures and rhetorical exaggeration, which actors had so often used in the past, were not acceptable within an aesthetic that demanded reality. The external approach to creating a character through exterior forms made way for a more internal approach, a technique of building a character from within.

To satisfy these needs, actor-director Konstantin Stanislavski at the turn of the twentieth century developed in Moscow the idea of encouraging actors to "live through" the characters they played. His psychological acting technique was designed to help the actor find the inner life of his character, so that he could portray him honestly, truthfully, and true-to-life. In this new technique emotions were central: what mattered was what moved the soul.

Central in this idea was that the actor should employ his own emotions when he portrays the feelings of his character, but that he must do so without losing control over himself. So mind and emotion became equal partners, balancing each other within the actor's being. This was a revolutionary step forward, one that seemed to overcome Diderot's paradox for good.

Stanislavski's "method" quickly became all the rage. He had the luxury of having his own theater, with an ensemble of actors he could train and with whom he could rehearse for years. Soon the Moscow Art Theater gained enormous fame,[5] and its work had a profound influence on theater history. One must not forget, however, that Stanislavski's "system" actually took several decades of experimentation to develop. His most important notes on acting were published for the first time in English in 1936, in his famous book *An Actor Prepares*.[6] But by then Stanislavski had already changed many of his observations and refined his ideas.

Realism as a Style and a Convention

Although the new science of psychology supported his view of human behavior, Stanislavski's starting point was actually the physical action of the actor. He and his colleagues must have felt how difficult it was to use the vast space and increased freedom of movement that actors now had. He himself had been an actor before he became a director, and he must have sensed how hard it was to lend truthfulness to a character while declaiming the text and using large, demonstrative gestures. In Chekhov's letters we can read hints about stiff and wooden movements of the actors and their thundering voices, which didn't really help the naturalness of their actions.[7] Preferring "minimization" and understatement, he criticized loud and exaggerated naturalistic overtones.[8]

Psychologically based realism in acting, together with the visual realism behind the fourth wall, led to a style of acting and of theater making that has been called *realism,* or *psychological realism,* or *naturalistic realism.* The inherent "realism" of theater—the human need to control reality through magic rituals—disappeared behind this new style of realism. One could call this style *representational realism.* It aimed to present not an image of reality, but reality itself, down to the smallest detail: both the external reality of the world around us and the internal reality of the people who inhabit that world.

With the introduction of this explicit "representational realism," the need for realism seemed to be satisfied. This style defined all elements of the form, from acting to stage design, to costumes and lights. And inevitably, "representational realism" itself became a fixed *convention* with "rules" and "laws" that still dominate the stage today.

One might think that, with the invention of representational realism, theater had found its perfect form and final destination. After 2,400 years, the theater had finally lost its artificiality, or rather it had tried, more or less successfully (with the help of rapidly improving technical means), to do so. However, three problems remained:

- In spite of all the seeming truthfulness of "realistic" acting, the paradox of the actor wasn't resolved. On the contrary, it became even more paradoxical than when Diderot had tried to get it under control more than a century earlier.
- The new rules and laws of the convention of realism made the actor himself virtually invisible: he disappeared behind his role.
- The audience was excluded.

Identification and Identity of the Actor

When actors began to allow and acknowledge that their own feelings could be the source of their character work, the experience must have been very liberating. "Identification" is the condition for and the result of the method of psychological realism: identification of the actor with his role, and identification of the audience with the character.

The truthfulness that resulted also must have contributed to the social emancipation of the actor, for now the actor gained not only self-respect and self-confidence, but also the respect and esteem of the public: he attained the same social status as the audience watching him. Later he grew into a "star."

However, the actor's ability to identify with the character he played also became a cause of great confusion about his own identity. This confusion is widespread, even today. Firm pronouncements like, "Who I am is not relevant," or "I am serving the play," usually cover it up, meaning that the actor feels his job is merely to serve the playwright or to enable the vision of the director. But deep in his heart the actor knows that this is just false modesty. When he says such things, the actor (falsely) reduces himself to a mere instrument or a vehicle for the creativity of others, and he undoes his own emancipation.

"When I act," the actor in realistic theater often declares, "I am the character." His inner emotional life is as important as what he does, perhaps even more important. He acts as the character would act; he thinks the thoughts the character would think, he feels the emotions the character would feel; he walks as the character would walk and he talks as the character would talk. He seems to *transform into* the character he plays: he is one with him.

In a television interview I once saw two actresses who effortlessly switched from saying "I" meaning themselves to saying "I" meaning the character they played. For me it was confusing: if I hadn't known the play they were talking about, I wouldn't have known whom they were referring to: were they talking about their own problems or those of their characters? Similarly, audiences often use the name of the actor when they talk about the role he's playing, Though, in the back of their mind both the actor and the audience actually know the difference. The actor knows that he is consciously embodying the requisite character emotions. And the audience needs only to be reminded in order to make the necessary distinction. And yet it is a telling confusion.

For centuries the technical difficulties of theatrical performance, the traditions of acting, and the architecture of the theater had all prevented the audience from identifying the actor with the role he played. But with the introduction of the fourth wall, and the psychological realism of Stanislavski's acting technique, this visible distinction disappeared. Nowadays the actor is encouraged to use his own emotions to play the feelings of his character, but at the same time he must hide this fact from the audience. Or rather: what he must hide from them—even more now than in Diderot's age—is whether or not he *is* using his own feelings.

Illusion of Reality

In traditional psychological realism, the actor *portrays* or *imitates* reality. Today the word *imitation* may sound a little negative, but in fact the "imitation of reality" was exactly what the nineteenth-century realists were aiming at. And behind the fourth wall, the technique of acting "as if" was just what the actor needed.

This imitation is twofold: the imitation of the fictitious character himself, as he appears in the text and the stage directions of the play, and then the imitation of the reality surrounding the action. For the performance of *The Lower Depths* by Maxim Gorki,[9] for instance, Stanislavski's actors went into the sewers of Moscow to study the models of their characters.

This "illusion of reality" on stage profoundly changed the actor's environment. The illusion required as precise and meticulous an imitation of everyday reality as possible. Most sets were made of cardboard and other shallow structures, which led to problems of the kind actors still struggle with when entering: how not to have the whole wall shake when you slam the door too hard, or how to ignore the fact that when you switch on a light, it comes on a second too late or too early. These kinds of absurdities can undermine the truthfulness of the situation. Of course, "truthfulness" is what it is all about, not only for the audience, but also for the actor. Over time, sets became more solid, but the problem has not disappeared.

Formerly, an actor simply came out of the wings; now he had to come out of the bathroom. To be truthful, he must wear a bathrobe, or if he has just taken a shower, his hair must be wet. Moreover, what happened in the bathroom, or what he was thinking about under the shower, now has to be visible in the way he opens the door and enters the living room. Everything he does has to be justified.

A realistic set is supposed to give the actor the feeling of a natural environment, one in which he can feel comfortable. Stanislavski went so far as to use sets that continued beyond the visible space into the wings, so that the actors in the third act of *The Cherry Orchard* (1904) wouldn't have to stop dancing, even when they were invisible for the audience.

The Virtually Invisible Actor

The role an actor plays makes him potentially invisible to the audience, giving him a kind of pseudoabsence. It doesn't make a difference whether he hides himself behind a mask, as in the Greek and Roman theater, or behind the way he speaks the text of the character he plays, as in the rhetorical tradition, or if he turns his back to the audience and withdraws in a simulated but true-to-life nineteenth-century salon, putting on the clothes of the period, as in the convention of realism. In each case, the audience only sees one figure, one body, on stage.

In Stanislavski's psychotechnique both the outer environment and the physical action have an inner justification. One problem with this technique is that an actor attempting to work this way can begin to feel that he must find the *inner* justification for his actions in the *outer* environment: the bathroom can become more important to him than the state he is in. He can even begin to "need" the bathroom . . . to be able to act truthfully, and in all this confusion, he may start to lose himself. What is meant to be a *technique* to achieve truthfulness can easily become an aim in itself.

The actor, after all, has only his own instrument, his own physical, emotional, and mental tools, with which to embody the character he plays. To be truthful, his physical actions have to be in harmony and in balance with his inner life. That is a big step forward, but within the fourth wall it becomes extremely difficult, if not impossible, for the actor to show the audience that he is, in fact, *not* the character he embodies. An acting technique has been created that allows the actor to identify with his character. But the fact that the actor himself is instrumental in this process becomes invisible: in the eyes of the audience, the actor has become identical with the character he plays. And that can be another problem. Behind the fourth wall, the actor operates in an autonomous, introverted world, while he himself becomes *virtually invisible* even as the character becomes more and more visible, and the "truthfulness" of the character becomes more important than ever.

Semblance of Perfection and Accomplished Facts

While the actor became invisible for the audience, at the same time the audience became almost invisible to the actor. The theater architecture in which the convention of realism flourished was largely responsible for this break in communication. The so-called *proscenium arch theater,* even in the newest theaters, hardly differs in its construction principles from the original Italian Baroque theaters upon which it is based. But the Baroque architecture had been designed for the creation of optical and pictorial illusions, which had the *semblance of perfection,* not for the real locations of recognizable daily life, populated with recognizable and believable people.

Theater architecture thus, quite literally, concretized the paradox of the actor, for it placed the actor inside an *unreal* illusion of reality. Centuries ago the new drama of Shakespeare and the French classicists had had no influence on the architecture of the theaters, or the styles of the acting. But now there arose a new drama and a new way of acting within a theater architecture that had to change its function but could not alter its construction. The pursuit of truthfulness demanded a new *illusion of reality,* which was even more unattainable than the eye-pleasing dreamlike illusions of the past.

This had far-reaching consequences: life, if it was to be portrayed on stage in a recognizable and believable manner, must seem perfectly and completely real. So just like Wagner's "total theater," this new theater form acquired a quality of *absoluteness* and *inaccessibility.* The "perfectly real" events on stage and the completely believable characters on that stage gave the audience the sense that what they were witnessing was *inescapable, unavoidable, unalterable and irrevocable.* The new theater presented the audience with *accomplished facts.* And on stage, any mistakes or imperfections had to be covered up.

The old Aristotelian "laws" of unity of time, place, and action were reconfirmed by the fourth wall and reinforced by the determinist cause-and-effect dramaturgy of the plays written at the time. Plays like *Ghosts, Hedda Gabler,* and *The Wild Duck* by Ibsen all show characters pursued by their past who can't escape their man-made fate, in the same way Oedipus couldn't escape his tragic fate, which was determined by the gods. It was an oppressive sort of theater for the audience.

Because of the semblance of perfection, the characters seemed to live in their own closed world. It is not accidental that playwrights like Ibsen, Schnitzler, and Shaw give lengthy and detailed descriptions of the sets in which the dramatic actions were to take place. The world they portrayed needed to be clearly recognizable, and the characters inhabiting that world must be people the audience might see everywhere, and "recognize." But the irrevocability of these characters' fate seemed to be determined right from the start—perhaps, and hopefully, not so much for the actors who were merely the executioners of these fateful events—for the audience that had to watch the inexorable events unfold.

It is striking that this development was in stark contrast to other developments of the time, a reality that was on the move in all respects.

Modern tragedy, which was epitomized by its "irrevocable perfection," was created within a world whose social and political ethos promised freedom and revolution.

Stanislavski did not succeed in resolving Diderot's paradox. On the contrary, since his time, and owing to factors beyond his method of acting, the paradox has only grown larger. One of the factors that maintained this paradox is the unchanged nature of theater architecture. Another is the birth and rapid development of new media like film and television, which encourage people to believe that live theater is a nineteenth-century relic that will soon become extinct. They would rather watch a movie in which everything seems "real."

Film

The new medium of the film, born around the same time Stanislavski invented his psychotechnique of acting at the beginning of the twentieth century, achieved the optimal semblance of perfection and completion. In the first decades of its existence, film was very theatrical and melodramatic: the exaggerated acting style was borrowed from the theater, whose actors and directors did not yet realize that a camera required an actor to do much less acting. At first the lack of sound, the black-and-white reproduction, and the often obviously cardboard studio sets all looked very artificial and nonrealistic. But with the introduction of sound, color, and filming on location, film, and a little later television, became a medium in which reality could be convincingly, photographically reproduced.

For film, the actor needed to bring his acting in accordance with the realistic environment of the film. This demanded an even higher level of realism in the acting technique. Elaborating Stanislavski's psychotechnique, Lee Strasberg developed his *method,* which helped the actor to reach and employ his own deepest emotions for the portrayal of the characters he plays. In the Actors Studio[10] the actor was trained to achieve the utmost in truthfulness. Strasberg's "method" was first and foremost meant for film actors.

Perfect realism is possible only in film. But of course this doesn't mean that what is shown in the film is reality. The truthful reproduction of reality in film, like truthfulness in acting, is created by artificial means. In film, reality just looks like real. In film, even more than on the stage, reality is skillfully manipulated, for example on the cutting table.

In film, as in much of modern theater, the audience is presented with a semblance of perfection and completeness. But unlike the audience of a stage performance, the audience of a film actually is completely cut off from the performance. The events on the silver screen really are irrevocable and impervious to the presence of the watchers. These events are fixed in the celluloid, the videotape, or the digital recording, and they are presented to the audience in exactly the same way at every screening: accomplished facts in celluloid. Only a new cut or a new digital arrangement can change that. In film everything is fixed forever.

Rational Distance and the Instinctive Identification of the Audience

In the theater the disconnect between audience and actors is merely imposed by convention. Cut off from each other's realities, the audience and actors in most theaters experience two different times: the time of the play and the time on the clock in the lobby and the green room. The audience may instinctively identify with the characters on the stage, or be sympathetic with them, but there is no direct communication between them. This allows the audience to distance itself, to think: "This is the fate of these characters. It has nothing to do with me." Or: "These are people from a different time period. Their adventures and vicissitudes don't interest me; I have other concerns." The audience can be deeply moved by what happens to the characters they see on the stage, be affected by them, and still turn away thinking: "How sad for *them!*" For the actors, however, the situation is much more difficult: lost within their characters, it can be impossible for them to measure the effect of what they are doing.

Reaction

The difficulties and paradoxes created by the conventions of realism did not provoke protests from the excluded audience, nor from the virtually absent actors, but it did from the theater-makers: the directors and set designers and to a lesser degree from the playwrights of the time. From the beginning of the twentieth century to the present time, even as realism has continued to dominate the stage, a countercurrent of resistance to realism has questioned its principles without ever managing to replace them.

Those who searched for alternatives to realism maintained that theater was not life itself but an artifice. Vsevolod Meyerhold, a pupil of Stanislavski's, developed a technique called *biomechanics,* an almost acrobatic approach to acting that aimed at magnification and exaggeration. Edward Gordon Craig in England, more a stage designer than a director, dreamed of the *Über-Marionette,* a larger-than-life puppet-actor; stage designer Adolphe Appia in Switzerland and France created spaces and abstract sets for the "mood" of a play. Playwrights Maurice Maeterlinck in Belgium and August Strindberg in Sweden began to write "symbolist" plays that portrayed a dreamlike and symbolic, rather than a realistic world; expressionists, like Georg Kaiser in Germany, tried to show enormous emotions as an expression of a rebellious inner life. Antonin Artaud in France argued—rather more theoretically than practically—for a return to the religiously based ritual origin of the theater.[11] In the 1920s and 1930s the *epic theater,* first invented by the technically innovative and socially inspired theater of Erwin Piscator,[12] and further developed by Bertolt Brecht, led to a style of production and acting that also eschewed realism.

All these innovators emphasized the *truthfulness* of theater, not its *verisimilitude,* the photographic representation of reality. They all sought to create theater that would be a locus for *images of reality.* For, they maintained, the theater derives its truthfulness—and its entertainment value—from its artificial theatrical form and from the artistic skill with which this form is presented: they wanted to demonstrate that what was called realism (or naturalism) had restricted the meaning of the word *truth,* that truth is something other than "realistic." Their proposals for another form of expression also implied the restoration of the immediate communication between the actors and the audience.

But plays and performances, whatever their intention might be, easily become victim to the iron laws of the proscenium arch when they are performed in such a setting. For the power of this dominant theater architecture is much greater than theater makers are usually aware of. On a proscenium arch stage, innovations can be very difficult to realize. Many innovators have learned this the hard way. Moreover, new forms, new ways of acting, and new acting techniques are easily incorporated into the ruling style of realism, and can be soon forgotten.

New theaters are usually designed and built for the existing demand, which means that in many cases they have to be able to house legitimate theater as well as opera. It also means that theaters with big prosceniums and open thrusts are usually built according to the (slightly adjusted) principles of the Italian theater: most lights are frontal and the actors are blinded. Theater entrepreneurs and city councils usually dream of big audiences, without knowing or caring too much about how the edifices they build might affect the art of acting. And architects don't know enough about acting to be able to understand the relationship between the actor and his environment.

Brecht and the Epic Theater

Of all the innovators after Stanislavski, Brecht was the most successful in creating an alternative to the theater of realism.[13] He was the most influential theater innovator in the first half of the twentieth century, especially for the development of the art of acting.

There are three reasons for this: First of all, Brecht was very outspoken in his criticism of the "emotional eruptions" in which some actors indulged. He also dared to criticize the audience for allowing itself to be carried away by these histrionic outbursts. Like Stanislavski, he had the time to develop his concept of acting by working consistently with a cohesive group of actors for almost a decade, his famous Berliner Ensemble, which exists till today.

Stanislavski's acting system itself was not used in the German theater until after his death. Although *An Actor Prepares* was first published in English in 1936, it wasn't available in German until after World War II. So when Brecht created an acting method based on his concept of "alienation," he did so quite independently, and not as a reaction against Stanislavski's teachings. What Brecht criticized was not Stanislavski but what he called the "dramatic theater" or "Aristotelian theater," by which he meant the cause-and-effect dramaturgy of the plays of his time and the way they were performed. Later, when Brecht specifically began to criticize the kind of acting that demanded that the actor identify his own inner life with that of the role he played, he referred to this emotion-filled style of acting not as "Stanislavski-esque" but as "illusionist realism."

It was only after the Nazis forced Brecht into exile that he discovered Stanislavski and his system. At first Brecht disparaged this work, which he maintained was rooted in bourgeois individualism, even though it had become the "standard" style of acting in the Soviet Union. It was only toward the end of his life that Brecht discovered and acknowledged the value of Stanislavski's work, especially his ideas about "physical action."

Brecht's concept of the *alienation effect* was, from its inception, originally not simply a criticism of a theater and acting technique. It was a critique of society at large. The German Weimar Republic was highly politicized and polarized, and Brecht's ideas, though they may have started as an attack on bourgeois aesthetics, soon acquired a political and social content. For Brecht theater, like the other arts, could be used as an instrument in the Marxist-inspired struggle for a better, more just society. Moreover, Brecht came to the theater as a playwright, not, like Stanislavski, as an actor. It was only because he was so deeply dissatisfied with the current theater practice in his country that he became a director—and proved to be the best director of his own plays.

In the non-Communist world, however, Brecht's ideas about the theater were mistrusted, misunderstood, and dismissed as "theoretical." During his life these ideas became victims of the Cold War, though even now, after Communism has failed and largely disappeared as a political ideology, his ideas remain controversial. But in fact Brecht actually experienced strong government opposition even in Soviet-dominated East Berlin of the 1950s. The reason for this was Brecht's conviction that theater should replace "realism" with a nonrealist theatrical form. For this idea the cultural apparatchiks accused him of "formalism." They demanded socialist realism, a realism based on the socialist ideals. In spite of these controversies, however, Brecht remains one of the most performed playwrights in the world, and theater-makers to this day still struggle to understand what "epic acting" means and how it should be done.

Alienation Effect

According to the "Aristotelian" and "determinist" laws of cause and effect, the convention of realism showed man as unalterable, caught in inevitable dramatic situations and condemned to an irreversible man-made fate. What Brecht hoped to achieve with his epic theater was to make the audience into "observers" who would be capable of deciding for themselves what is right or wrong about the events they see on stage.

Of course, plays written and performed in the realistic tradition, and within the proscenium arch, are capable of inspiring people to think about the events shown on the stage, including thinking about important social issues. Plays like Ibsen's *A Doll's House* and Gorki's *The Lower Depths* have contributed considerably to the political debate on the subjects of women's emancipation and social injustice, at least on the level of the literary and theater critique. But Brecht's irritation was caused by the general "culinary" consumerist attitude of the audience, who indulged in emotions and cried in sympathy with the misery they witnessed, rather than being challenged by, or actively involved intellectually, or even physically, with what they saw happening on the stage.

Brecht wanted to show his audiences that *reality is alterable.* With its social aims, its alienation effects, and its acting technique, one could call his epic theater *reflective realism,* as opposed to the *representational realism* of the late nineteenth century.

The purpose of the alienation effect was to *interrupt the emotional involvement of the audience,* and to provoke in them *thoughts about the alterability of man,* so that they might begin to think about alternatives and social change. He sought to achieve this not simply by the kind of "reversal of morality" one sees in his early, satirical plays, like *Man Is Man* (1925) and *The Three Penny Opera* (1928), but also by the use of dramaturgical and theatrical devices that interrupted the flow of dramatic action on stage.

But the unalterability of man and the inevitability of his fate, which seemed so intrinsic to the conventions of realism, were not only the result of realistic playwriting and of the psychological realism in acting; they were also caused by the unalterability of the stage itself: the isolated reality that had for so long been moved behind the fourth wall of the proscenium arch. This problem was something Brecht may have been aware of, but it was not one he was able to overcome with his epic theater.

In order to undermine the mystification and emotionalism of theater, Brecht added to the canon of alienation effects an almost bare, nonillusionist stage, harsh white light, and sets and costumes that were reduced to their essentials. The result was that they acquired a *symbolic* and *emblematic* function, rather than the *exemplary* functions Brecht had originally envisioned.

Together, these stylistic elements became the artistic trademark of the Berliner Ensemble. Brecht had dreamed of big public spaces, like sport palaces for boxing or cycling for his theater. But after he returned from exile in the United States to Europe in 1947, he was offered a proscenium arch theater in East Berlin, then the capital of East Germany. In this theater, the Theater am Schiffbauerdamm, he was forced to make compromises with the realities of existing theater architecture.

Stylization

If Brecht had not been a stage director himself, his innovative ideas might have remained literary or theoretical. But as a practicing stage director at "his" Berliner Ensemble, he was able to put them into practice, and show by example how his theories could work on stage. Because of this, his model of the epic theater became the most important countertrend to Stanislavski's psychological realism.

Within the conventions of the epic theater, the actor usually embodies his character in a highly stylized form. Brecht believed that the unrealistic nature of such an artificial theatrical form would ensure that there was a clear distinction between the actor and the role he played. This might have been true for the actor, but for the audience the actor and his role can still appear to be one and the same: both of them stylized. This is why many people think that Brecht's epic theater is cold and rational. An additional obstacle to the understanding of Brecht's concept has been the traditional circumstances under which the epic theater is usually produced. Brecht's ideal, that theater should truly engage its audience and be entertaining at the same time, was—and continues to be—difficult to realize in a theater with a proscenium arch, where the actors can easily hide behind the mask of their roles.

The limitations of the proscenium arch and the fourth wall prevented Brecht's actors from showing the gestus of the acting itself, and made it difficult for the audience to observe it. The physical distance between the stage and the audience, the use of the fourth wall and the separation of the actors from the audience, instituted by Wagner's pit and Edison's spotlights, was simply too great for the actor, without a special acting technique, to look at himself—as he might in Chinese or Japanese theater, or in the circus—and show the audience that he was the mediator between them and the role he was playing. Though the ancient, but still prevailing, Noh, Kabuki, and Bunraku theaters in Japan are large, and circus tents are enormous, their audiences are not separated from the performers: they are all in one space, and the lights are always on. The distance created by the proscenium theater and the fourth wall separated audience and performer and made interaction between the two practically impossible. It doesn't allow the actor to show that he is "real" and his character isn't. The actor can exhibit the gesture with which his character acts, feels, and thinks, but he himself disappears behind the form. The light may have been clear and white, but the actors were still blinded by it, so the stage remained an introverted world, inaccessible to the audience. It is significant that actors who have been trained in the epic theater often claim that they themselves are not important: they humbly serve the author and the text.

Nevertheless the reduced and minimalist gestures of the actors, as in Brecht's *Galileo* and parts of *Mother Courage,* and the magnified theatrical forms, sometimes even to caricature, as in Brecht's productions of *The Caucasian Chalk Circle* and *The Good Woman of Setzuan,* were refreshingly new and a real answer to the pseudorealistic acting style of his time. Brecht's Berliner Ensemble in former East Berlin became famous.

The stylized gestures of the epic actor were highly artistic and precise. Brecht had an excellent ensemble of actors, and the Berliner Ensemble contributed greatly to the modernization of the German theater and the art of acting.

But with his *stylized realism* and all his theatrical innovations, Brecht was not successful in his desire to change the theater from a place of "illusions of reality" into a place for a "reality of illusions." What a pity! In his theoretical writings, which are often very practical, he came close to describing a solution for the problems he observed in common theater practice. But the material conditions of the existing theater architecture presented Brecht with insuperable obstacles. Unable to change the architecture of his theater, he was never able to break down the fourth wall.

Again Innovations

In order to restore the sense of direct communication between the stage and the audience, some fundamental changes need to be made:

- A different acting style
- A different theater architecture
- A different design for the stage

New theater conventions can best be invented and flourish outside the confines of traditional theater. As early as the late 1950s and the middle of the 1960s, theater-makers all over the world stepped out of the proscenium arch. In the United States, the Living Theater of Julian Beck and Judith Malina and the Open Theatre of Joseph Chaikin[14] came to world fame with their innovations in acting and performance techniques. In the 1960s the Polish director Jerzy Grotowski[15] created yet another technique of *physical acting,* based on the purest physical expression of an inner life, a life so intense that his (rare) performances had the character of a ritual. Grotowski wanted to exchange the usual theater building for other locations. His performances took place in intimate spaces for small audiences, which would make the performance experience as direct and immediate as possible. In the few performances he created, he sometimes had his actors play in the midst of the audience.

In Paris, Peter Brook's Centre International de la Recherche Théâtrale[16] became an ensemble that created a much-envied alternative. In West Berlin Peter Stein established the Schaubühne am Halleschen Ufer, presenting a modern alternative for the worn-out Berliner Ensemble in East Berlin. They, and many others all over the Western world, discovered new forms of theater making and theater production and developed new acting techniques.

In Holland theater-makers, encouraged by a short-lived but spectacular protest action,[17] were inspired to overthrow the privileged, subsidized theater system and replace it with a more flexible structure. Many actors turned their backs to the traditional proscenium arch theaters and formed companies like the well-known Werkteater (Worktheater), Onafhankelijk Toneel (Independent Theater), and Baal (named after Brecht's first big play and the group's first production). They began to perform in new, open, nontheater spaces: factories, slaughterhouses, greenhouses, railway stations, abandoned churches, auction halls and water-pumping stations, in which they could freely experiment and develop new forms, and for which they had to design new plays and a new way of acting. *Site-specific* theater became one of the enduring forms of the modern Dutch theater. Theater directors began to write their own plays, which fit the new circumstances. This required new acting techniques, in which actors became more central in the performance. In what I now call *real-time* theater, the technique of *acting in real time* became prevalent. This acting form is now practiced in many theaters throughout the country and taught in schools.

The "Second Metaphor" and the Presence of the Actor as Himself

As Brecht's epic theater experiments made plain, stylizing the form of theater is not sufficient to overcome the principles of realism. The actor's need to justify his presence and his actions on stage stems from the convention of realism, but these needs do not disappear simply because the play is performed in a stylized fashion—especially when the actor must still perform within the closed space behind the proscenium arch. Even when the proscenium arch is replaced by an open space, as Peter Brook has demanded, the actor's need for justification remains very strong. To overcome this problem, one needs to find a new way of acting.

One of the central elements of real-time theater is that the actor is *present on stage as himself.* This is a principle I discovered during years of directing. Other theater-makers in Holland and Belgium discovered the same principles through other approaches.

After my first brush with Brecht's plays, *The Measures Taken* (see the introduction to this book), I directed many more of his plays. For *The Exception and the Rule* (Frankfurt am Main / Berlin, 1976), the British director Albert Hunt[18] encouraged me to apply a *second theatrical metaphor* as a vehicle for images in the play. As was also Hunt's experience, it was possible with this second theatrical metaphor to overcome the need for realism and to have the actors *demonstrate* the characters of the play instead of *becoming* them. Instead of using Brecht's alienation effects to interrupt the action of the play, this second metaphor became an alienation effect, which continued throughout the whole play, opening many possibilities for actors to distance themselves from the action of the play and from identification with the characters. The second metaphor provided a vehicle for images that were alien to the play, but not to its subject matter. This required the actor to create a second character, an artificial *theatrical persona* who performed the character in the play. Therefore we chose clowns to play the characters in *The Exception and the Rule,* and the location was a small one-ring circus. In *Fear and Misery in the Third Reich* (Toneelacademie Maastricht, 1981/1983), the actors were stand-up comedians, singers, and striptease dancers in a nightclub cabaret. In *The Bread Shop* (Schlicksupp teatertrupp, Frankfurt am Main, 1981) the actors were modern vagabonds, city nomads: half homeless people, half street musicians. We played *The Breadshop* in all sorts of venues, from a former slaughterhouse to an empty wharf, but rarely within a "real" theater. In these productions, the artificial theater personae *performed* the characters within the play. This required the actors to be in technical and artistic command of these personae. The actors could then allow these second personae to be in direct communication with the audience.

But there was still a problem: This second persona provided the actor once again with a justification for his presence on the stage and for playing the character he played. Now the actor no longer hid behind the mask of the character in the play but behind the mask of the second theatrical persona. He had to act within the strict "rules" of the form we had established. So in *The Exception and the Rule,* for instance, each actor had to be a clown at every moment. That was hard and fun at the same time: it's a wonderful thing to master a highly accomplished technique that brings about a very theatrical show. It was with *Fear and Misery* that I realized that the actor could simply be present on stage as himself, that there were other ways to display highly accomplished acting techniques, and that there were moments when there was nothing for him to "act," nothing that he needed to do except watch the other actors. In these moments, I realized, the actor could make the story of the play into *his* story, and show the audience how he himself related to the narrative of the play. This discovery I had already made with *The Measures Taken,* but now, eight years later, the watching actor became the *narrator* of the role he played and of the whole play, just by being there as himself.

The second metaphor was an essential step toward the creation of a pure theatrical form in which the actor finds an expression for the action of the character he plays. Without the second metaphor, the actor could simply be present as himself, and "stage" himself directly in the role he was playing. And at this point of the development, the element of *play* began to exist next or parallel to, and even simultaneously with the acting. Present on the stage as himself, staging himself in the role, the actor could begin to *play* again. Through this reintroduced element of play, the actor as himself became truly free to communicate directly with the audience about the role he performed. And he could do this even through the role he played. The greatest, most exciting discovery was that this direct communication between actor and audience took place in the *here and now,* in *real time:* the time of the actual performance of the play, which is the same for the actors as for the audience. Empowered by this element of play and by the acknowledgement of his own presence, the actor could rediscover his lost relationship with the audience. Many actors I have worked with in performance or in workshops have refound the joy of playing that had brought them into acting in the first place.

This discovery was possible not only because of the chosen theatrical form (circus, nightclub cabaret, the street), but also because of the *location* of the performances, which were often open, nontheater spaces. We at first found ourselves inventing cumbersome theatrical devices to make exits and entrances in these spaces, imitating a "real" theater, but soon I discovered that this was awkward, superfluous, and even silly, as if an audience needed to be lured into an illusionary dramatic situation by a curtain that opened to reveal a stage. In the end, I realized, these devices were simply not necessary. And so exits and entrances were not necessary! Just as "going to black" before the performance begins isn't really necessary.

Real-Time Acting: A Form and a Technique for Postmodern Theater

The open form of real-time theater allows all sorts of different theatrical forms and acting techniques to coexist within one performance.

For instance, a serious emotion-laden performance can include a tap dance or an operatic aria, which are not necessarily part of the ongoing dramatic action and break the performing style of the previous scenes. Such "alien inserts" can add to the narrative of the play not merely by illustrating the emotional state of mind of a character in song, as they do in musicals ("when the words are not enough, sing it"), but also by applying theatrical devices that need not be justified in any way by the dramatic action of the play, but *illuminate* them. Sometimes these can be purely theatrical actions, like changing the scene or operating a sound system; sometimes they can be more artistic, like breaking into dance when the rhythm of the performance "needs" a dance, even when the story itself doesn't call for dancing.

This quality is brought forward by the real-time acting technique, which is based on the acknowledgement of the *presence of the actor as himself* (not as the fictitious/illusionary character he plays), and of the *reality of the stage and the theater* (not of the dramatic situation of the play).

In real-time theater, the *actor, who doesn't represent anything but himself,* "presents" the character he is playing to the audience. It is he who tells the story of the play, he who publicly "creates" the dramatic situations, he who chooses the character's actions, he who "quotes" the character's words, and he who publicly puts all this into the required (and rehearsed) theatrical form.

Stanislavski's physical and dramatic action can still have an important place in the technique, mainly for the preparation of the actor, and for the technique required to connect with himself. Psychology and emotions are not taboo in real-time theater, but they are part of the action. Stylization of the action, as in epic theater, isn't a taboo either. It is an applicable and useful form, especially because of its precision.

The space and freedom that the actor acquires in this way can bring new meaning to Brecht's alienation and montage techniques. Real-time acting is a tool to *break up* a closed dramatic text, and to allow all the other theatrical elements to tell the story of the play. This is what happens in *postmodern* theater: the drama (the story) is *deconstructed* by using performance elements other than the imitation of the actions of the characters. Elements that are not part of the original play can be added to the text, and "alien" theatrical elements can help to shed light on the story. In the United States the Wooster Group is one of the greatest examples of this postmodern theater.

Because of the deconstruction process, cause and effect are practically eliminated from real-time theater. Situations are offered to an audience, and the audience must make connections themselves. Both the writing and the directing of real-time plays work this way. Stage reality interrupts dramatic reality; past and present can be thrown together; the dead can be on stage with the living; real people—characters who really existed—can appear with imaginary people. On stage the realest person is the actor himself.

The technique of real-time acting is based on four main elements:

- The actor must be present as himself, both while he is playing his role and when he is not acting. He and his acting are real. But the play and the character are an illusion: They are *really acted* rather than *acted for real.*
- The actor must stage himself in the theatrical forms, of which the physical expression of his character's actions is a part.
- The theater space is a real space in which the imagination of the actor can unfold: the theater space is real. It is the space *where* the actor acts, and Now is the time *when* the actor acts: in *real time.*
- The theater is a public place, where actors and audience are equal, and where they can be in direct contact with each other.

Real-time acting eliminates the seeming perfection of the impenetrable realistic stage; it replaces the intangible and unalterable nature of the theatrical reality by something just as imperfect as life itself, something as tangible and alterable. The real-time actor restores a kind of immediacy of communication between himself and the audience.

In this concept of real-time theater, something that has been hidden for a long time becomes visible again: the actor and the reality of the stage itself. In this theater, the actor is no longer absent, lost somewhere behind the fourth wall. *The four constituent elements of theater—the play, the actor and his acting, the theatrical space, and the audience—no longer exclude each other but exist together as one.*

The Flat-Floor Theater, the Transparent Actor, and the Magic of Theater

Without radical changes in the usual theater architecture, it is almost impossible to experience theater as a reality in its own right, rather than as an illusionary reality, or as a substitution for real reality. The optimal performance space for real-time acting is a *flat- or level-floor* theater, one in which the audience risers begin on the same level as the acting space, permitting no separation between actor and audience. In an open space like this, lighting can be installed on a grid covering the whole ceiling of the space. Such lighting does not blind the actors, and it allows them to make eye contact with the audience.

Unlike a child, an actor knows that he is performing. In the setting of the flat-floor theater, the real-time actor shares this "knowledge" with the audience. He is not inhibited by this knowledge, as a child becomes self-conscious when he knows people observe him; on the contrary, it *liberates* him, and he is able to fully dedicate himself to his performance and to his imagination.

But like a child he has space and time to "play" as well. By making eye contact with the audience while he stages himself, allowing them to look through his eyes into the soul of the character he plays, the now "transparent" actor invites the audience to share this "playing" with him. In this sharing, both the actor and the audience can find the true magic of theater.

NOTES

Introduction

1. Konstantin Stanislavski (1863–1938) was the founder of the Moscow Art Theatre (1898), where he developed his ideas for psychological realism.

2. The reader will find a more detailed definition of these terms in Part III of this book.

3. In this book, when I speak about acting, I use the verbs "to act," "to perform," and "to play." And what I am speaking about is stage acting, not film or television acting. To avoid awkward grammar, I use the word "actor," and the pronoun "he" to mean both male and female actors.

4. Bertolt Brecht (1898–1956) was the founder of the Berliner Ensemble in East Berlin (1949), where he tested his theories of epic acting.

5. *The Measures Taken* was first published as *Die Massnahme* (Berlin: G. Kiepenheuer, 1930). It belongs to a small group of so-called didactic plays. Eric Bentley's translation was first published in the *Colorado Review* in 1956–57. Another translation by Elizabeth Hanunian was published by the U.S. Government for the House Committee on Un-American Activities' case against Brecht in 1947, causing him to leave the United States, where he had been living in exile from Nazi Germany since 1942.

6. The original play was meant for so-called workers' choirs—big organizations affiliated with the unions or the Communist Party. Eisler, too, had been living in exile in the United States, was indicted by the House Committee on Un-American Activities, and had to leave the country.

7. We discovered this in the newly available German edition of the complete works of Bertolt Brecht, *Gesammelte Werke*, 20 vols. (Frankfurt am Main: Suhrkamp, 1968). In the Dutch text the Young Comrade is listed as one of the other characters, equal to the Agitators and the Chorus. Also in Bentley's trans-

lation the Young Comrade is listed as one of the characters, which easily leads to the misunderstanding that he is the main character and the tragic hero of the play. This leads to the misunderstanding that this role will be cast in the traditional way.

8. Hanns Eisler's original score was for a workers' choir of four hundred amateur singers. The actors in the first performance of the play, directed by Brecht in 1930, were professionals. One of them was Brecht's wife Helene Weigel, another the famous actor Ernst Busch.

9. The other "giants of the modern theater" are Jerzy Grotowski and Peter Brook.

10. Joseph Chaikin, *The Presence of the Actor* (New York: Theatre Communications Group, 1972).

Chapter 1

1. Denis Diderot, *Le Paradoxe sur le Comédien,* written in 1773 (Paris, 1830), trans. Geoffrey Bremner as *The Paradox of the Actor,* in Denis Diderot, *Selected Writings on Art and Literature,* (London: Penguin, 1994). *The Paradox* is a discourse *on* the subject of acting truthfully. The content of the discourse is in fact the paradox *of* the actor.

2. Among Pirandello's most famous plays are *Six Characters in Search of an Author* and *Henry IV,* trans. Mark Musa (London: Penguin, 1995), and *Tonight We Improvise,* trans. Marta Abba (New York: Samuel French, 1988). Pirandello received the Nobel Prize for Literature in 1934.

Chapter 2

1. Aristotle, *Poetics,* around 350 B.C, trans by S. H. Butcher (New York: Hill and Wang, 1961).

2. Konstantin Stanislavski wrote several books about his system, of which *An Actor Prepares* (New York: Theatre Art Books, 1936) is the most influential. His later books, *Building a Character* (New York: Theater Art Books, 1948) and *Creating a Role* (New York: Theater Art Books, 1961), only appeared in English long after Stanislavski had died.

Of the many books about Stanislavski, I would recommend especially Sonia Moore's *The Stanislavski System: The Professional Training of an Actor,* 2nd ed. (New York: Penguin, 1984); and Jean Benedetti's more recent *Stanislavski and the Actor* (New York: Routledge, 1998).

3. See also the section "The Actor's First Paradox: What Is Real?" in chapter 1.

4. Ton Lutz (1919–2009), Dutch actor, director, acting teacher, and the artistic director of several big theater companies in the Netherlands.

5. Lee Strasberg (1901–1982), the cofounder and later director of the Actors Studio in New York (1947), developed the substitution and emotional memory techniques further into what became known as the Method: "sense memory" became a cornerstone for "method acting."

6. Strasberg originated the word *beat* for every bit of text where the actor can define the action of the character by a verb. Anecdote has it that Strasberg actually used the word *bit,* which in his pronunciation of the English language sounded like "beat." That nobody has corrected him might have to do with the musical and rhythmical implication of the word *beat,* which is so applicable to a dramatic text.

Chapter 3

1. Brecht's thoughts on acting theory are recorded in his *Writings on the Theater (Schriften zum Theater).* The most important volumes of this seven-volume work are *Notes to the Opera "Rise and Fall of the City of Mahagonny,"* 1930 and 1938; *Alienation Effects in Chinese Acting,* as part of *Der Messingkauf,* 1937–51; *Small Organum for the Theater,* 1948; *A New Technique of Acting,* 1949–55; and *Stanislavski Studies,* 1951–54. All these works are translated and published by John Willett in *Brecht on Theatre: The Development of an Aesthetic* (1964). Another book on Brecht is John Willett, *The Theater of Bertolt Brecht* (1959). Willett is one of the few who were able to balance Brecht's artistic merits as a writer and director with his work as a theoretician.

2. Cf Willett, *Brecht on Theatre,* 121–28. The original title of the "Street Scene" is "Die Strassenszene," in *Schriften zum Theater,* vol. 4 (Frankfurt am Main: Suhrkamp, 1950).

3. *Gesammelte Werke,* vol. 2, *Schriften Zum Theater* (Frankfurt am Main: Suhrkamp, 1968), 754. Also in his *Theaterarbeit* (Berlin, 1950). Brecht gives several examples of the meaning of gestus. In *Theaterarbeit* Brecht describes several performances he created as models for future productions.

4. The performance at the Deutsches Theater led to the establishment of the Berliner Ensemble, Brecht's own theater in East Berlin in 1949, which kept the production of *Mother Courage* on its repertoire long after Brecht's death in 1956.

5. Therese Giehse was one of Brecht's favorite actresses. Like the production with Helene Weigel at the Deutsches Theater, Brecht directed the production at the Munich Kammerspiele in 1950 himself. The difference in interpretation demonstrates the "not this, but that" principle very clearly. Giehse had played Mother Courage at the world premiere of the play in the Zurich Schauspielhaus, 1941, which emphasized the tragedy of war.

Chapter 4

1. The fourth wall is the invisible, "virtual," wall of the proscenium arch, the stage opening of the traditional theater. Actors can't see through this wall, because they are blinded by frontal lights. (See also Part III.)

2. Over the years I have directed *Mephisto* several times. When I refer to these different performances in this book, I give them a number. This performance of the play is called *Mephisto (2).* Similarly, I number my two *Ivanov* productions, and the two *Man Is Man* productions I directed.

3. Ariane Mnouchkine is the founder and artistic director of the avant-garde Théâtre du Soleil in Paris (1964).

4. George Bernard Shaw, the Irish-English playwright (1856–1950) who wrote more than sixty plays mostly dealing with social problems, was also a journalist with a very sharp and witty pen. As a political activist he was a member of the Fabian Society, which furthered the causes of the working class, social justice, and equal rights. He received the Nobel Prize for Literature in 1925. Many of his plays are still being performed. His play *Pygmalion* was adapted into a musical and a film: *My Fair Lady.*

5. Japanese filmmaker Akira Kurosawa (1910–1998) acquired world fame with such films as *Rashomon* and *Seven Samurai.* For *Ran* he won the Palme d'Or at the Cannes Film Festival (1985).

6. Arthur Schnitzler (1832–1931), Austrian playwright-novelist and contemporary of Sigmund Freud, often provoked the upper class of the Viennese society he was part of, by the choice of his themes, and the sharp psychological depth he gave to his characters. Of his plays *Reigen* (*La Ronde*) is most famous, in part because of the several movies made of it. Stanley Kubrick made a film of his short story "Dream Story" with the title *Eyes Wide Shut* (1999).

7. Jean Genet (1910–1986), French experimental playwright-novelist, vagabond, and thief, whose literary talents saved his life. His play *The Maids* is often performed.

8. The Wooster Group, one of the longest-living experimental theater groups in New York, of international renown. The group emerged from Richard Schechner's Performance Group during 1975–80, with Liz LeCompte as its artistic director.

9. Cf. note 5, chapter 2. Elia Kazan, Cheryl Crawford, and Robert Lewis founded the Actors Studio in 1947. They were, like Strasberg, founding members of the Group Theatre, the first actors' collective in the United States (1931). Strasberg became the director of the studio in 1951. His approach became known as the Method, which met with both approval and criticism. Robert Lewis wrote a critical book about it: *Method—or Madness?* (New York: Samuel French, 1958).

10. Exercises on active seeing and looking can be found in chapter 6.

11. Exercises on active hearing and listening can be found in chapter 6.

12. Exercises on active rest, grounding, relaxing, and connection can be found in chapter 6.

13. Viola Spolin, *Improvisation for the Theatre,* 3rd ed. (Evanston, IL: Northwestern University Press, 1999).

14. Keith Johnstone, *Improvisation and the Theatre* (London: Methuen, 1979).

15. Related approaches to improvisations on space are discussed by Anne Bogart and Tina Landau in *Viewpoints: A Practical Guide to Viewpoints and Composition* (New York: TCG, 2006), and by Mary Overlie, the originator of View-

points, in her chapter "The Six Viewpoints," in *Training of the American Actor,* ed. Arthur Bartow (New York: TCG, 2006).

16. In his *Short Description of a New Technique of Acting Which Produces an Alienation Effect* (Willett, *Brecht on Theatre,* 138), Brecht recommends transposing the text of the character into the third person. He also recommends transposing the text into the past and speaking the stage directions out loud.

17. Peter Brook, *The Empty Space* (New York Touchstone, 1968).

18. *Die Dreigroschenoper* premiered in 1928 under the direction of Erich Engel at the Theater am Schiffbauerdamm in Berlin, the later Berliner Ensemble, with Lotte Lenya as Jenny.

19. Louis Andriessen (1939), leading contemporary Dutch composer and the father of a new modern music culture in Holland, whose work is performed all over the world.

20. Heiner Goebbels (1952), one of the most important contemporary German composers, whose compositions are theatrical events that he directs himself.

Chapter 5

1. Heinrich Böll (1917–1985) was one of the most important postwar German authors. He received the Nobel Prize for Literature in 1972.

2. Erwin Piscator (1893–1966) was the first to use the term *epic theater* for a genre of social-political theater. In his book *The Political Theater* (1929) Piscator provided a theoretical basis for his ideas. He was the influential artistic director of the Volksbühne (People's Theater) in Berlin, and the so-called Piscator Bühne. He emigrated to America in 1939 and established the influential Dramatic Workshop at the New School in New York.

3. Cf Willett, *Brecht on Theatre,* 138.

4. Occasionally I have conducted the workshop with student directors, as well.

5. From 1979 to 1989 this workshop was a permanent part of the curriculum of the Theater School in Maastricht, always followed by a performance of a play. Since 1985 I have taught the workshop at the Department of Acting of the Theater School in Amsterdam, at times in combination with the Director's Department, sometimes by itself, and sometimes followed by the performance of a play. Since 1995 I've also conducted this workshop with students of the Summer Drama School of New York University in Amsterdam, always followed by solo performances by the students. In 2005 I gave the workshop at the Theater Program of Princeton University, for the first time followed by a montage performance.

6. In 1978 I did an intensive workshop with all the actors of the Theater am Turm in Frankfurt, followed by the performance of Brecht's *Saint Joan of the Stockyards.* Out of this workshop and performance Schlicksupp teatertrupp was formed as a "free" professional theater group. I led the workshop several

times with the actors of this group, followed by the performance of plays we created. I have also conducted the workshop with the actors of other theater groups, including Het Vervolg, in Maastricht, and DNA and Southern Comfort, both in Amsterdam, and with actors of the Theater Center in Tel Aviv.

7. Cf. Willett, *Brecht on Theatre*, 121–29.

8. The term *sense memory* is an essential part of "method acting." It means the memory through the five senses. Cf. chapter 2, note 5.

9. Cf. the "inside-outside" exercise developed by Joseph Chaikin with the Open Theatre. See for this Chaikin's *The Presence of the Actor*.

10. Dario Fo (b. 1924), actor, director, and playwright, is as a satirist highly critical of the political situation in his country and the world. For his work as a playwright he received the Nobel Prize for Literature in 1997. *Mistero Buffo* is one of his most famous plays, translated into many languages and performed all over the world.

11. Brecht compared his ideal audience with spectators in sports stadiums. Cf. Willett, *Brecht on Theatre*, 6.

Chapter 7

1. Cf., for instance, Phyllis Hartnoll, *A Concise History of the Theatre*, 3rd ed. (New York: Thames and Hudson, 1998).

2. Cf. note 1, chapter 2.

3. Three books—published long ago, but still unsurpassed—analyze in depth the subjects I speak of in the following sections: James George Frazer, *The Golden Bough*, ed. Theodore Gaster as *The New Golden Bough*, 3rd ed. (New York: Criterion, 1968); Johan Huizinga, *Homo Ludens* (Haarlem, 1936); Benjamin Hunningher, *The Origin of the Theater* (Amsterdam, 1955; Westport, CT: Greenwood, 1978). In Hunninger's book I found the inspiration for my ideas about the significance of the relationship between child's play, ritual, religion, and theater. It also supports my theory about the distinction between play and acting.

A fourth, more recent book, which critically analyzes the findings of scholars who have been looking for an answer to the intriguing question of the origin of theater, confirms in great lines my own theory: Eli Rozik, *The Roots of Theatre*, Iowa City, University of Iowa Press, 2002.

I have largely refrained from citing from the work of these and other distinguished scholars and theater-makers, although many of their books and articles have added to my understanding of theater and acting, and have served as a background for this otherwise nonacademic book.

4. Hunningher, *The Origin of the Theater*, 12.

5. Hunningher, *The Origin of the Theater*, 12.

6. The primitive ritual lives on in Shintoism and in certain tribal, mostly isolated, communities in remote areas of Africa, among Indian tribes in North and South America and Southeast Asia, where the gods are still everywhere and in everything.

7. Eric Bentley in *The Life of the Drama* (New York: Atheneum, 1964), quotes E. M. Forster, describing the difference between story and plot as fol-

lows: "The King died and then the Queen died" is story. "The King died and then the Queen died of grief" is plot.

8. Peter Schumann is a Vermont-based puppeteer and theater-maker of international renown, whose performances always feature oversized puppets. A famous example is *The Cry of the People for Meat* (1968)

9. Cf. B. L. Joseph, *Elizabethan Acting* (London: Oxford University Press, 1951).

10. See for more references to theater architecture the invaluable book by Allerdyce Nicoll, *The Development of the Theatre,* 5th ed. (London: George G. Harrap, 1966).

11. The Teatro Olimpico has, miraculously, been preserved ever since its construction. It is still in good condition and can be visited via guided tours.

12. Inigo Jones (1573–1652) was the first great English architect, who designed still existing buildings in the classicist style, such as Whitehall and Covent Garden.

13. Oliver Cromwell overthrew King Charles I, who was beheaded in 1651. In his crusade against Catholicism, Cromwell started two civil wars and led the English republic until his death in 1658. He also "cleaned up" English society with a moral revival.

14. *L'Orfeo,* first performed in Mantua (1607).

15. *The Children of Paradise* (1945), taking place in the Paris of courtesans, actors, thieves, and aristocrats at the beginning of the nineteenth-century, has become an all-time classic.

16. The Age of the Enlightenment, the eighteenth century, is also called the Age of Reason. Reason became the basis of all thinking, science, and culture. The Enlightenment is the beginning of modernity.

17. Cf. note 1, chapter 1.

18. Victor Hugo (1802–1885) is best known for his novels. Among them: *The Hunchback of Notre-Dame* and *Les Misérables.* Like other writers of his time he was an advocate of social justice.

Chapter 8

1. Charles Darwin (1809–1882) is the father of the evolution theory, which proclaims that all life-forms are a result of natural selection. After long studies he published his ideas in *On the Origin of Species* (1859). They are largely uncontested among scientists today.

2. Emile Zola, *Le Naturalisme sur le Théâtre* (Paris, 1880).

3. Antoine founded his Théâtre Libre in 1887, where he used the technical innovations for the new dramas of his time, such as *Ghosts* by Ibsen and *Miss Julie* by Strindberg.

4. In a television documentary (2001) on the Toneelgroep (Theater Group) Amsterdam, the leading theater company in the Netherlands, the actors explained—seriously or as an ironical joke (it wasn't quite clear)—that they measured the success or failure of a play by how much the audience had coughed.

5. The Moscow Art Theater was founded by Stanislavski and his dra-

maturge friend Nemirovich Danchenko in 1898. It exists still today and has in its repertoire productions from the time of its founding.

6. Cf. note 2, chapter 2.

7. *The Selected Letters of Anton Chekhov,* ed. Lillian Hellman (New York: Farrar, Straus and Giroux, 1984); *Anton Chekhov's Life and Thought: Selected Letters and Commentary,* ed. Simon Karlinsky, trans. Michael Henry Heim (Evanston, IL: Northwestern University Press, 1999).

8. Cf. Marc Slonim, *Russian Theater* (New York: Collier, 1962).

9. Maksim Gorki (1868–1936), Russian playwright who, even before it happened in 1917, became the voice of the Russian Revolution with his style of "socialist realism," which became under Stalin the only form in which artists were allowed to express themselves.

10. Cf note 5, chapter 2.

11. Antonin Artaud (1896–1948) was a visionary of a new, physical theater that found its roots in old rituals and our collective subconsciousness. His book *Le Théâtre et Son Double,* in which he unfolded his theories about the Theater of Cruelty, trans. M. C. Richards (New York: Grove-Weidenfeld, 1958), exerted an enormous influence on modern theater innovators like Peter Brook, Joseph Chaikin, Richard Foreman, and many others.

12. Cf. note 2, chapter 5.

13. Cf. note 1, chapter 3.

14. Chaikin, *The Presence of the Actor.* On Joseph Chaikin and his Open Theatre see also Eileen Blumenthal, *Joseph Chaikin* (Cambridge: Cambridge University Press, 1984).

15. Jerzy Grotowski (1933–1999) was the founder of the Laboratory Theater of 13 Rows in Opole and Wroclaw. His book on his philosophy and theater work, *Towards a Poor Theatre,* ed. Eugenio Barba (London: Methuen, 1969), inspired a new generation of theater-makers in Europe and the United States.

An elaboration of Grotowski's acting technique can be found in Stephen Wangh's book *An Acrobat of the Heart* (New York: Vintage, 2000).

16. Cf. Peter Brook, *The Empty Space* (New York: Touchstone, 1968).

17. In 1969, audiences in Dutch theaters revived the ancient tradition of loudly voicing their displeasure with what they saw on the stage. When they began to throw tomatoes at performances in Amsterdam, their "Tomato Action" marked the beginning of many changes in the theater system in the Netherlands.

18. For his play *The Cuban Missile Crisis* (Bradford Art College, 1968), Hunt used the films of John Ford, such as *Gunfight at the OK Corral,* as a theatrical metaphor for the story. The main characters in this political comedy, the Kennedy brothers and Nikita Krushchev, were played as John Wayne–like cowboys. See Albert Hunt's *Hopes for Great Happenings* (London: Eyre-Methuen, 1976).